Catholic Theological Formation Series

General Editor: Kevin Zilverberg

The Catholic Theological Formation Series is sponsored by The Saint Paul Seminary School of Divinity, the graduate school of theological formation for Roman Catholic seminarians and laity enrolled at the University of Saint Thomas in Saint Paul, Minnesota. As a premier institution of theological formation for the region and beyond, The Saint Paul Seminary School of Divinity seeks to form men and women for the task of fulfilling the specific call God has for them, a call grounded in their common baptismal vocation to serve one another in Christ.

As an institution of the Archdiocese of Saint Paul and Minneapolis, the school is intentional in its commitment to priestly and diaconal formation. As an institution of graduate theological education, the school prepares the laity for the equally compelling task of making Christ known and loved in the world. Although the students prepare for diverse ministries, all enroll in a curriculum of theological formation within the context of holistic and integrated Catholic formation.

It is this challenge of theological formation—the challenge to faithfully inform one's understanding—that serves as the focus of this series, with special attention given to the task of preparing priests, deacons, teachers, and leaders within the Roman Catholic tradition. Although the series is academic in tenor, it aims beyond mere academics in its integrative intellectual approach. We seek to promote a form of discourse that is professional in its conduct and spiritual in its outcomes, for theological formation is more than an exercise in academic technique. It is rather about the perfecting of a spiritual capacity: the capacity on the part of the human person to discern what is true and good.

This series, then, aims to develop the habits of mind required of a sound intellect—a spiritual aptitude for the truth of God's living Word and his Church. Most often, it will draw from the more traditional specializations of historical, systematic, moral, and biblical scholarship. Homiletics and pastoral ministry are anticipated venues as well. There will be occasions, however, when a theme is examined across disciplines and periods, for the purposes of bringing to our common consideration a thesis yet undeveloped.

Despite the variety of methodologies and topics explored, the series' aim remains constant: to provide a sustained reflection upon the mission and ministry of Catholic theological formation of both clergy and laity alike.

The general editor of the Catholic Theological Formation Series, Fr. Kevin Zilverberg, serves as assistant professor of sacred Scripture and the founding director of Saint Paul Seminary Press at The Saint Paul Seminary School of Divinity.

Augustine's *Confessions* and Contemporary Concerns

Edited by

David Vincent Meconi, SJ

**SAINT PAUL
SEMINARY PRESS**

SAINT PAUL, MINNESOTA • 2022

Cover image: St. Augustine of Hippo, All Saints' Church, Laughton, Lincolnshire, UK
Window by Burlison & Grylls, late 19th to early 20th century
Photo by Philip Wright
Cover design by Willem Mineur

Published 2022 by
Saint Paul Seminary Press
2260 Summit Ave., Saint Paul, Minnesota 55105

Library of Congress Control Number: 2022931512
LC record available at https://lccn.loc.gov/2022931512

Catholic Theological Formation Series

ISSN 2765-9283
ISBN 978-1-953936-05-9 (paperback)
ISBN 978-1-953936-55-4 (ebook)

spspress.com

Contents

Abbreviations

an. quant.	*De animae quantitate*
c. Jul.	*Contra Julianum*
CCSL	Corpus Christianorum. Series Latina
ciu. Dei	*Du ciuitate Dei*
conf.	*Confessiones*
contra acad.	*Contra academicos*
de or.	*De oratore*
en. Ps.	*Enarrationes in Psalmos*
Enn.	*Enneades*
ep.	*Epistulae*
Gn. litt.	*De Genesi ad litteram*
Io. eu. tr.	*Iohannis Euangelium tractatus, In*
leg. Man	*Pro lege Manilia* or *De imperio Cn. Pompeii*
lib. arb.	*De libero arbitrio*
nat. b.	*De natura boni*
OSHT	Oxford Studies in Historical Theology
rep.	*De republica*
retr.	*Retractationes*
s.	*Sermones*
sol.	*Soliloquia*
trin.	*De trinitate*
Tusc.	*Tusculanae Quaestiones*
uera rel.	*De uera religione*
WOSA	The Works of Saint Augustine

Introduction

Augustine never wrote as a person limited by the constraints of late antiquity. In telling his life's story, he muted the particulars so as to stress the perennials and perennial he became. His homilies still feed the Christian soul, his teachings on the nature of God and human heart still illumine the searching, and his *Confessions* above all continue to show us what each of our life story is becoming. It is the truths contained in this omnibiography, this story of every human soul before God, which these pages set out to unfold. For it was Augustine's intention to tell a story that could be read at any time by any one and still bear fruit that is eternal.

That is why, in the summer of 2019, scholars from around the United States gathered at Saint Paul Seminary in St. Paul, Minnesota, to discuss how each book of the *Confessions* could be read today. Every generation brings a new story with which to read Augustine's story and the narrative of the twenty-first century is yet again that of a generation unrestful and unsure. We are a people who fear but remain unawed, who question but do not seek, who wander but make no pilgrimage. As such, the cultural emptiness of the twenty-first century offers a space where Augustine's voice can be heard anew. That is the goal with which each author below was tasked: What does this particular book of Augustine's *Confessions* say to us today?

The occasion for Augustine's sitting down to compose the *Confessions* still remains a debated point. Some think it was his roundabout way of explaining the story of the North African Church to Bishop Paulinus of Nola—particularly the story of his and Paulinus's common friend Alypius. Was he trying to show

1

the schismatic Donatists that their accusations that he was still a secret Manichee were unfounded? Was he appealing to a larger audience to show that his conversion to Catholicism was in fact authentic? Remember, when he left the shores of North Africa, he went to work for the pagan emperor, had a live-in concubine, and still belonged to a New Age-type cult. His story had to be told.

In thirteen pre-planned books, then, Augustine set out to narrate the beginnings of the "restless heart" to the Church—where the collective body of praise proves to be the eternal remedy—and all the blessings and burdens of the intervening years. Whereas books 1 through 9 read more autobiographically, they are held together by the more philosophical books—book 10, which treats the memory able to unify these years of varied experiences; book 11, which treats the time which memory traverses; and then books 12 and 13, which bring us back to the original beginning, the Book of Genesis. As such, each of our authors takes up one of these books to see how it might speak to us today.

We begin with John W. Martens's look at book 1, where Augustine alludes to Matthew 19:14, writing, "It was only the small stature of a child that you mentioned with approval as a symbol of humility, O Lord our king, when you declared of such is the kingdom of heaven" (1.19.30).

Martens's essay shows why Augustine seemed to miss Jesus' theological point about children and to reduce them to little sinners not model disciples. To understand Augustine's view of children and childhood, the author compares ancient Roman views of childhood with current views of child development. Augustine gives us insight into the ways of the Roman world through his recollections of his own childhood but also through his adult observation and knowledge of children.

Augustine's insights align with what we know of Roman antiquity and its understanding of childhood, with one important proviso. Although what he has to say about children and how he understands them reflects the dominant view of children and childhood in antiquity, there was a counternarrative, represented by Jesus' own teaching, which was also found in some pagan thought of the time. The counternarrative about children in pagan antiquity is that of pure children, who functioned as conduits to the divine and even guides for rituals and liturgy. This seems to be the model that Jesus points to in his own teaching.

In many ways, our culture today has overreacted to Augustinian views of childhood and education and portrays childhood as filled with innocence and goodness. Augustine might be able to offer us balance in how we raise and educate children. That is, while Augustine turns against a positive view of the spirituality of childhood as taught by Jesus, he also warns against the temptation seen in much modern culture that children ought to be arbiters and judges of their own lives.

On the other hand, without challenging Augustine's views of original sin, it should be noted that his willingness to attribute sinful motives, scheming and conniving, to infant behavior originates in his culture's lack of knowledge about human development. Ancient doctors and moralists looked at development in physical terms and not in terms of emotional, mental, or moral development. Even if they understood that the age of reason was reached at the age of seven, for instance, they did not examine how children were shaped by environment, trauma, or culture, nor did they understand neurocognitive brain development.

Augustine's assessment of infants as sinful schemers overstates the reality. Adults shape children, for good or ill, and one of the most significant ways in which the impact of human sinfulness can be tempered or accentuated is how we discipline and educate our children. Children are born with a propensity to sin, but it was not "only the small stature of a child that you mentioned with approval as a symbol of humility, O Lord our king" (1.19.30), it was the goodness inherent in children, which the adults who bring them into the world, raise and educate them, must cherish as Jesus himself did.

In book 2, Augustine explores the eerie depths of the mystery of iniquity. Saint Louis University's Fr. David Meconi, SJ, sets out to show how an acid joy is somehow contagious and thus habitual to the sinner. Augustine so famously steals those pears one summer night, confessing that they were not at all enticing or alluring. In fact, he had better fruit at home. He was neither hungry nor thinking how some pilfered produce might be to his advantage. He stole the pears simply because he was divided in soul and had fallen in love with his own ruin.

This is the modern malaise we see in so many harmful habits, from the self-harm of cutting and eating disorders to suicide itself. When such is freely taken on out of an unwillingness to be known and to be loved, the divided soul refuses the solace of community and is forced to turn in only on itself. Here, Augustine knew, the broken psyche refuses healing and grows comfortable with the uncomfortable, finding its own destruction somehow pleasing.

The remedy is the Cross. Before that crucified love, the stony heart can finally melt and thus receive the healing for which all stand in need. Augustine learned early on that unless one feels accepted and known and loved for who he or she is, that individual will have no choice but to find solace in his or her own sin. It is an abuse of the self that no one really wants, but often it is all one allows him or herself to have. It is the documentation behind every act of domestic violence: first remove the victim from her support system, friend group, and routine, and then, in that isolation, the hurt can ensue and the bruises can be hidden from the eyes which really care. The pear-tree scene taught Augustine this twisted allure and provided him with an experience with which he came later on to know the power of the Cross.

With book 3, the University of Dallas's Jeffrey S. Lehman turns our attention to Augustine's youthful embrace of the pagan classics. By examining Augustine's reading of Cicero together with its immediate and broader context in book 3, Lehman argues that the *Hortensius* episode reveals the beginnings of a third "way of life" proposed by Augustine, one grounded in an intimate, personal encounter with the triune God who is Truth and Love. Lehman begins by considering the first two books of the *Confessions*, noting how certain passages prepare us for the nascent pedagogy we see developing in book 3. He then examines the *Hortensius* episode within the context of book 3, revealing the close connection between this episode and what precedes and follows it in that book. Finally, he considers the third way as a fruitful contribution to effective pedagogy today.

Book 4 is famously about friendship and grief. Erika Kidd from the University of St. Thomas takes an unusual approach, opening her essay not with Augustine's tender portrait of grief, but with his whole-hearted preoccupation with beauty. Augustine claims in book 4 to be a great lover of beauty. He writes a youthful book in which he explains what makes beautiful things beautiful, and he struggles to understand his attachment to beauty, even as he finds this attachment coming up short. Kidd proposes that Augustine's attachment to beauty frames and illuminates Augustine's book 4 account of his own grief. Augustine is not neutral about that grief; he confesses it, implying it is somehow problematic.

Kidd argues Augustine finds fault with himself not for choosing the wrong object of love, nor for loving creatures too much. Instead, Augustine confesses his failure to love created beauties well. Drawing on Augustine's rich analogy between syllables and creatures, Kidd suggests the meaningfulness of creation emerges out of a joint recognition (Augustine's and God's) of the beauty of what was lost. She concludes that the beauty of creatures is, for Augustine, not a trap nor a distraction, but a revelation, one that invites Augustine into deeper intimacy with God and with the beautiful creatures they both love.

Writing on book 5, Christopher J. Thompson, the Academic Dean of St. Paul Seminary, invites readers to reflect on the broader context of psychological integrity, both in its descriptive and prescriptive modes. Thompson suggests an Augustinian model of identity that adequately "describes" the perduring dissonance of ordinary human experience. Thompson then identifies the "prescriptive" or normative defense of that same identity, narrated from the vantage of the Church's theology of Christ and creation.

James J. O'Donnell says that Augustine's anxieties appear evident on every page of the *Confessions*. With distinctions about the kinds of anxiety known today, Fr. Andrew Hofer, OP, Professor of Theology at the Dominican House of Studies in Washington, D.C., offers "Augustine's Anxiety and Ours." Hofer looks at Augustine's anxiety in book 6, and uses that book as a mirror to reflect to us what we need in our own culture so ridden with anxiety. In the chapter's first part, we see that Augustine features his mother Monica and his spiritual father Ambrose as models of faith for his anxious heart. After comparing his life as orator at the imperial court with a drunken beggar on the streets, he reviews his friendships and lusts in the presence of God, who alone can give rest. In the chapter's second part, we then make explicit something of our own state seen in book 6's mirror: models of faith needed to steady us in turbulent times, comparisons of worldly success and failure in searching for happiness, as well as our friendships and lusts. In the chapter's end, we allow Augustine the bishop to preach to us about the joy of the Lord's presence, a certainty that can overcome our anxiety.

Sight has a particularly pronounced place in book 7. Ave Maria University's Gerald P. Boersma uses book 7 to ask what the gift of sight delivers to Augustine, while also looking into how mortal sight fails. Boersma argues that the liminality of Augustine's state of conversion is expressed in the language of unconsummated vision. He demonstrates that the overwhelming question of book 7, namely, how to understand the nature of the divine substance, is described as a deficient quest to see. With the aid of divine illumination through the mystical vision(s) at Milan, Augustine does receive intellectual clarity about the divine substance. As such, the ecstasy of book 7 highlights the restored sense of spiritual sight. Nevertheless, the vision of Milan is short-lived; Augustine is left dissatisfied, a feeling that underscores the book's liminal character and the inability of sight to deliver, at least in this life, a vision of God. These experiences of book 7 offer substantive cognitive payoff.

Augustine becomes intellectually certain (*certus*) of the faith he received from Monica and Ambrose, and his quest to understand the nature of the divine substance and the origins of evil finds a degree of resolution. At this point, we still await the momentous moral conversation of book 8 and Augustine's entry into the sacramental life of the Catholic Church in book 9, such that the apogee of his autobiography occurs at Ostia with his mother, Monica. As such, the narrative of the *Confessions* presents the vision of Milan as penultimate rather than ultimate. Book 7 has a liminal place in Augustine's conversion; in book 7,

Augustine sees, but in a manner that is incomplete and unsustained. The perspective of faith governs his outlook, but it is a faith that, by his own admission, is as yet unformed. His vision needs to be healed and strengthened, and that is the journey of book 7.

Saint Paul Seminary's Paul Ruff puts Augustine's account of his moral conversion in book 8 into dialogue with the contemporary psychology of transformation, particularly as presented in the phenomenological theory of Diane Fosha. Ruff reviews Fosha's map of the key relational, affective, and cognitive processes that are the drivers and markers of transformation back to our True Self. He overlays this map onto the detailed, dramatic, phenomenon reported in Augustine's account of his conversion process in book 8, showing striking parallels. He compares these dramatic "natural" and "supernatural" processes, noting what they have in common and what might distinguish them from each other. Ruff concludes with a discussion of the importance of Christians being open to and accompanied through the disruptive, tremulous experience of transformative conversion led by the heart. He also highlights the need for the converted to find their place in the body of Christ. Augustine's accounting of integrative, embodied conversion grounded in the community of the body of Christ speaks powerfully to our post-modern, dissociative, atomized, world.

Saint Michael's College's John Peter Kenney, having spent his life studying Augustine's mystical theology, takes book 9 to consider Augustine's autobiographical account of contemplative transcendence in light of contemporary naturalism. Drawing on the work of Charles Taylor, Kenney considers salient characteristics of scientific naturalism, including its commitment to an anti-transcendental account of reality, its representation of the human self as sharply individuated and "buffered," and its commitment to the "objective perspective" of the natural sciences, what Taylor calls the "view from nowhere." The resultant nihilism of this account is then underscored.

That prolegomenon sets the ancient transcendentalism of Augustine into relief. Augustine's *Confessions* attributes his discovery of the very idea of transcendent reality to his reading of ancient Platonism, especially Plotinus. There he discovered a philosophical account of an infinite One, at once transcendent of the material world and ontologically immanent within all finite reality. The human soul must thus be regarded as suffused with the inherent presence of the One. Nor could the soul be a spectator of the infinite. The soul could achieve a kind of knowledge of the One through inner contemplation, recovering and intensifying the interior presence of the divine.

Now the reader is better prepared to understand book 9's "vision at Ostia," where two descriptions of Christian contemplation by Augustine and Monica are simultaneously offered. Each of these texts is reviewed with particular attention to the "participatory" knowledge that these two very different souls achieve. This immediate, interior participation in the reality of divine Word is the foundation of Augustine's commitment to transcendence, understood in Christian terms. The chapter concludes with some final observations on the differences between the nihilism of secular materialism and Augustine's Christian transcendentalism.

When treating Augustine's amazing book 10 on self-identity and the power of recall, Saint Louis University's Hilary Finley considers the role of technology in reshaping human memory, which Augustine depicts throughout the book as the vehicle for Divine communication. In light of the prevalence of technology in modern society, Finley examines the potential diminishing of human openness to Divine communication in two fundamental areas, as technology mimics Divine authority and seems to command human activity: first, in terms of how humans come to know God through meditation on personal experience and knowledge, as Augustine explains, which reflection occurs less frequently as a result of the ubiquitous availability of social media, keeping human activity in a short-term holding pattern; and second, how an abundance of particular technological images are now absorbed by the human brain and become the fodder of human memory, upon which humans then meditate to know God—but the images are fleeting colors on pixels, removed from the natural world, which for centuries has represented more directly the Divine presence in the world.

In "Sacramental Time or the Never-Ending News Feed?," Veronica Roberts Ogle of Assumption University explores Augustine's meditation on time, drawing out its relevance for our age of distraction. Arguing that Augustine endeavors to divest us of our tendency to think about time in terms of a timeline—a spatial metaphor that conceals the true relationship between time and eternity—Roberts Ogle shows how he does this in order to help us rethink the nature of eternity and to rediscover its pull. In brief, Augustine argues, spatial time flattens our horizon so that passing things more easily occupy us and take our attention away from our eschatological goal. By dissolving down to a vanishing point the time that is, Augustine draws the reader's attention to the simultaneous reality and ephemerality of the temporal present, and so makes it possible for that reader to conceive of eternity as the true reality of the present: that which the temporal "now" fails to fully be. In glimpsing the true nature of eternity, Augustine hopes, we give ourselves knowledge that we can constantly recollect, using it to enliven our desire for eternity, and so to persevere on the journey home.

Thus, Augustine's meditation is both philosophically rigorous and pastorally tailored to our fallen state. Deeply aware of our tendency to fall into *distentio*, the state of being pulled apart by fractured desire, he shows us how our attempts to flee this fragmentation by drowning ourselves in distraction is futile. Augustine, in forcing us to sit still, recalls our attention to ourselves and helps us clearly see our true restlessness—and where it points. Roberts Ogle considers the power of this message for contemporary culture and concludes by exploring the use and abuse of social media in its light. By observing that Augustine helps us see that we have, as a society, plunged headlong into time alienated from eternity, the author ends her essay on a note of hope. If Augustine can shows us how we have strayed, he can also show us a way home—through the recovery of sacramental time.

Margaret Blume Freddoso, who comes to the conference from the University of Notre Dame, in her essay covering book 12 develops the metaphysical understanding of contemplation that Augustine sets forth in that penultimate book of the *Confessions*. Contemplation is not some state of absorption into the divine, but rather a soul's anticipatory participation in the realm of the blessed, who freely and perpetually gaze upon eternal Wisdom. Next, Blume Freddoso shows that for Augustine, contemplation cannot be achieved by intellectual or psychological techniques. Throughout the *Confessions*, Augustine reveals that the way to contemplation is daily incorporation into Christ's Body through the sacraments and meditation upon Scripture in communion with the Church, which bears fruit in works of charity. It is the way of a penitent pilgrim who continually confesses his sin, his misery, and his longing to return home, as well as his faith, love, and trust in the Savior who will bring him there.

In the final part of her essay, Blume Freddoso compares Augustinian contemplation to the popular contemporary practice of Centering Prayer. Although Centering Prayer's proponents present it as traditional Christian contemplation transposed into a modern key, she shows that the practice itself is quite different from the practices that constitute the way to Augustinian contemplation. Indeed, in practice, Centering Prayer most closely resembles Transcendental Meditation, which has its roots in a metaphysics directly contrary to the metaphysics of contemplation that Augustine articulates in book 12.

In his analysis of book 13, Joseph Grone, a doctoral candidate at Saint Louis University, considers Augustine's prolonged exegesis of the Hexaemeron as a corrective and remedy to the stark individuality that pervades the modern West. At a time when individuals are increasingly turning away from churches and other religious communities, book 13 offers a vision of human fulfillment which comes only through a communion prepared by God from the very beginning. For Augustine, the creation of the heavens and the earth is also a foreshadowing and preparation for their future re-creation—God not only wills the being of his creatures but also their well-being. Thus, seen in the light of Christ, each creative act in the Genesis 1 account recalls God's redemptive actions through the Church on earth.

Grone begins with Augustine's account of God's creation, restoration, and illumination of rational beings. The goodness which God bestowed in creation was not forfeited as humanity fell into darkness; rather, Augustine suggests, by baptism, God has drawn fallen persons out of darkness to share in his eternal light. Those who have been baptized have been created as spiritual and material members of his Church—the heavens and the earth—who are continually drawn deeper into their union with God. With this introduction, Grone traces the details of Augustine's exegesis, demonstrating his reading of creation as God's work of redeeming fallen humanity through the mystery of Christ's Church. Scripture, sacraments, miracles, the apostles, the preachers of the Word, the saints, the spiritual and material persons on earth, and more find expression in Augustine's reading of Genesis, as each element participates in God's saving activity in time. From here, Grone recounts Augustine's additional commentaries on the commandments and provisions of God's grace, the fruits of virtue, and the exceeding goodness of created things. Finally, Grone describes Augustine's treatment of the seventh day, in which the human is finally able to share in God's eternal rest. This is the rest which the restless heart from the beginning of the *Confessions* is finally able to receive, and it is, Grone emphasizes, only in the dynamics of divine grace in the Church that this rest is able to be found.

Fr. David Vincent Meconi, SJ
Saint Louis University

A Typical Child of the Fifties

John W. Martens

1. Introduction

At the end of book 1 of the *Confessions*, Augustine alludes to Matthew 19:14, writing, "It was only the small stature of a child that you mentioned with approval as a symbol of humility, O Lord our king, when you declared *of such is the kingdom of heaven*" (1.19.30).[1] The Gospel passage in full reads, "Then children were brought to him that he might lay his hands on them and pray. The disciples rebuked them, but Jesus said, 'Let the children come to me, and do not prevent them; for the kingdom of heaven belongs to such as these.' After he placed his hands on them, he went away" (Matt 19:13–15).[2]

Augustine's reference to a "symbol of humility" also suggests another Matthean passage, when "the disciples approached Jesus and said, 'Who is the greatest in the kingdom of heaven?' He called a child over, placed it in their midst, and said, 'Amen, I say to you, unless you turn and become like children, you will not enter the kingdom of heaven. Whoever humbles himself like this child is the greatest in the kingdom of heaven. And whoever receives one child such as this in my name receives me" (Matt 18:1–5). Given that the Bishop of Hippo is a careful and incisive reader of Scripture, this paper is an attempt to

1. All citations of Augustine in English are from Augustine, *The Confessions*, ed. John E. Rotelle, trans. Maria Boulding , WOSA vol. I/1 (Hyde Park, NY: New City Press, 2018).

2. All biblical citations are from *The New American Bible Revised Edition* (New York: Oxford University Press, 2012).

understand why he seemed to miss Jesus' theological point about children, reducing them to little sinners rather than model disciples. In order to understand Augustine's view of children and childhood, we will need to examine ancient Roman views of childhood and compare these, when appropriate, with current views of child development.

2. Models of Childhood

In the Hebrew, Greek, and Latin worlds of antiquity, cultures commonly delineated the ideal stages of human life. People paid careful attention to the physical growth and development of human beings and ordered it by stages marked by specific years of age. Our concern here is only with the stages that separate childhood from adulthood in Roman thought. With respect to the stages of childhood found in the Latin sources,

> According to Roman medical texts a girl reached puberty at the age of fourteen, but according to Roman legal and literary texts a girl could marry at age twelve and boys at age fourteen. These dates align with the second stage of human development recognized in Roman law and thought, that of the *impuberes*, whose limit was reached at twelve for girls and fourteen for boys. Prior to this came the age of the *infans*, literally "the one who does not speak," a child until the age of seven. Reflected in this terminology we find the view that the first period of a person's life is one of basic growth and development, particularly with regard to the child's teeth and thus its capability of using language. Once a child had acquired a basic command of language, the second phase of childhood, or *impuberitia*, was characterized as *pueritia*, from age seven to fourteen. It marked the onset of puberty and the accompanying ability to procreate.[3]

For our purposes we need only examine the stages of the *infans* (Greek *pais*), a child under the age of seven, and the *pueritia* (Greek *hēbē*), a young person from age seven to fourteen. *Infans* and *pueritia* are used to describe Augustine's childhood throughout book 1.

3. Cornelia Horn and John W. Martens, *"Let the Little Children Come to Me": Childhood and Children in Early Christianity* (Washington, DC: Catholic University of America Press, 2009), 15–16. For the stages in Greek thought, see John W. Martens, "Methodology: Who Is a Child and Where Do We Find Children in the Greco-Roman World?" in Julie F. Parker and Sharon Betsworth, eds., *T & T Clark Handbook of Children in the Bible and the Biblical World* (London: T&T Clark, 2019), 223–243. On the six (or five) stages in Augustine's thought, see James Joseph O'Donnell, *Augustine: Confessions,* vol. 2, *Commentary* (Oxford: Clarendon Press, 1992), 52–56. On the fact that actual "adulthood" might be reached for men only in their thirties or forties, see Shaw, "The Family in Late Antiquity: The Experience of Augustine," 40–41.

It is important to stress that the stages of childhood described here, and which Augustine will describe, are based on the types of childhood experienced by freeborn boys with some family wealth or status.[4] There is not a single type of ancient childhood, just as there is not a single type of modern childhood. The kind of childhood one experienced depended on the reality of one's birth. A poor child, an enslaved child, or a female child would have much different stories to tell than Augustine simply by virtue of gender, socioeconomic status, or birth.

Childhood was especially short for enslaved persons, who might begin working at the age of five, but not much longer for poor boys and girls who had to begin work or apprenticeship at much the same age.[5] Girls in general, especially if highborn, left childhood for marriage at a young age.[6] Knowing these stages is helpful in understanding that what Augustine is presenting to us would have been a typical boyhood only for those of a certain class, and it was not the worst childhood the ancient world offered.

2.1. Infancy (Infans)

St. Augustine was born in the 350s, a time of transition from an old to a new world, from the age of antiquity shaped by the Roman Empire and Roman paganism to an age shaped increasingly by Christianity, which was legalized only in the century in which Augustine was born. A new world was struggling to be born, but in terms of child development, child rearing, and education, the old world was alive, healthy, and thriving.

Augustine gives us insight into the ways of this world not only to the extent that he can recall his own childhood but also through his adult observations and knowledge of children. His observations regarding the unworthiness or wretchedness of children and childhood aligns with what we know of Roman antiquity and its understanding of childhood, with one important proviso—there was also a counter-narrative regarding the value of children.[7]

---

4. Horn and Martens, *"Let the Little Children Come to Me,"* 171–173. See Brent D. Shaw, "The Family in Late Antiquity: The Experience of Augustine," in *Past & Present* 115 (May 1987), 8–10 on the upper class nature of Augustine's family.

5. Horn and Martens, "Let the Little Children Come to Me," 166–171.

6. Lauren E. Caldwell, *Roman Girlhood and the Fashioning of Femininity* (Cambridge, UK: Cambridge University Press, 2015), 6.

7. Charles T. Mathewes claims that Augustine is not writing autobiography but *anti-autobiography* in the *Confessions*. Augustine, says Mathewes, wants us to see our lives as unintelligible as our own creations. See Charles T. Mathewes, "Book One: The Presumptuousness of Autobiography and the Paradoxes of Beginning" in Kim Paffenroth and Robert Peter Kennedy

The counter-narrative could be found among Jews, Greeks, and Romans, and most profoundly in Jesus' teaching, that children were connected to God somehow due to their purity, which allowed them to function as conduits to the divine and even guides for rituals and liturgy.[8] For instance,

> religious rites in Athens were a core aspect of family life. Some elements of such rites centered on children, who had specific responsibilities in performing religious rituals. Children not only participated in the rites of the household gods, the gods of the hearth, i.e., the *lares*, but were also seen as mediators between adults and the divine world.[9]

Augustine understandably rejected pagan rites, but the pagan understanding of the closeness of children to the divine aligns with Jesus' teaching on children as model disciples. A number of early Christians of Augustine's age and prior also saw children as exemplars of humility and holiness.[10] It is, therefore, less understandable why Jesus' own sayings about children are ignored by Augustine.

In many ways, our culture today has overreacted against Augustinian views of childhood and education, instead portraying childhood as filled with innocence and goodness, but Augustine might be able to offer us balance in how we raise and educate children. Although Augustine turns against a positive view of the spirituality of childhood as taught by Jesus, he also warns against the temptation seen in much modern culture that children ought to be arbiters and judges of their own lives (especially with respect to education), with adults standing on the sidelines as cheerleaders for childish choices. Such a reconsideration of our cultural views also involves engaging Augustine's theological teaching on the sinfulness of children to consider how that aligns with, or is at odds with, the current understanding of human development of the child.

The beginning of book 1 is concerned with the centrality of remembering

eds. *A Reader's Companion to Augustine's Confessions* (Louisville, KY: Westminster John Knox Press, 2003), 8–9.

8. See Mark Golden, *Children and Childhood in Classical Athens* (Baltimore, MD: Johns Hopkins University Press, 2015), 30–32; Thomas E. J. Wiedemann, *Adults and Children in the Roman Empire* (New Haven, CT: Yale University Press, 1989), 177; and Jenifer Neils, "Children and Greek Religion" in *Coming of Age in Ancient Greece: Images of Childhood from the Classical Past*, eds. Jenifer Neils and John Oakley (New Haven, CT: Yale University Press, 2003), 140–159.

9. Horn and Martens, "Let the Little Children Come to Me," 33.

10. "Inspiration for such a valuation of the monk as spiritually equivalent to the child was provided by the various biblical texts that held up 'becoming like a child' as the goal and ideal of the Christian life (Matt 18:3–4; Mark 10:14–15; 1 Pet 2:1–3)." Horn and Martens, "Let the Little Children Come to Me," 326.

for human beings. Particularly in the context of infancy, Augustine recognizes that to understand his own infancy and personhood, he must either rely on others to remind him or observe infants in his own day.[11] Part of this remembering is cast in Augustine's trying to understand his, and all humanity's, origin from God, and yet not knowing who God is.[12] That lack of knowing, however, is at the same time a lack of self-knowledge. For the infant who has become a man (or woman), there is no remembrance that can bring our infancy back to us. I formulate Augustine's unstated question to be something like, "Who am I if I do not know who I was and will never know?"[13] This is the problem, or reality, of infancy both then and now.

Augustine states that "I do not know where I came from," but he was welcomed ("for so I have been told") by parents who showed him "the tender care of your mercy," including such practical examples as "the comforts of human milk" (1.6.7). This milk came not just from his mother, but from wet nurses who might have been free women hired for the task or enslaved women who resided within the family home.[14] All of this nurture, says Augustine, came from God, but "at that time I knew only how to suck and be deliciously comforted, and how to cry when anything hurt my body, but no more" (1.6.7).

Although Augustine is struggling theologically to make sense of his lost infancy, a modern understanding of human development can aid us in understanding. Whereas his musings about infancy and about our human origin in God are central to the development of his theology—concerning such questions as whether humans have a primordial memory of God, or how infants can have a past if they cannot recollect it—these questions do not account for the needs of evolutionary and biological development.[15] Some of what Augustine ponders about infancy, which does not undermine the significance of his

11. Mathewes, "Book One: The Presumptuousness of Autobiography and the Paradoxes of Beginning," 9.

12. Mathewes, "Book One: The Presumptuousness of Autobiography and the Paradoxes of Beginning," 12.

13. Mathewes, "Book One: The Presumptuousness of Autobiography and the Paradoxes of Beginning," 10–12.

14. Horn and Martens, "Let the Little Children Come to Me," 22; Sandra R. Joshel, "Nurturing the Master's Child: Slavery and the Roman Child Nurse," *Signs* 12.1 (1986), 3–22; Shaw, "The Family in Late Antiquity: The Experience of Augustine," 41–42.

15. Robert J. O'Connell, *St. Augustine's Confessions: The Odyssey of Soul* (New York: Fordham University Press, 1989), 42: "Did we then pre-exist? If so, we have forgotten it; having forgotten it, we resist the thought of counting it part of our life in any sense. Understandable, but the same logic would lead us to deny we were ever infants, yet here we have no doubts whatever."

theological reflection, is better understood at a basic, animal level as necessary for human development.

Infancy is a developmental stage, essential for human brain development and later human flourishing. The infant, overwhelmed by stimuli it cannot comprehend, has been given tools, such as crying, to increase its chances of survival. In this period of intense physical, emotional, and neurocognitive growth, the child learns through basic reflexes, senses, and motor responses to the world around it.[16] In response to environmental stimuli and basic human needs, the infant sucks, grasps, reaches, looks, cries, and listens. About all of this, Augustine admits, "I have been told, and I believe it on the strength of what we see other babies doing, for I do not remember doing it myself" (1.6.8). The theological questions regarding the origin of humanity and our relationship to God are central, but we should not marginalize basic human developmental activities. Yet Augustine's reflections attribute guilt to infant children, each of whom come into the world guilty and whose disordered desires weaken the will. Infants are not just prone to sin, but are actually guilty.[17]

As a result, Augustine is willing to attribute sinful motives, scheming and conniving, for his and all infant behavior. The reason for this goes beyond his view of original sin and originates in his culture's lack of knowledge about human development.[18] It is not that we ought to expect an ancient Piaget or Erikson, for ancient doctors looked at development in physical terms and not in terms of emotional, mental, or moral development.[19] Even if they understood that the age of reason was reached at the age of seven, for instance, they did not examine how children were shaped by environment, trauma, or culture, nor did they understand neurocognitive brain development.[20]

---

16. See John H. Flavell, *The Developmental Psychology of Jean Piaget with a Foreword by Jean Piaget,* The University Series in Psychology (Princeton, NJ: Van Nostrand, 1963), especially chapters three through five.

17. O'Connell, *St. Augustine's Confessions,* 43: "no child is truly innocent therefore. We are not only born but 'conceived' in iniquity."

18. In fairness, modern commentators find Augustine's descriptions of infant motivations and concupiscence convincing. Margaret R. Miles, "Infancy, Parenting, and Nourishment in Augustine's *Confessions,*" in *The Journal of the American Academy of Religion* 50 (1982), 352 says that infants seek "not only the need for necessary nourishment, but fantasies of power over the parents and possession of the nourishing breast (I, 7)."

19. O'Donnell, *Augustine: Confessions,* vol. 2, 44, "an infant is a small adult," that is, children were born as small versions of their adult selves.

20. Though Augustine acknowledges the influence of environment when he discusses a free child and an enslaved child born at different times and in different circumstances, which will certainly lead to different sorts of lives (7.6.8), he does not consider how different expe-

What ancient psychology did not consider is the impact of abuse, trauma, and environment on children. A child was who he or she was by birth—whether enslaved or free—but the impact of what a child experienced in its own life was not factored in to how the child was shaped. Augustine agrees with ancient medical and scientific culture that the adult in totality already exists like a seed in the child, and so Augustine finds it reasonable to attribute to the little child motives, schemes, and sinfulness that one might properly attribute to forty-year-old, eighteen-year-old, or even ten-year-old Augustine. As O'Donnell states, for Augustine the infant is "lacking various powers but experiencing the world just as an adult would. He cannot speak or make his *indignatio* efficacious, but he is capable of all the emotions and the velleities that arise from them. Such a view of the infant is eminently compatible with a doctrine of infant baptism, but is philosophically problematic."[21] More than philosophically problematic, it is wrong from the point of view of child development, as we know from medicine and psychology. Motives, schemes, and actual sins cannot be attributed to the infant Augustine or any infant.

In infancy, the newborn baby until at least eighteen months is learning to regulate itself at a most basic level.[22] As Claire Kopp writes, a child goes through stages of "*neurophysiological modulation, sensorimotor modulation, control, self-control,* and *self-regulation.* The first signifies neurophysiological and reflexive adaptations to the environment, the second denotes sensorimotor adaptations in response to perceptual or motivational cues."[23] Kopp adds that "the third, fourth, and fifth phases represent instances in which children use their cognitive abilities to intentionally control their own behavior with

riences shaped the individual characters of the children in question. See Dietsje D. Jolles and Eveline A Crone, "Training the Developing Brain: A Neurocognitive Perspective," in *Frontiers in Human Neuroscience* 6.76 (9 Apr. 2012), 1–13.

21. O'Donnell, *Augustine: Confessions,* vol. 2, 44. The Roman age of seven was the equivalent of our age six; see Shaw, "The Family in Late Antiquity: The Experience of Augustine," 40.

22. "Self-regulation does not appear spontaneously during childhood; rather, there is a developmental progression from earliest infancy through childhood that gradually results in the ability to voluntarily monitor and modify ongoing behavior." Brian E. Vaughn, Claire B. Kopp and Joanne B. Krakow, "The Emergence and Consolidation of Self-Control from Eighteen to Thirty Months of Age: Normative Trends and Individual Differences" in *Child Development* 55.3 (June 1984), 991. See also Claire B. Kopp, "Antecedents of Self-regulation: A Developmental Perspective," *Developmental Psychology* 18.2 (1982), 199–201; and Claire B. Kopp, "Development in the Early Years: Socialization, Motor Development, and Consciousness" in *Annual Review of Psychology* 62 (2011), 165–87, and Flavell, *Developmental Psychology of Jean Piaget,* 86–108.

23. Kopp, "Antecedents of Self-regulation: A Developmental Perspective," 201.

an awareness of caregiver wishes and expectations," but these developments are achieved only throughout a three-year period of development.[24] Full consciousness, or will, is not available to the infant, because it requires

> young children's ability to describe their own mental states, reveal awareness of their own self-conscious emotions, engage in social interactions and narratives that indicate concern for others, remember their own actions with others, and recognize that what others know and want may differ from what the self knows and wants.[25]

This ability is not available to the young infant. Moreover, for it to arise, developmental growth in the prefrontal cortex is necessary and this follows developmental stages that occur, then as now, on an evolutionary timetable.[26]

Augustine writes that there is no one to remind him of "the sin of [his] infancy," adding,

> (for sin there was: no one is free from sin in your sight, not even an infant whose span of earthly life is but a single day); who can remind me of it? Some little mite who is a tiny child now, in who I might observe conduct I do not remember in myself? What was then my sin at that age? (1.7.11)

He acknowledges that we give up these infantile "habits" he calls sins as we grow up, but since he has never seen "any sensible person throw away good things when clearing out," we cannot suppose the infant's actions were good (1.7.11). Indeed, these are sins according to Augustine because "the only innocent feature in babies is the weakness of their frames; the minds of infants are far from innocent" (1.7.11).

It seems clear that Augustine is here counting an infant's conduct as sinful, not simply encapsulating the propensity to sin, but this forces us to categorize the instinctual desire for life, crying out for milk or comfort, as sinful. This is a state Augustine links with the time spent in his mother's womb, hearkening back to Ps 51:5, and even there "if I was conceived in iniquity, and with sin my mother nourished me in her womb, where, I beg of you, my God, where was I, your servant, ever innocent? Where, Lord, and when?" (1.7.12). For him to describe this time of his life as a "collection" of sin seems, even considering the effects of original sin, a category error in which instinctual natural behaviors are

---

24. Kopp, "Antecedents of Self-regulation: A Developmental Perspective," 201.

25. Kopp, "Development in the Early Years: Socialization, Motor Development, and Consciousness," 177.

26. Kopp, "Development in the Early Years: Socialization, Motor Development, and Consciousness," 177.

made into something that they cannot be in infancy. Infant crying as a means to demand comfort or food is not the product of an individual's sin, but the means by which human infants must make their needs known. This makes normal human development into a strange dark mix of infant sins for Augustine, though he also acknowledges that God "implanted in him all the urges proper to a living creature to ensure his coherence and safety" (1.7.12).

Yet, it also brings us back to the role of memory, which Augustine describes as "the dark blank" (1.7.12). If we cannot remember, how do infant behaviors belong to us? Can they be classified as sin? Or, rather, do they belong to the human process of development? How does memory play into sin? How can one sin without knowledge or memory? These questions, including the question of our origin or pre-existence, make theological sense, but these behaviors also denote the process of human development and growth in which earlier stages, and the achievements of them, are integrated into the developing human being.[27] The notion of original sin gives us theological insight into our alienation from God, and why we are born alienated from God, yet it is not helpful for understanding the earliest stages of child development.[28]

To attribute conscious sins to a nursing infant does not aid us in understanding human development. A child who wants his mother's (or nurse's) breast is responding to the physiological needs of the body. Admittedly, it is hard to know how a breast-feeding infant would nurse in a non-fallen world. Even so, the child's cries tell us not about the rampant will of an infant, but about how infants communicate needs. Augustine explains too much by recourse to personal sin that is better understood as the process of human development. On the other hand, moral behaviors develop quite early in children, as recent research at the Infant Cognition Center at Yale University has demonstrated, and there is no doubt that as children grow, so, too, does the human will and the choices for and against moral behaviors.[29] Augustine can, indeed, remember his sinful boyhood.

2.2. Augustine's Boyhood (Pueritia)
The literal meaning of an *infans* is one who is not able to speak. Augustine's discussion of boyhood (*pueritia*) begins, literally, with the subtitle of the next

27. Flavell, *Developmental Psychology of Jean Piaget*, 202–223.

28. Kopp, "Antecedents of Self-regulation: A Developmental Perspective," 199–214; and Kopp, "Development in the Early Years: Socialization, Motor Development, and Consciousness," 165–87.

29. Links to the research at the Infant Cognition Center are available online at https://campuspress.yale.edu/infantlab/.

section, *Learning to Speak.* Augustine says, "Infancy did not depart, so what happened to it?" (1.8.13). But as Augustine learns to speak, is it true that infancy did not depart? Infancy is subsumed in the development of the boy, whether we call it departure or something else.[30] The reality of emotional, moral, and mental development is the integrated self.[31] For ancient and late antique thinkers, there was little sense that the child was being changed and shaped by how he or she was nurtured, by the child's culture, and by the child's own experiences, neither was there consideration for how the experiences of the infant and the child were integrated into the maturing adult. Such maturity is not simply shaped by genetics, but by all of the experiences a child undergoes.[32] That is, the child is not a fully formed person at birth waiting only to grow into adult stature.

Augustine now became "a boy who could talk" and, by paying attention to what his elders around him said and did with glances, facial expressions and pointing, he "gradually built up a collection of words" (1.8.13). This is a time he can remember, and he presents his memory of his own activities, people's movements, tone of voice, and words, though he adds that he was not yet free since "I was still subject to authority of parents and the guidance of my elders" (1.8.13). Though not directly acknowledging it, he is indeed being shaped and formed by those around him, for good and ill. From his point of view, he looks back and reflects that he was not able to do what he really wants to do. He is not independent, but seeking a true authority.[33]

2.2.1. SCHOOL

It is the lack of independence that most troubles Augustine. He complains that he had to "obey my mentors" by going to school and learning letters and other things so that he could succeed in the world, although he "could see no point in them" (1.9.14). What is particularly grievous for him, and with good reason, is that he "would be beaten," and "was lazy about learning" (1.9.14). What must be kept in mind about this grievous time in Augustine's life is that very few boys would have had this opportunity for learning that he had. Not many boys went to school and fewer girls. Most boys and girls, therefore, would be working at this age, either in the trades they would learn from their fathers, if boys,

---

30. Flavell, *Developmental Psychology of Jean Piaget*, 202.

31. Michael Lewis and Jeanne Brooks-Dunn, *Social Cognition and the Acquisition of Self* (New York: Basic books, 1979).

32. Richard E. Tremblay, Daniel S. Nagin, Jean R. Séguin, Mark Zoccolillo, Philip D. Zelazo, Michel Boivin, Daniel Pérusse and Christa Japel, "Physical Aggression During Early Childhood: Trajectories and Predictors" in *Pediatrics* 114.1 (July 2004): e43–e50.

33. O'Donnell, *Augustine: Confessions*, vol. 2, 59.

and in the domestic arts, particularly weaving, if girls.[34] Another percentage of children, perhaps thirty percent, would be enslaved and their work would have started at a young age, such as 5, 6, or 7, though some slave girls and slave boys were also apprenticed—apprenticeship itself consisting of work, but of a finer variety.[35] This does not diminish Augustine's own suffering at school, with its harsh corporal punishment, but alerts us that the punishments of daily labor for other children and the corporal punishments of slavery, as well as hard work, were shaping the other children in Augustine's world. That is, while many children still experience trauma today, almost every ancient child was shaped and formed by trauma which is no longer imaginable as a part of daily life (neither is it legal) in many parts of the world today.[36] How did this regular trauma affect the growth and development of ancient or late antique children and the development of Augustine's theology?[37]

Corporal punishment was a part of school, yet Augustine knew that this punishment was cruel.[38] Augustine began to pray to God to be freed from such beatings at school, but God did not listen to his prayer "lest by hearing it you might have consigned me to a fool's fate" (1.9.14). Looking back on his pain, therefore, Augustine says that the beatings had value which he could not have known at the time, which must be why the intent of his prayers for release from beatings later seemed to him as a plea for a "fool's fate." These beatings he suffered, however, allow us to ask, what is the value of forming a child with discipline, and what should be the limits of such discipline? This encapsulates the most significant question for this stage of life: what is the best formation for a child? How much discipline is too much?[39] On the one hand, it was understood that children were who they were from infancy, but on the other that

---

34. Horn and Martens, "Let the Little Children Come to Me," 166–173.

35. Horn and Martens, "Let the Little Children Come to Me," 167–171.

36. Horn and Martens, "Let the Little Children Come to Me," 213–251.

37. Horn and Martens, "Let the Little Children Come to Me," 221, 239–250. For some modern studies of the impact of trauma, which are numerous, see Lansford, et al, "Physical Discipline and Children's Adjustment: Cultural Normativeness as a Moderator," 1234–1246; Candice Feiring, Lynn Taska, and Michael Lewis, "Adjustment Following Sexual Abuse Discovery: The Role of Shame and Attributional Style" in *Developmental Psychology* Vol. 38.1 (Jan 2002), 79–92.

38. O'Donnell writes that "such punishment was common and disdain for it conventional." See O'Donnell, *Augustine: Confessions*, vol. 2, 61,

39. Lansford et al acknowledge that how children respond to physical discipline is dependent upon its normativeness in the culture in which it is practiced, but that discipline at some point crosses over into abuse that scars a child. See Lansford et al, "Physical Discipline and Children's Adjustment: Cultural Normativeness as a Moderator," 1244–1246.

they should be held in check by degrees of violence and punishment that every child needed.[40]

Augustine described his elders and even his parents laughing at "my stripes," people who "would not have wished anything bad to happen to me. But bad it was, and very dreadful for me" (1.9.14). Such physical punishment, which the forty-three-year-old Augustine remembered as "dreadful," is, to answer my own question, too much discipline. Augustine begged God not to let him be beaten. In his childish imagination, he thought of God as a "great personage" (1.9.14), but apart from his pleas to God, he was beaten, and his parents only laughed at the torment. He compares it to genuine tortures—racks and hooks—and wonders how his parents could make light of what genuinely terrified him and his peers (1.9.15). In this remembrance, we are finding what today we would call trauma and we ought to look at the education system of this time as creating trauma, of which we now know the long-lasting effects on children through studies of children who experienced war, child refugees, and sexually and physically abused children.[41] Augustine was, by modern terms, a physically abused child.[42]

Still, the question of guidance, discipline, and formation is not fully answered here. Children do need guidance, children do need direction, and children do, at times, need punishment (as do adults, a point Augustine will make also). Augustine says, "All the same we were blameworthy!" (1.9.15). Why? The children did not focus on their studies.[43] Yet, Augustine does not want to let the adults, including himself, off the hook, nor does he want to

40. Shaw outlines the beatings, abuse, and trauma that were at the heart of Augustine's family particularly through the violence of his father Patricius. Although this paper focuses on the violence Augustine endured at school, it should be noted that Patricius beat Monica regularly and others in the household. The relationship between violence and respect was woven into the fabric of his family and deeply embedded in the whole society. See Shaw, "The Family in Late Antiquity," 12–24, 29–32.

41. Kathleen Gallagher Elkins, "Children and the Memory of Traumatic Violence," in *T & T Clark Handbook of Children in the Bible and the Biblical World*, eds. Julie F. Parker and Sharon Betsworth (London: T&T Clark, 2019), 181–197.

42. Lansford, et al, "Physical Discipline and Children's Adjustment: Cultural Normativeness as a Moderator," 1234–1246. On the use of the language of abuse to define the experiences of ancient children, while dealing specifically with sexual abuse, see John W. Martens, "Do Not Sexually Abuse Children: The Language of Early Christian Sexual Ethics," in *Children in Late Ancient Christianity*, eds. Cornelia B. Horn and Robert Phenix (Tubingen: Mohr-Siebeck, 2010), 227–254. See O'Donnell, *Augustine: Confessions*, vol. 2, 62.

43. O'Donnell writes, "It never occurs to him that the child's idleness could be anything but culpable. The right of the teachers to punish this sin, on the other hand, is brought severely into question." See O'Donnell, *Augustine: Confessions*, vol. 2, 64.

forget his abuse: "Are we to assume that any sound judge of the matter would think it right to be beaten because I played ball as a boy?" (1.9.15). Augustine's point is a serious one about discipline for adults too because Augustine says he was only being prepared for an "uglier game" by school, that of worldly success (1.9.15). And it was the same teachers who beat him who were upset by their own petty academic losses.

Children need play, they need study, and they need discipline. The move away from corporal punishment in schools has been important because too often, not just in antiquity, it led to children being hurt and traumatized due to the disorder of their teachers, who themselves needed discipline to control themselves.[44] Our move away from corporal punishment, however, has also led to a move away from any formation or discipline. The "frivolous pursuits of grown-up people" are "business" (1.19.15) and the grown-ups were no better than the children in their desires, except that they had more power and control (1.10.16) and used it, by societal consent, to hurt children.[45] Here one could reflect not only on Jesus' teaching about children as models in Matthew 18 but also on his teachings portraying them as little ones who need to be cared for, as in Matthew 19 and Mark 9. Abuse, whether of children or adults, is one manner in which the effects of original sin are made manifest in the lives of those who are affected. Abuse victims come to believe they "deserve" what happened to them, or that it was "my fault." This is why Augustine can say that he "deserved" this punishment, though it was clearly out of proportion for the good and flourishing of a child, as he knew.[46]

Although he was disobedient to parents and teachers, he was able to "make good use of the lessons my relatives wanted me to learn" as he grew up (1.10.16). But a big part of Augustine's issue with his education, apart from corporal punishment, was that the things he was being prepared for in his culture, especially to view public shows that were basically pornographic displays, were a lot worse than ball games played by little boys.[47] The adults of his day, including parents

---

44. O'Donnell, *Augustine: Confessions*, vol. 2, is correct to say Augustine's education system "was profoundly disordered and ungodly" (64).

45. Mathewes, "Book One: The Presumptuousness of Autobiography and the Paradoxes of Beginning," 21. O'Donnell, *Augustine: Confessions*, vol. 2, 61–63, 84.

46. Shaw says that the link between "the imagery of God the Father, a celestial paternal figure who inflicts terrible punishment only to correct and in a spirit of love" emerges from actual relations between fathers and sons or, more broadly, between fathers and their households. See Shaw, "The Family in Late Antiquity: The Experience of Augustine," 24.

47. O'Donnell, *Augustine: Confessions*, vol. 2, 65–66. Mathewes, "Book One: The Presumptuousness of Autobiography and the Paradoxes of Beginning," 19–21.

and teachers, were "quite prepared to see those children beaten for watching similar shows when it was to the detriment of their study" (1.10.16), but their long-term hope was for their children to be successful enough to mount such shows for the community. The discipline Augustine experienced might have been contradictory, even hypocritical, as well as too severe, but without discipline children's behavior can spiral out of control, as can that of adults. In some form, the discipline of antiquity has something to teach us today, namely, however much children can embody goodness, it is not the whole story, and children need formation.

2.2.2. BAPTISM DEFERRED

Augustine certainly felt that his own education was lacking, not just in terms of what he physically suffered, but in terms of what was absent: teaching about God. This absence was not only at school—for most education still followed a pagan curriculum—but also at home. He had learned about eternal life and "was regularly signed with the cross and given his salt even from the womb of my mother" (1.11.17). The salt was intended to drive out demons on the birth of the child.[48] When Augustine the boy became ill with a fever, he begged to be baptized. His mother did not do it, however, when he recovered from his illness, for "it was held that the guilt of sinful defilement incurred after the laver of baptism was graver and more perilous" (1.11.17). It is worth pondering that the parents of Augustine approved of formation through beatings, but not through baptism.

Deferring baptism not only indicates a broad theological position about sin—that it is necessary to let children sin so not to imperil their eternal life later—but also serves as an early Christian commentary on the limits of transformation through baptism. As much as a theological position, though, it is a commentary on the restlessness and defiance of youth. Augustine's father allowed his mother to raise him in the faith, but Augustine believed that an error was made in not having him baptized. His mother "anticipated" the waves of temptation to come and "thought it better to risk them in the clay from which I would later be molded than in the new-formed man himself" (1.11.18). Better to sin prior to baptism than after baptism since children will inevitably sin.[49] Once again, however, there is no sense of continuity in human development here. Instead, there is a belief that the habitual sins of the youth would not

---

48. On the salt rite, see O'Donnell, *Augustine: Confessions*, vol. 2, 66–68.

49. On infant baptism in the early Church, see Horn and Martens, "*Let the Little Children Come to Me*," 273–291.

shape the newly baptized man but would be put aside after baptism. That each stage of a human life disappears and does not influence the new stage is easily disproved by Augustine's own life.[50]

Yet, as noted earlier, even as Augustine was not being compelled in the faith, he was compelled in his childhood studies. He was forced to study and "the people who forced me were not acting well either, but good accrued to me all the same from you, my God" (1.12.19). At the same time, Augustine says "I learned only under compulsion, and no one is doing right who acts unwillingly, even if what he does is good in itself" (1.12.19). Nevertheless, Augustine sees that God put his education to good use later in his life, even if the intentions of his teachers were not good.[51] He says that he deserved punishment for he was a "great sinner for such a tiny boy" (1.12.19).

Augustine's notion of his boyhood self as a "great sinner" suggests he has taken responsibility for the excesses of unjust punishment imposed on him by his teachers. Unless we understand his point more generally, that all of us in our disobedience to the divine teacher are great sinners, it seems he has projected some measure of childhood blame on the sinfulness done to him. I suspect, though, in light of his view of original sin, Augustine did have this unrealistic view of his childhood sins, and, in light of the physical abuse he suffered, found reasons as to why he was, like the other children, so cruelly treated.[52] The study of children who have been abused finds that it is common for children to attribute abuse to their own behavior.[53]

2.2.3. LATIN AND GREEK STUDIES

Augustine famously hated Greek and loved Latin, something that he has a hard time understanding even as an adult, though he admits that his early lessons in "reading, writing, and arithmetic had been no less boring" than his later study of Greek (1.13.20). Augustine attributes his attitude here to "the sinful, inane pride in my flesh," asking "what other reason could there be" for it (1.13.20)? Sinfulness, perhaps exhibited as stubbornness or laziness, might account for our not doing schoolwork as a child or adult, but is sinfulness behind our preferences? People have talents and abilities that prefer one topic or task more than another, but Augustine alerts us that there might

---

50. Flavell, *Developmental Psychology of Jean Piaget*, 201–203.

51. O'Donnell, *Augustine: Confessions*, vol. 2, 73–75.

52. O'Donnell states that "Augustine's past remains unintelligible to him except as a history of self-will." See *Augustine: Confessions*, vol. 2, 75.

53. Lansford, et al, "Physical Discipline and Children's Adjustment: Cultural Normativeness as a Moderator," 1234–1246.

be another reason as he goes on to reflect upon his learning as a boy prior to attending school.

Augustine finds that the impact of his primary education was better than that of memorizing passages from the *Aeneid*. Basically Augustine sees this as a matter of the superiority of learning skills over giving in to his emotions and weeping over Dido's suicide (1.13.20). His concern over his weeping might be grounded in crying over a pagan text rather than a Christian one. It is not clear if emotion itself was suspect or if properly ordered emotion, such as over his waywardness from God, would have been seen as valid to him: "I put up with myself with never a tear" (1.13.20.).

Education matters in general, but in retrospect it also mattered to Augustine to be taught correctly, by which he means that he was taught subjects that ordered the whole of learning and his life. Augustine attended schools with a pagan curriculum not a Christian one. It is possible that a Christian school would have met with his approval more readily, if he had cried over his sin and waywardness from God not Dido and Aeneas.[54] It raises significant questions, however, about how novels, TV shows, YouTube, video games, and movies teach our children and shape their emotions as well as minds.

Even if he might protest too much about the lack of fittingness of the *Aeneid*, Augustine's complaints take us back to the formative value of education and shaping it according to educational and moral norms in tune with Christian thought. Augustine seems to reject the study of pagan Latin classics outright—"how insane it is to regard these studies as more civilized and rewarding than the elementary lessons in which I learned to read and write" (1.13.21)—but it seems possible that he would approve of a Christian curriculum which ordered his emotions to the highest goods.

When Augustine bemoans having preferred the "frivolous tales," questions about formation are raised. Was it "sin" to prefer those tales to "much more useful attainments" (1.13.22)? I cannot say that was the case, since emotion, imbued with a proper sense of justice and truth, is not inherently bad, and is something that will emerge at this early-teen age at any rate.[55] But this is why it is essential to think seriously about the sort of literature or stories, on the screen or off, which shape our children. And the screens are shaping our children's emotions today.[56]

---

54. On Christian education in the early Church, see Horn and Martens, "*Let the Little Children Come to Me*," 116–159.

55. Flavell, *Developmental Psychology of Jean Piaget*, 203–205, 223.

56. Jim Taylor, "How Technology Is Changing the Way Children Think and Focus," at *Psychology Today* (December 4, 2012), at www.psychologytoday.com/us/blog/the-power-prime/201212/how-technology-is-changing-the-way-children-think-and-focus.

The sin is not found in the preference for compelling tales that shape children's emotions properly, but in adults who do not choose proper tales for their children. Still, Augustine argues, the primary education "is better in every respect" (1.13.22) than "those poetic fantasies."

Augustine then segues to the best way to learn, which was "by paying attention, without any fear or pain at all, amid the cuddles of my nurses, and teasing, and playful, happy laughter" as he learned Latin words (1.14.23). He acknowledges that "the free play of curiosity is a more powerful spur to learning than is fear-ridden coercion" (1.14.23). This sounds rather heavenly, yet Augustine then states that

> in accordance with your laws, O God, coercion checks the free play of curiosity. By your laws it constrains us, from the beatings meted out by your teachers to the ordeals of the martyrs, for in accord with those laws it prescribes for us bitter draughts of salutary discipline to recall us from the venomous pleasure which led us away from you. (1.14.23)

This whole passage, especially in light of the professed joys of learning with pleasure, sounds like a man suffering from trauma within a society that understood harsh discipline as essential to check pleasure.[57] Yet, here, his memory serves to remind us that being taught gently succeeds. Does trauma explain his theological rejection of his fond memories of learning with pleasure?

Kathleen Gallagher Elkins, in her article "Children and the Memory of Traumatic Violence," deals with the concept of trauma as a methodological lens in understanding events in antiquity. She acknowledges that scholars debate the "usefulness and application" of the notion of trauma to the ancient world, asking, "Is it appropriate to use a modern, psychological concept to analyze ancient, pre-psychological texts, events, and figures?"[58] It is a fair question. Gallagher Elkins surveys a number of responses, ranging from scholars who see the inherent validity of understanding the past through the lens of trauma to those who argue against "retrospective diagnoses."[59]

Three reasons lead me to employ the language of trauma. One, Christian theology ought to proclaim the basic integrity of human beings across the ages. Violence and coercion impact people across the ages in fundamentally the same

---

57. On the violent culture embedded in Augustine's home life and the society he lived in, see Shaw, "The Family in Late Antiquity: The Experience of Augustine," 17, 31.

58. Elkins, "Children and the Memory of Traumatic Violence," 184.

59. Elkins, "Children and the Memory of Traumatic Violence," 184.

way.[60] I have argued elsewhere that the Christian neologism *paidophthoreo* ought to be translated as "sexual abuse of children," even though no such terminology existed prior in antiquity, because Christians perceived that *paiderasteo*, the commonly used Greek term for the sexual love of children, did not capture how these forms of sex harmed children.[61] Two, trauma lasts throughout one's lifespan, and the rawness with which Augustine describes these events of violence still affect him as a man over thirty years later. This is in line with the lingering impacts of trauma throughout the life cycle seen today.[62] Three, Augustine remembers his own psychological state after being beaten, and though he may not always remember his past clearly, these events maintain the ring of truth.

Why does Augustine claim that learning must necessarily be coerced by teachers or by God? Because "bitter draughts of salutary discipline" are necessary "to recall us from the venomous pleasure which led us away from you" (1.14.23)? Yet Augustine acknowledges that such bitter draughts led him to pray for release, and God did not answer his prayers, with the result that Augustine strayed further away from God. The bottom line is that there is no need for cruel corporal punishment in learning. Although Augustine might have perceived the hand of God, what he experienced was simply at the hands of fallen human beings. God does not demand such cruelty in teaching and forming children. Bitter punishments just create bitterness. An adult looking back at properly ordered discipline, even if he or she perceived it as cruel at the time, would not recall it in bitterness and pain as Augustine remembered his punishment at school.[63]

As a man, Augustine prayed that God would grow sweeter to him than all of his studies and to let all the things he learned as a boy be useful "to you now Lord" (1.15.24). He is too harsh on his childhood self, and in his view childhood seems to have no inherent value in itself, except as preparation for adulthood. He studiously ignores Jesus' teaching on children as model disciples, worthy

60. On the differences in the impact of physical discipline in different modern cultures, see Lansford, et al, "Physical Discipline and Children's Adjustment: Cultural Normativeness as a Moderator," 1234–1246.

61. John W. Martens, "Do Not Sexually Abuse Children: The Language of Early Christian Sexual Ethics," in *Children in Late Ancient Christianity*, ed. Cornelia B. Horn and Robert Phenix (Tubingen: Mohr-Siebeck, 2010), 227–254.

62. On the impact of trauma across one's life, see Feiring et al, "Adjustment Following Sexual Abuse Discovery," 79–82.

63. Hebrews 12:4–11, though, might be in Augustine's mind as he considers his past punishments, but God's ways are not the ways of human teachers.

in themselves, having value in themselves. Augustine on this issue really is an ancient Roman man: childhood is just preparation, a stage to pass through to adulthood, void of its own value or goodness. He also seems to ignore the fact that play, having fun, enjoying goodness is a sign of God's kingdom as well. Not everything, or everyone, needs "bitter draughts of salutary discipline to recall us from the venomous pleasure which led us away from you" (1.14.23). Children, like adults, learn best with joy.

As a boy, Augustine had to learn about pagan gods and their sexual sins (1.16.25–26), but this does not mean that literature for pleasure in itself is sinful. Although he might be right that "it is simply not true that such words are more conveniently learned from obscene stories of this type" (1.16.26), he did mention earlier how much easier it was to learn Latin as a boy in the midst of pleasure. And in the case of the stories of the gods, if the boys did not learn them, they were caned, yet Augustine acknowledges, "Wretch that I was, I learned these things eagerly and took pleasure in them; and so I was accounted a boy of high promise" (1.16.26). So it seems that Augustine did learn easily and well when pleasure was found in learning—it did work—even if the content was not what a Christian would choose ideally. But dissatisfaction with the content of a classical pagan education, is not an argument against pleasure in learning.

Augustine's learning, though he bemoans it—"What did it profit me, O God, my true life, that my speech was acclaimed above those of my many peers and fellow students?" (1.17.27)—serves him well all through his life. What did it profit him? We might ask, what does it profit us? He wrote the *Confessions* and numerous other classic works based to a large extent on the quality of his education. And that he learned best with pleasure might be kept in mind in terms of our own education of students today. Striving to instill greater joy in learning ought to inform our own educational choices for children. Augustine felt that his educational models were not worthy, focusing more on proper pronunciation of syllables and spelling and "neglecting the eternal rules directed to unending salvation" (1.18.29), yet certainly both can be done in education. One can learn about syllables and to love God.

2.2.4. CHILDISH SINS

Augustine's own childish sins did not allow him to assess properly God's love or the goodness of his education. In the last section of book 1, Augustine describes "the moral standards of the world at whose threshold I lay, a wretched boy" (1.19.30). Augustine was in a "whirlpool of disgraceful conduct," earning disapproval by "the countless lies" by which he deceived the enslaved person who took him to school, as well as his parents and teachers, because he just wanted to play and "gawk at worthless shows" (1.19.30). Was Augustine's sinful behavior really the worst of the worst? This is not to reject Augustine's own categorization of himself as sinful, or to reject his repentance for those sins, only to reject his view of himself as the most wretched of boys. Sin rests in all of us, and it manifests itself in a variety of ways, influenced by how we are raised, the experiences we undergo, as well as by our own character and the processes of moral, emotional, and mental maturity. This includes experiences of trauma.

Augustine says, for instance, of Jesus' teaching on children, that "it was only the small stature of a child that you mentioned with approval as a symbol of humility, O Lord our king" (1.19.30). This is where Augustine is engaged in building a narrative that suits the rhetorical, theological, and perhaps psychological needs of an adult bishop, not a little boy. Jesus presents children as models of the kingdom not due to their height, but because they are models for all disciples in a number of ways, such as humility, vulnerability, and dependence upon God. In fact, Augustine's own *Thanksgiving* at the end of book 1 directs us to the inherent goodness of children, not their perfection, and childhood itself, even his own, when he says, "I would still thank you even if you had not willed me to live beyond boyhood" (1.20.31). Here Augustine gives us access to the goodness of his boyhood—that he was alive, that he experienced the world, that he was being educated, that he did have friends, that he played and enjoyed it. All this came from God: "I thank him for all those good gifts which made me what I was, even as a boy" (1.20.31). This should be the takeaway of his life and should influence his view of childhood in general. It is no different than the inherent goodness of any other stage of life except for the leaps and bounds we make in knowledge, understanding, and human growth and development. How much, we need to consider, did the violence of his boyhood shape his theology when he reflects on his sinfulness and the sinfulness of childhood in general?

Augustine should have been a little gentler on himself—especially in his description and understanding of himself as an infant sinner and as the worst of sinners as a boy—and so should we be on all children with respect to normal human growth and development. We should also, as readers, acknowledge the profound impact that the violence of ancient life had on all children, including Augustine. His harsh assessment of himself as a most sinful boy overstates the reality. It points to the significant role adults have on shaping children though, for good or ill. One of the most significant ways in which the impact of human sinfulness can be tempered or accentuated is how we discipline and educate our children. To the best of our ability, we should seek out the best education possible to form our children, which is not simply a formal education, and we should think seriously about the ways in which they can be deformed. And, taking a cue from Augustine when he remembered learning on the knees of his nurses, children should be allowed to learn with joy, without considering themselves the worst of all sinners and deserving of brutal punishment. Children are born with a propensity to sin, but it was not "only the small stature of a child that you mentioned with approval as a symbol of humility, O Lord our king" (1.19.30), it was the goodness inherent in the child, which the adults who bring them into the world, raise and educate them, must cherish as Jesus himself did.

The Acidic Allure of Self-Loathing

David Vincent Meconi, SJ

Contemporary culture is filled with a prevalent yet undetected sense of self-loathing. We have more than enough and yet hate ourselves for our plenty. We starve ourselves, we cut ourselves, we numb ourselves. We have more data bombarding our senses than ever before, but still chill under the surface. We enjoy thousands of virtual friends but crave for intimacy. This is summed up in so many hints in popular culture. Think, for example, of a line from the country rock band Lady Antebellum and their song "I Need You Now": "Guess I'd rather hurt than feel nothing at all." Or recall the Goo Goo Dolls' "Iris," a chart-topper from years ago, "When everything feels like the movies / Yeah you bleed just to know you're alive . . ." Examples abound in any popular outlet. Think of the old NBC program *30 Rock*. At one point the arrogant CEO Jack Donaghy walks into the darkened office of a depressed and frantic Liz Lemon, superbly played by Tina Fey, and Donaghy smugly inquires, "Lemon, what tragedy happened in your life that you insist upon punishing yourself with all this mediocrity?"[1]

Book 2 of Augustine's *Confessions* knew about this tendency toward self-destruction well before Hollywood and Nashville ever did. Augustine understood sin as an unfathomable self-sabotage that seeks to keep the self at the center of one's own reality: I know that this depravity will not bring me wholeness, but at least it is *my* depravity. The iconic theft of the pears reverberates

---

1. *30 Rock*, season 1, episode 6.

through every sin which results in a type of self-loathing. "I was in love with my own ruin," Augustine recalls, sensing the ironic desire for destruction and disappearance in his malfeasance. Augustine understands the essence of sin to be a freely chosen autonomy and alienation, resulting in the loathing and destruction of self. We sin when we remove ourselves from interpersonal communion and inevitably establish ourselves as our own sovereigns, thereby producing the sort of self each needs to destroy. For Augustine, sin produces internal fragmentation and, as we shall see, the divided will rebels against itself, intent not only on distance from the Good but destruction of any Good that demands the soul's allegiance or speaks of its own deformities. The more I can destroy the beautiful, the better I can feel about my own ugliness.

This contrast between sin as self-alienation and destruction on the one hand, and salvation as relationship and interpersonal communion, helps us make sense of a very serious and important strand of thought running throughout most of Augustine's treatises, letters and homilies. Here he is theologian and pastor, spiritual wisdom figure and humble confidant. He is constantly exhorting his listeners to love themselves by loving Christ. In order to do this, he must first invite us to examine ourselves to see what it is we truly love. In the end, we shall learn from this master of the heart that love is an all-or-nothing affair. For in the end we shall see that we love either God or ourselves, the first being worthy of the name charity, the latter resulting in the pains of hell. These divergent destinies are, however, not some future realities but the choice facing each of us even now: "Do you love the earth? You will be earth. Do you love God? What shall I say? That you will be God? I don't dare to say this on my own. Let us listen to the scriptures. . . . You are gods and sons of the Most High (Ps 82:6)."[2]

But if the choice is so clearly set before us, becoming like God in all perfection or being reduced to that which is moribund and base, why do we continue to snuggle up to that which we know brings only shame and disappointment? Augustine is not too proud to use his own experience to examine this mystery of iniquity, and this commentary on book 2 of his *Confessions* will provide the closest answer Augustine can provide for the mystery of iniquity, why we consciously choose our own ruin.

Accordingly, this paper is divided into four main sections. The first is to take up the context of what John Cavadini calls the metanarrative window unto sin for Augustine, the famous pear-tree scene (2.1–4). Here the stage is being

---

2. St. Augustine, *Homilies on the First Epistle of John* 2.14, trans. Boniface Ramsey, WOSA, vol. I/14 (Hyde Park, NY: New City Press, 2009), 51.

set and Augustine begins to examine his past as a one who is entering adulthood among the timeless trials of the human condition along as well as the demands of a young man growing up in late Christian antiquity. The second section turns to *conf.* 2.5–10 and our author's early acknowledgment that sin is a freely chosen embrace of our own eradication, a way of wishing we simply did not exist. If wholeness is drawing near to God, dissipation is moving far from him and in our sinful actions, we are really telling ourselves it is better if we did not exist. Our third section then goes outside the pages of the *Confessions* to examine the grammar of self-love in Augustine. How do we love ourselves without loving ourselves wrongly? How do we love God yet still love self and neighbor? The fourth and final section looks to the Crucified Christ as the only real antidote to loving oneself wrongly. Only the vulnerable Christ can descend into our own woundedness and make us beautiful, for love always takes the initiative for Augustine, and this crucified and resurrected love alone can quiet our restless hearts.

1. Contextual Prelude (2.1–2.3)

Having left his infancy and boyhood behind, Augustine admits that he is now of the age where it is right and meritorious to "call to mind the foul deeds I committed, those sins of the flesh that corrupted my soul." What prompts him to make this courageous move? It is the love of God that propels him—"not in order to love them, but to love you, my God" (2.1.1). Such confession is the first step in the wholeness now desired, "a coherent account" of his "disintegrated self." This fragmentation is the result of having turned away from God and seeking his own dissolution. Yet this perspicacious adolescent knows that what drives him away from the fullness of life is his own burning hunger to be filled with hell itself, *satiari inferis*. What an irony, what a sad paradox, to hunger for that which starves, to yearn for that which leaves empty. Yet there has to be some allure, there has to be some attraction.

At this time in Augustine's life, all that matters to him is: "only loving and being loved" (2.1.1). Here there is only the thrill of romance and the magnetism of eros. There is no face involved in such love, there is no "other," but only the needed object for Augustine to act out his own "fog of lust." In order to squelch these flames a bit, Augustine rues how no one thought fit to "arrange a marriage" for him, but even here his subjunctive verbs imply that even a wife would not have been able to satisfy his insatiability—"Some bounds might have been set. . ."; "Or again, if I had been able to find tranquility. . ." (2.2.3). Even at this point in his maturation, Augustine was naturally attuned enough to know that sex and children are inextricably related, distinguishing lust from love by the role procreation must play in the latter: "content to use my sexuality to procreate children as your law enjoins." But this invitation seemed repulsive for one so hormonally charged, one "far too impetuous," and even though he retrospectively admits that the Lord was showering him with disappointments and desolations, Augustine refused to change the path he was on, eschewing marriage and pursuing the worldly career for which he was sent to school in the first place.

Providence working the way it does, however, Augustine's life is upturned and he must leave Madaura and return to Thagaste, his father no longer able to afford school fees that year. Here he is placed face-to-face with Patricius, a father whose lack of intellectual care and immersion in the fleshiness of late antiquity is all too obvious. In a scene cringeworthy to most undergraduates, Augustine remembers how his father commented on his naked teenaged body, now showing forth pubic hair and possible tumescence, in the public baths. This "ripening sexuality," as Augustine calls it, strikes many readers as nothing other than an unfortunate memory of an embarrassed pubescent, but it actually proves to be a providential foreshadowing. For the next paternal figure who will see Augustine emerge unclothed from the waters is Ambrose, one who will be presented as his true father in book 6.

The last image Augustine stresses before turning to that notorious night of theft is once again to recall his "various disreputable amours" (2.3.8). This seems to have been a constant, what Augustine calls, a straying (*irem abs te longius*) in that there was no telos, no goal, no real purpose to his dalliances. His heart yearned for wholeness but his hands seemed content with a "dark fog" (*caligo intercludens*) which Augustine knew was cutting him "off from your bright truth, my God, and my sin grew sleek on my excesses." The restlessness of Augustine's heart which so famously opens this volume is now understood as a dis-ease manifested as libidinous unquenchability. Augustine is raging inside prowling like a feral brute seeking satisfaction, if only for a fleeting moment. His life is no more liquid than now, the strength of his youth sensing its inevitable transience. The fragmented self is gasping for fullness, and it will be this very disquiet that leads to a night of carousing with a like-minded group intent on nothing other than the immediate, albeit fleeting, thrill of aliveness.

2. The Pear Tree (2.4–2.10)

Augustine was at least in his young forties when he sat down to compose the *Confessions*. Looking back at his early life, one sin stands out as eerily diabolical. One moment of early dusk weakness still seems to haunt him, the stealing of some measly fruit from a neighboring vineyard. It is no wonder that other thinkers mock him for his overly sensitive scruples or childish fixation on such a seemingly innocuous act. Friedrich Nietzsche, for example, pours forth sorrow for one so emotionally stunted, "Oh this old rhetor! How false he is and how distorted his vision! How I laughed (e.g., about the 'theft' of his youth, basically a student story)."[3] Oliver Wendell Holmes wrote his friend Harold Laski in the same tone, "Rum thing to see a man making a mountain out of robbing a pear tree in his teens."[4]

However, by using 2.4–8 as the narrative window through which we see how Augustine understands sin, this episode becomes much more than just a frozen scrupulosity. This relatively harmless memory continues to haunt our convert not because of the matter at stake, but the motive. It is not the pears that still psychically disturb Augustine, but the reason behind the acid joy experienced in such degradation. Let us now quote at length this pivotal scene of book 2:

> Beyond question, theft is punished by your law, O Lord (Ex 20:15; Dt 5:19), and by the law written in human hearts (Rom 2:14–15), which not even sin itself can erase; for does any thief tolerate being robbed by another thief, even if he is rich and the other is driven by want? I was under no compulsion of need, unless a lack of moral sense can count as need, and a loathing for justice, and a greedy, full-fed love of sin. Yet I wanted to steal, and steal I did. I already had plenty of what I stole, and of much better quality too, and I had no desire to enjoy it when I resolved to steal it. I simply wanted to enjoy the theft for its own sake, and the sin.
>
> Close to our vineyard there was a pear tree laden with fruit. This fruit was not enticing, either in appearance or in flavor. We nasty lads went there to shake down the fruit and carry it off at dead of night, after prolonging our games out of doors until that late hour according to our abominable custom. We took enormous quantities, not to feast on ourselves but perhaps to throw to the pigs; we did eat a few, but that was not our motive: we derived pleasure from the deed simply because it was forbidden.
>
> Look upon my heart, O God, look upon this heart of mine, on which you took pity in its abysmal depths. Enable my heart to tell you now what it was seeking in this action which made me bad for no reason, in which there was no motive for my malice except malice. The malice was loathsome,

3. *Briefwechsel: Kritische Gesamtausgabe*, vol. 3 (Berlin, 1982) 3.34, quoted in Robin Lane Fox, *Augustine: Conversions in Confessions* (New York: Basic Books, 2015), 66.

4. Oliver Wendell Holmes in *Holmes-Laski Letters: The Correspondence of Mr. Justice Holmes and Harold J. Laski, 1916–35*, ed. Mark DeWolfe Howe (Cambridge, MA: Harvard University Press, 1953), 300.

and I loved it. I was in love with my own ruin, in love with decay: not with the thing for which I was falling into decay but with decay itself, for I was depraved in soul, and I leapt down from your strong support into destruction, hungering not for some advantage to be gained by the foul deed, but for the foulness of it. (2.4.9)

Were Nietzsche and Wendell Holmes correct? William Mann calls this section "one of the most philosophically perplexing passages" in all of Augustine's writings.[5] Scott MacDonald similarly pillories this passage as "Augustine's most extreme piece of self-flagellation. He appears to scourge himself mercilessly for what might best be described as a bit of late-night adolescent mischief."[6]

Let us examine this central scene of book 2 with five brief observations. The first is the significance of the tree. In the Christian story, trees and gardens provide the backdrop for all central moments: from Eden, through Calvary, to Mary Magdalene's confusion that the Risen Christ might in fact simply be the gardener (John 20:15). Early on in Augustine's own story, a tree stood as a portal to the Manichean heaven:

> Manicheans believe that trees spring from the semen of demons and are a rich source of particles that have escaped the Kingdom of Light. A Manichean would never pluck their fruit and even if he did so accidentally, he would ask of the Manichean elect to ingest it to release the light. From a Manichean perspective, giving the fruit to an animal ("we did throw some to the pigs") would increase the disgrace of the crime, embedding the goodness of the particles in it in creatures lower in the chain of being than trees.[7]

Is Augustine's focusing our attention on a tree an anti-Manichean move? Is he showing the lowliness of what his former brothers were still honoring? Is it Augustine's way of showing that the battle between good and evil is not to be found in the fruit but in each of our own souls?

Of course, the tree for any Christian thinker is a refraction of the cross of Christ:

> Hence, Adam is the symbol of Christ. They ask: In what way is he the symbol? As Adam became the cause of death for those who are born from him,

5. William E. Mann, *God, Belief, and Perplexity* (Oxford: Oxford University Press, 2016), 27.

6. Scott MacDonald, "Petit Larceny, the Beginning of All Sin: Augustine's Theft of the Pears," *Augustine's Confessions: Critical Essays*, ed. William E. Mann (Lanham, MD: Rowman & Littlefield, 2006), 46.

7. Carl G. Vaught, *The Journey Toward God in Augustine's Confessions*, books I–VI (Albany, NY: SUNY Press, 2003) 55.

though they did not eat from the tree, so Christ has become for those who are born from him, even if they have done nothing righteous, the source of the righteousness which he gave to all of us through the cross.[8]

Second, Augustine's strong recalling that this event occurred at night is not insignificant. Nighttime is a natural opportunity for furtiveness and isolation, the perfect metaphors for Augustine's theology of sin. Our author thus makes sure we all realize that his theft from the pear tree happened in the night. Here he tells God that he has come to imitate the first Adam, who had become "like that servant of yours who fled from his Lord and hid in the shadows" as well (2.6.14). In a very early sermon (c. 391), the young priest preached how

> this life, in fact, should rather be called the shade or shadow of life. Nor is it without significance that Adam the fugitive, after the offense of his sin, hid from the face of the Lord by covering himself with the leaves of trees, which provide dark shady places—like one fleeing his Lord, as it says, and reaching shade.[9]

As we shall see, if sin is understood as separation and the turn away from others and into the self as the epicenter of all, nighttime serves as the perfect medium in which to highlight the essence of heterotelic aversion.

The third observation worth exploring is the imagery and taxonomy of the Prodigal Son from Luke 15 woven into Augustine's own story of wandering. Early in the *Confessions*, Augustine realizes that he too is recalling a story involving a departure from his heavenly Father only to realize that the life he has chosen for himself is ignoble and sordid compared to the glories offered to him in his intended home. This is the goal of the *Confessions* entire, to find one's way back to the Father by first returning to oneself:

> He first returns to himself in order to return to the one from whom he had fallen, in falling from himself. He had fallen from his father, he had fallen from himself. He had gone away from himself to things outside. He comes back to himself and sets off to his father, where he can keep himself in the utmost security.[10]

Augustine again finds himself rejecting that security and consequently reverberating the Prodigal's resistance to sonship, the filiality to which all are called. He instead finds himself in the sty of sin, cavorting with swine and the filth involved in a life apart from the father.

---

8. *c. Jul.* 1.27, Teske, *Answer to the Pelagians* II (WOSA vol. I/24) 286.
9. s. 351.3; Hill, *Sermons* (WOSA vol. III/10), 121.
10. s. 96.2; Hill, *Sermons* (WOSA vol. III/4), 30.

In the secure embrace of their father, however, we children can finally learn the lesson that is the purpose of the pear-tree scene. We cannot love ourselves without loving our own ruin; we can love ourselves only by loving rightly with the love of Christ. For he alone is love and in loving him we are thereby empowered to love self and neighbor truly. This is a hard lesson the prodigals often learn through suffering:

> If your works are not praise offered to God, you are beginning to be in love with yourself, and to join the company of those people whom the apostle predicts, They will be lovers of themselves (2 Tim 3:2). Find no pleasure in yourself, and let him be your delight who made you; because what you find displeasing in yourself is what you yourself brought about in you. . . . Give back to him his own gifts; do not try to snatch a share of your inheritance and go off abroad, there to squander it on harlots and feed pigs.[11]

The harlots and pigs are not nothing, so they are to some degree metaphysically attractive. Every sinner knows it. To find such uncomfortable things comfortable, however, our passions must become twisted and our desire remain fallen, the result of our turning from the Father.

A leap away from God, an imitation of Lucifer himself, a fall from grace, inevitably follows—the fourth point worth examining. Book 2 of the *Confessions* opens, after all, with Augustine's admittance that as an adolescent he could not wait to be filled with the fires of hell (*inferis*), and even relates this confession to the dynamic of a tree and the shadows that inevitably fall from it: "There was a time in adolescence when I was afire to take my fill of hell. I boldly thrust out rank, luxuriant growth in various furtive love affairs [*Exarsi enim aliquando satiari inferis in adulescentia et siluescere ausus sum uariis et umbrosis amoribus*]" (2.1.1). The terms *inferis* (lowly, hellish) *siluescere* (to run wild, woodsy) and *umbrosis* (shadowy, obscure) all capture the themes Augustine uses to advance his narrative of the pear tree. In a similar manner to the modern songs with which we opened, Augustine too knows that to be filled with hell may be a way to be fed but it is no way to be satisfied.

Finally, our author will later admit that this was an act he might not have done if he had been that night all alone. This act of "pear pressure" comes the closest to a reason why this night is memorable at all. Whereas the factors of the tree, of the dark and of the prodigal leap from faith all describe and add context, none of them provide a reason. Can a reason be given for evil? Is there an efficient cause or only one deficient? Even the excuse of wanting to fit in, that

---

11. *en. Ps.* 44.9; Boulding, *Expositions* (WOSA vol. III/16), 289.

youthful impulse to be "part of the gang," is written in a voice most hesitant: "I most certainly would not have done it alone." This confession is the closest we have to an intelligible reason for why this callow adolescent pilfered those pears, but it itself is not an explanation. Community and acting as one of many may have sweetened the crime, but it does not account for it.

To do that, we must step out of this vineyard into other places of growth for Augustine. When we move to his overall theological project, we see that the pear-tree scene is to be understood in terms of, first, a search for the deified life which is built into every human soul for Augustine and, second, how the love of Christ is the only antidote that keeps us from searching for divinization wrongly. As such, let us now turn to these two answers to why the pear tree continued to disturb Augustine's soul, and whom he realized was the sole remedy.

3. The Theological Problem and Solution

Nowhere does Augustine provide a logical and coherent account for his thievery. What he does describe is something much darker, more sinister. It is something quite shocking and scary, to which we can all relate. The self-loathing involved in sin is something Augustine tried to dissect in many ways. What baffled him is how he could be in love with his own ruin, in love with what will only prove to be unlovable. "The malice was loathsome, and I loved it. I was in love with my own ruin, in love with decay: not with the thing for which I was falling into decay but with decay itself, for I was depraved in soul" (2.4.9). What may seem a very extraordinary and even cosmic confusion, this act of loving our own loathsomeness is really behind every sinful thought, word, and deed.

Augustine's way of illuminating this darkness can be examined in three ways. The first is our attempt at finding godliness apart from God. The second lies in our fallen tendency to destroy the good and beautiful, and the third is a form of inverted self-love which results in separation.

Deification of Self. Why do any of us return to the disappointment of our habitual patterns of sin most days? Why too do we do that which we deep down realize will bring only sorrow and shame, disappointment and perhaps even distance between us and those we love? Augustine's answer is rooted in the opening of the Judeo-Christian story: having been made in God's image and likeness, we are made to become like God. It is this thirst for participatory divinity that drives the human psyche, that unrests the human heart. It is therefore the one reality Satan knew he could exploit to tempt us all: you too can be "like God" (Gen 3:5). One cannot be tempted by what one already possesses nor by that about which one has no desire. Becoming godly was thus the one thing Satan knew he could hold out before our first parents.

In Augustine's flow of text, this answer is cursorily given immediately after he catalogs fourteen other more noticeable sins: pride, honor, ferocity, flirtatiousness, stupidity, sloth, luxuriousness, extravagance, greed, envy, anger, timidity, and inordinate sorrow (2.6.13). Underlying all of these confessable delicts is a more primal aversion of the good, namely, a self-divinization which seeks to make oneself whole by keeping oneself at the center of all that is. Augustine thus writes: "All those who wander far away and set themselves up against you are imitating you, but in a perverse way . . . trying to simulate a crippled sort of freedom, attempting a shady parody of omnipotence" (2.6.14).

This answer is not new. Augustine has consistently thought of the first sin, that of pride, as a way of seeking divinity without the divine. It is a safe yet doomed-to-fail attempt at making oneself complete on one's own power. It is an attempt at wholeness without the risk of transparency and vulnerability, seeking not the other but simply the projections of one's own poverties. Having been made in the image and likeness of our Triune Creator, the human person cannot help but seek that same perfection. Yet in our fallenness, we sink back into thinking of God not as a community of other-centered love, but of a potentate whose power is somehow greater than his goodness, and in our concupiscence, that is the perfection we seek:

> What else, after all, is man seeking in all this but to be the one and only, if that were possible, to whom all things are subject, in perverse imitation, that is to say [*peruersa scilicet imitatio*], of almighty God? And to think that he would have submissively to imitate God by living according to his commandments, and he would have all other things made subject to him and would not sink to such baseness as to be afraid of that beastie who wants to have humanity at his beck and call! So then, pride too has a kind of appetite for unity and omnipotence. [*Habet ergo et superbia quemdam appetitum unitatis et omnipotentiae.*][12]

It is a perversion to think that a creature can be the one to whom all things are subject. But it is also the mark of perversion to be attracted to a sort of power disassociated from charity and goodness.

This is the tenebrous power so alluring in the garden that dusky evening. This is the power of alienation in refusing the embrace of another and the intimacy involved in surrender. Having been created *ex nihil*, Augustine portrayed

---

12. *uera rel.* 45.84; Hill, *On True Religion*, as in *On Christian Belief* (WOSA vol. I/8), 87; CCL 32.243.

life as a drama teetering between the fullness of the divine life and the nothingness from which we also come. This is why these pears still gnaw at our author. They stand as a very concrete reality and reminder that every created existent carries traces of both God and nothing. Or, as Oxford's Carol Harrison so insightfully wrote, creatures endowed with the gift of free will are at every moment either moving "towards God or turn[ing] away from him into nothingness."[13] Consequently, in trying to reach for God without God's initiative and grace, the self-divinizing creature falls back into as close to a nothingness a creature can go: "Human beings like God? *O God, who is like you?* Nothing. . . . But as for me, says wretched Adam—and Adam is every one of us—look what became of me when I perversely tried to be like you! I am reduced to crying out to you from my captivity. . . And how did I fall away from you? By seeking in a perverted way to be like you."[14]

Fallen Tendency to Destroy. In this perversion, we are torn between wanting to be like God but also knowing deep down that we never can be. It is an attraction toward a love of which we refuse to think is possible. It is a view of sin as a form of self-sabotage, for us fallen souls who hear the enemy's voice that says we are not worthy of the Father's love, not worthy of care and compassion, and that our infidelities are somehow greater than God's mercy. Such disintegration is one of the sure signs of hatred, of finding ways to make oneself or the other go away. Hatred seeks to obliterate any signs of those we have come to hate. This is precisely what Augustine thinks those who move from vice to vice choose to do: they allow themselves to be fooled that their choices will not result in anything unfortunate and in their immediate success(es) they continue to fall deeper and deeper into a world of deception. Augustine thus continues his gloss on Psalm 129:

> This is what happens to people deeply sunk in sin: they are successful in their wrongdoing, and plunge yet deeper in measure that they regard themselves as lucky. Illusory fortune is in truth a greater misfortune. Then such persons proceed to another argument: "I have let slip the chance to do all the bad things in my power?" This is the attitude adopted by desperate robbers: "If the judge is going to execute me for ten murders in exactly the same ways as for five, or even one, why shouldn't I do whatever I like?" This is what scripture means by the words, *A person devoid of reverence goes deep into sin and is defiant.*[15]

13. Carol Harrison, "Augustine and Religious Experience," *Louvain Studies* 27 (2002): 105.
14. *en. Ps.* 70, exp. 2.6; Boulding, *Expositions* (WOSA vol. III/17), 442–43.
15. *en. Ps.* 129.1; Boulding, *Expositions* (WOSA vol. III/20), 128.

Since I have already sinned, Augustine's pastoral advice senses, what is one more fall, one more binge, one more rush? It is akin to what social psychologists back in the 1980s coined the "Broken Window Theory."

The broken window became a metaphor in 1982 for what psychologists James Wilson and George Kelling argued was the direct link between isolation and destruction. The theory argues that if a window is broken in a given neighborhood or automobile, other destructive actions inevitably not only occur but even explode and proliferate. When brokenness is apparent, perpetrators gain confidence that their actions will go unnoticed and violence increases. Conversely, when no window is broken, no crimes of vandalism are committed. Reporting on the experiments done by Wilson and Kelling, the *Atlantic Monthly* reported this:

> Consider a building with a few broken windows. If the windows are not repaired, the tendency is for vandals to break a few more windows. Eventually, they may even break into the building, and if it's unoccupied, perhaps become squatters or light fires inside. Or consider a pavement. Some litter accumulates. Soon, more litter accumulates. Eventually, people even start leaving bags of refuse from take-out restaurants there or even break into cars.[16]

When feeling invaded and broken, the fallen soul likewise tends to destroy itself through further failings. All traces of that person are henceforth to be removed and we work hard to banish that one from our lives and memories.

In the 1999 film *Fight Club*, men struggling with the sterility of suburbia form a clique centered around brutal beatings and the thrill of carnage. They eventually begin to undertake other senseless acts of violence and vandalism. At one point during an evening bout, a minor character Jack, played by the sad Edward Norton, goes absolutely mad and tears unnecessarily into his opponent's quite handsome face. Ripping Jack off his opponent in shock, Jack's counter-ego, played by Brad Pitt, asks, "Where did you go, Psycho Boy?" To which Jack responded, "I felt like destroying something beautiful." Is that the essence of every sin? The marring of the beautiful, the destruction of the good?

---

16. George L. Kelling and James Q. Wilson, "Broken Windows: The Police and Neighborhood Safety," *The Atlantic Monthly*, March 1982, 31. This phenomenon is also obvious throughout a study by John T. Cacioppo and William Patrick in *Loneliness: Human Nature and the Need for Social Connection* (New York: W.W. Norton & Co., 2008), e.g., "Those who felt depressed withdrew from others and became lonelier over time. So here too was the mechanism of loneliness and depressive symptoms we had postulated, working in opposition to create a pernicious cycle of learned helplessness and passive coping" (90–91).

In those obviously painful years of seething adolescence, Augustine came to hate himself and, consequently, to make himself go away by destroying himself.

> In contrast, the brothers Cain and Abel did not both have the same desires for earthly gains. Nor did the one who killed the other feel envious of his brother because his own dominion would be restricted if they both held rule at once, for Abel did not want to have dominion in the city founded by his brother. Cain's envy was rather the diabolical envy that the evil feel toward the good simply because they are good, while they themselves are evil. For a person's possession of the good is by no means diminished when another comes or continues to share in it. On the contrary, goodness is a possession that spreads out more and more widely insofar as those who share in it are united in undivided love. In fact, anyone who is unwilling to share this possession will find that he does not possess it at all, but the more he is able to love the one who shares in it with him, the greater he will find that his own possession of it becomes.[17]

Only by destroying any good apparent in himself, could he feel better about his own malice. By ruining all the beauty in him, he could more easily cozy up to his own cruelty.

Such sin for Augustine is a way of keeping others—the only source of our healing—at a safe distance. All relationship is risky, and Augustine learned early on that senseless acts of violence, perverted sexuality, and even cruel words were ways he could never be asked to submit truly to another. His sins allowed him to stay at the center of his world and never have to be jeopardized by allowing another to become important to him. As such, Gen 3:5 and the enemy's alluring us to become our own gods reverberates throughout all sin for Augustine, and the recklessness of such divinization extinguishes the demands of closeness. Yet in such extinguishing, a level of shame arises that even Augustine found difficult to articulate.

This particular evening of the pears still burns in Augustine's memory not because of what he did but why he did it. He engaged in this communal act of theft not because of any real reason—he had better fruit at home, he wasn't hungry, and so on—but simply because he loved tasting his own destruction. He commits a crime not for the normal reason—personal conquest, financial gain, long-awaited revenge, sexual satisfaction, or myriad other reasons any of us know all too well. Those kinds of sins are easy to understand, and that is precisely why he brings up the classic cases of Catiline's political intrigue and adultery precisely here (2.5.11). Augustine steals not out of inordinate love of some

---

17. *ciu. Dei* 15.5; trans. William Babcock, *City of God* (WOSA vol. I/7) 2.143.

perceived good, but out of a twisted fascination with evil, and such dissolution raises a very important question in Augustine's mind that he is still wrestling with decades later.

Inverted Self-love and Separation. Reading Augustine's own retrospective on this relatively innocuous act still sends shivers down one's spine: not in need of any fruit, actually possessing better fruit at home, he commits the sinful act of theft simply because he relished the feel of his own ruin. This is the foundational reason for sin as Augustine sees it, a form of self-divinization. Instead of seeking to rely on the one, true God, the sinner attempts to become one's own god. It is the seeking of utter separation, the result of the sinner's fleeing from the God of communion and cohesion, preferring to set him or herself up as a deity teetering upon one's own distortion of divinity. Deep down we may know that we are *not* God, but at least at this moment of maliciousness, I am in control, able to do what I want as I want with no real demands upon me. Ultimately, the theological problem here is one of wrongly aimed self-love. For alone, we cannot find any true rest, and only then do we realize deeply, viscerally, that our "first ruin was caused by love of self" [*Prima hominis perditio, fuit amor sui*].[18]

How does this happen? As Augustine here and many times elsewhere admits, one cannot not love him or herself by him or herself. Self-love is bidirectional, not unilateral. What one must learn to do is not to stalk himself and act against himself by loving himself wrongly. To do this one must learn not only what true love is but also what constitutes proper hatred. The irony in this transition is that to hate oneself rightly is to learn to love oneself in and through the other. Far from masochism, Augustine's call to hate oneself means that one comes to put aside that self who seeks isolation and destruction, that shadowy self which insists on relying on its own powers and asserting itself over all else. This is concupiscence for Augustine, a self-centeredness that replaces the divine as the arbiter and arranger of all reality with our own fictions and poverties. It is the young child who wishes to disappear by covering his eyes: so self-centered, he figures if I cannot see you, there is no way you can see me. That is the self, that self that wants to dominate and divinize itself which Christ tells us we must hate, that is the self the best of the Christian Tradition exhorts followers of Jesus to put aside and die to.

---

18. s. 96.2; Hill, *Sermons* (WOSA vol. III/4) 29–30: "Man's first ruin was caused by love of self. I mean, if he hadn't loved himself, and had put God before himself, he would have wanted always to be subject to God, and he wouldn't have turned away to disregarding God's will and doing his own."

This is how every act of domestic abuse begins: remove someone from communion, lock another up in some psychic or social prison and then insist that this is enough. There is no need for any other communion, no other contact to a world out of the one just constructed. Is this not the opening line documented in every case of domestic abuse? Isolation before destruction: the abuser first controls and cuts off the abused, isolating her from her friends and family, passions, and her heart's desires. The abuser alleges that he alone should be enough, that only he understands her and can thereby determine the reality in which she will now live. Psychic isolation inevitably results in ontological destruction. Seeing this helped me to understand why the internal alienation of the self that Augustine works out at *De Trinitate* 12 leads to questions of self-love and ruin in book 14. For if the memory, intellect and will are not turned fully upon the persons of the Trinity, the self collapses into itself and inevitably tears itself apart by trying to live on that which is not livable, to love that which is not loveable apart from Love himself:

> So the man who knows how to love himself loves God; and the man who does not love God, even though he loves himself, which is innate in him by nature, can still be said quite reasonably to hate himself when he does what is against his own interest, and stalks himself as if he were his own enemy. It is indeed a dreadful derangement that while everyone wants to do himself good, many people do nothing but what is absolutely destructive of themselves. The poet describes a disease of this sort that afflicts dumb animals:
>> Ye gods, for pious men a better lot,
>> this wild derangement for your foes preserve!
>> Their own limbs with unsheathed teeth they tore.[19]

Augustine never wavers from his position that whereas all desire the good for themselves, some have become so malformed, they do not actually realize what that good is. This is the dreadful derangement (*error horrendus*), to confuse self-love with self-destruction, to become one's own rival.

4. The Crucified Love of Christ

What Augustine needs to realize is how God too has become a horror. God too has "become sin" so in his lowliness he can be met by the stumbling sinner. This is why the Son of God empties himself of power and glory, so his lowliness can remedy our conceit and pride. Christian salvation therefore begins with the Son's descent into and assumption of humanity; but on humanity's part, it

---

19. *Trin.* 14.18; Hill, *On the Trinity* (WOSA vol. I/5), 384–85; citing Virgil, *Georgics* 3.513.

begins when the humble come to Christ—not in pretentious power or feigned faultlessness, but precisely in their wounds and ways they have turned away:

> Do you want to please him? You cannot please him as long as you are ugly, but what will you do to become beautiful? First of all, you must find your deformity displeasing, and then you will receive beauty from him whom you hope to please by being beautiful. He who formed you in the beginning will reform you. . . . If in your ugly condition you find yourself repulsive, you are already pleasing to your beautiful bridegroom. . . . What are you to do? Since your ugliness is offensive even to yourself, your first step must be to approach him by confession. . . Begin by admitting your ugliness, the deformity of soul that results from sins and iniquity. Initiate your confession by accusing yourself of this ugliness, for as you confess you become more seemly. And who grants this to you? Who else but he who is fairer than any of humankind?[20]

Naming one's deformities is not easy; it certainly is not in vogue. Yet, for Augustine, naming our depravities is the first step of confession. This can be done well and truly, only before the face of Jesus Christ. To name one's sins without Christ as interlocutor, as merciful priest, is instead to engage in self-loathing and the inevitable continuance of self-destruction. Only in Christ are all called to place our deformities trustfully in Jesus' pierced, bloody hands.

Given today's sensibilities, Augustine's pastoral advice on how to find ourselves displeasing may seem quite insensitive. We must pray to find ourselves displeasing: "Find no pleasure in yourself [*Displice tibi*], and let him be your delight who made you; because what you find displeasing in yourself is what you have yourself brought about in you."[21] When we read this closely, we see that was is "displeasing" is that which I have brought about in myself. This will prove to be Augustine's understanding of the theological anthropology of his later rival Pelagius, to think there is good in any of us which God did not put there. This is how to detect false love of self, to think that I can love myself only by and through myself. True love is ultimately God's nature and therefore, when I say "I love" without God proves in the end to be a perversion:

> "Let him deny himself, if he loves himself." By loving himself, you see, he loses himself; by denying himself, he finds himself. *Whoever loves his soul, he says, let him lose it* (John 12:25). . . . *Whoever loves, let him lose.* It is a painful thing to lose what you love. But from time to time, even the farmer loses what he sows. He brings it out, scatters it, throws it away, buries it. . .

---

20. *en. Ps.* 103, exp. 1.4; Boulding, *Expositions* (WOSA vol. III/19), 110–11.
21. *en. Ps.* 44.9; Boulding, *Expositions* (WOSA vol. III/16), 289.

So that's the meaning of "Let him deny himself"; let him not lose himself by crookedly loving himself [*ne perverse eam amando perdat se*].[22]

Self-denial thus means not destroying the good human person God himself created in his own image and likeness. To deny oneself healthily and whole-heartedly in the Christian tradition means to put away that sniveling self which refuses surrender and intimacy.

In a sermon preached in the same year Bishop Augustine started composing his *Confessions* (397), he used some feast of Catholic martyrs to make this same point. If we attempt to love ourselves by securing ourselves, we shall always miss the mark. We love ourselves only when we surrender to the love of God which in turn is poured into our hearts, transforming each of us into tremendous lovers:

> Where are you now, you that were busy loving yourself? Obviously you're outside. Are you, I'm asking you, are you money? Obviously, after loving yourself by neglecting God, by loving money you have even abandoned yourself. First you have abandoned, and then later on you have destroyed yourself [*Prius deseruisti, postea perdidisti*]. . . . But you do this because by leaving God out of your life and loving yourself, you have also gone away from yourself; and you now value other things, which are outside you, more than yourself. Come back to yourself; but again, turn upward when you've come back to yourself, don't stay in yourself. First come back to yourself from the things outside you, and then give yourself back to the one who made you, and when you were lost sought you, and as a runaway found you, and when you had turned away turned you back to himself. So then, come back to yourself, and go on to the one who made you. . . . That is what denying oneself means.[23]

C.S. Lewis saw this clearly in the theology of Augustine, as only he could do. Reflecting on our saint's sojourn, he ended up writing one of the most powerful and memorable lines in all of his works:

> There is no escape along the lines St. Augustine suggests. Nor along any other lines. There is no safe investment. To love at all is to be vulnerable. Love anything, and your heart will certainly be wrung and possibly broken. If you want to make sure of keeping it intact, you must give your heart to no one, not even to an animal. Wrap it carefully round with hobbies and little luxuries; avoid all entanglements; lock it up safe in the casket or coffin of your selfishness. But in that casket—safe, dark, motionless, airless—it will

---

22. *s.* 330.2; Hill, *Sermons* (WOSA vol. III/9), 186.
23. *s.* 330.3; Hill, *Sermons* (WOSA vol. III/9), 186–87.

change. It will not be broken; it will become unbreakable, impenetrable, irredeemable. The alternative to tragedy, or at least to the risk of tragedy, is damnation. The only place outside of Heaven where you can be perfectly safe from all the dangers and perturbations of love is Hell.[24]

We again see that love is an all or nothing drama: love rightly and it means heaven, whereas loving wrongly means the sad discovery that what one thought was "love" was, in the end, hell.

In recognizing the possibility of an eternal sickness, Augustine hopes the sinner will become the penitent, the worldly master become the humble patient. Only in surrendering to the doctor can our wounds then become healed and whole:

> You are not being told, "Be something less than you are," but "Understand what you are. Understand that you're weak, understand that you are merely human, understand that you are a sinner. Understand that he is the one who justifies, understand that you are defiled." Let the defilement of your heart reveal itself in your confession, and you will belong to Christ's flock. Because the confession of sins is for sure an invitation to the doctor to come and cure, just as the one who in his sickness says, "I am perfectly well, thank you," is not seeking the services of the doctor.[25]

In offering this sort of pastoral counsel, Augustine is sure to advise that we can look at our truest selves only in Christ because each of us is most truly ourselves only there.

This is the beginning of Christian salvation, when believers begin to see not only how humanity and divinity become one in the person of Jesus Christ, but even how they themselves are being offered the grace to become extensions of God's own perfect humanity as the body of Christ on earth:

> Now, however, I wonder if we shouldn't have a look at ourselves, if we shouldn't think about his body, because he is also us [*quia et nos ipse est*]. After all, if we weren't him, this wouldn't be true: *When you did it for one of the least of mine, you did it for me* (Matt 25:40). If we weren't him, this wouldn't be true: *Saul, Saul, why are you persecuting me?* (Acts 9:4). So we too are him, because we are his organs, because we are his body, because he is our head, because the whole Christ is both head and body.[26]

---

24. C.S. Lewis, *The Four Loves* (New York: Harcourt Brace, 1988; first published 1960), 121.

25. *s.* 137.4; Hill, *Sermons* (WOSA vol. III/4), 374.

26. *s.* 133.8; Hill, *Sermons* (WOSA vol. III/4), 338; s. 263A.2; *en. Ps.* 21.3, 40.6.

This is Augustine's *totus Christus*—the "whole Christ"—wherein perfect Love identifies himself with his beloved. Only here do our sins take on their true reality. Apart from the Body of Christ, our sins remain either mere peccadillos over which we hardly fret, or they become nothing other than fissures for further self-harm.

But, in his condescension Christ the Head chooses to see his own weal and woe in the condition of his Body. The central effect salvation in Christ has for creatures is that he now begins to identify himself with those who come to him. Phrases like "we are he" (*nos ipse*) and "we are in him" (*sumus in illo*) signal how intimate such identification is in Augustine's mind: "because in me they are also I" (*quoniam in me etiam ipsi sunt ego*). This is the essence of charity, the essence of the Church where the Lover longs to become so one with the beloved that there is no longer separation or division.

In fact, this union is so real that the persons involved begin to be identified with one another. This is what love does: love always identifies the lover with the beloved, and vice versa. This is the good news of the Christian story and this is precisely what Augustinian sin rejects, the interpersonal and mutual indwelling of humanity and divinity. In no uncertain terms, then, Augustine will rouse his congregants and use the theme of Johannine indwelling to teach them that their Christian life is to become much more than observance and obeyance. It is literally to become another Christ for the world:

> Let us congratulate ourselves then and give thanks for having been made not only Christians but Christ. Do you understand, brothers and sisters, the grace of God upon us; do you grasp that? Be filled with wonder, rejoice and be glad; we have been made Christ. For if he is the head, and we the members, then he and are the whole man. . . . The fullness of Christ, then, is the head and the members. What is that, head and members? Christ and the Church.[27]

Only in this unifying transformation, in this transformative union, can the sinful tendency to destroy ourselves be remedied. Nothing else can satisfy the images and likenesses made for eternal love, made for God. Other objects can allure and seduce, but only God can give the heart the *quies* for which it has been made. Only here can self-harm and self-loathing cease.

27. *Io. eu. tr.* 21.8; Hill, *Homilies on the Gospel of John* (WOSA vol. I/12), 379; also cited in Catechism of the Catholic Church §795.

5. Conclusion

Looking back over the whole of his life, Augustine chooses this scene from his sixteenth year—the stealing of some pears—to show posterity the powerful allure of decay. If this were just the rascally ruse of some bored youths, a carousing evening costing some local farmers a few measly pieces of produce, our author surely would not have given it another moment's thought, but it is still raw in Augustine's memory many decades later.

Midway in his teen years, Augustine commits what most of us today would consider a relatively innocuous act. Yet this still bothers him with such a raw intensity, that decades later he still includes it as the centerpiece of the second chapter of his life's history. To understand why this act gnaws at our author, we have to commit ourselves to how he sees reality—as that which teeters between the fullness of all being—God—and the nothingness from which God created all things. That is, for Augustine, every created existent carries traces of both God and nothing; for created persons gifted with free will, then, the ability to choose the fullness of reality or the utter emptiness of nothing is a constant possibility.

Augustine "derived pleasure from the deed," not because of some benefit gained but, "because it was forbidden." He came to find himself "bad for no reason" (*gratis malus*). Having leapt down from the Lord's strong support into his own self, he reaches the periphery of autonomy, where he longs to be above any restriction or commitment, and here he fell in love. He fell in love not with another, but, as he declares, "I was in love with my own ruin, in love with decay." And whereas every lover is famished, Augustine admits the same sense of craving—not for a beloved, but simply "hungering for . . . foulness itself." The pear-tree scene became symbolic because it represents our desire to choose nothingness itself, to find contentment in the only possible rival to God.

This gnawing persisted from North Africa, up to Rome, and even into Augustine's days in Milan. But there, through the witness and eloquence of members of Christ's body, Augustine came to learn the lesson that God's love was exponentially greater than his sins, that the wounds of Christ were more whole than his own self-imposed lacerations. Here Augustine began to heal. Here we are all invited to see in whatever pear tree we have in our lives, the beginning of wholeness. For when sin and disappointment are allowed to fester, the crevice they create in the human psyche are all too obvious today, in our popular culture and not to mention in our high rates of suicide and depression.

It is the love of the crucified Christ that alone can enter these wounds. Having become ugly in order to restore our beauty, the crucified one woos us simply by hanging on a tree. It is here that the human heart is supposed to melt and open itself up to a love that it could not imagine on any natural level. For on the human level, one is loved only where one is beautiful and strong, successful and agreeable. But what Augustine came to learn on that foggy night of theft was the greatest lesson his Catholic faith could and still does offer: that the spiraling of self-loathing not only ceases but is actually transformed into eternal glory once Jesus Christ is allowed therein.

Augustine's Pedagogy of Presence, Truth, and Love

Jeffrey S. Lehman

One of the most celebrated episodes in Augustine's recollection of his spiritual pilgrimage in *Confessions* is his reading of, and response to, Cicero's *Hortensius*. Reported in the middle of book 3 (3.4.7–8), Cicero's "exhortation to philosophy" proves instrumental in bringing about the first great "conversion" in the narrative of Augustine's return to God. At first glance, the *Hortensius* episode may appear to be principally (if not solely) an *intellectual* conversion that precedes a conversion of will in book 8. Such an interpretation gains credence from the way Augustine describes this encounter as the first stage in a more all-encompassing turning-away from eloquence pursued for the "damnably proud desire to gratify [his] own vanity" (3.4.7) and toward the pursuit of wisdom—not of "this or that school, but . . . wisdom itself, whatever it might be" (3.4.8).

Generally, scholars have identified two schools of thought and practice on the nature and purpose of education in the Western tradition.[1] The rhetorical school, advocated by Isocrates (436–338 BC) and his disciples, centers on the cultivation of the art of rhetoric and the public performance of this art. For the Orator, education's ultimate goal is to prepare students to take their

---

1. For a detailed treatment of these two schools and their interactions throughout the Western tradition, see Bruce A. Kimball's *Orators and Philosophers: A History of the Idea of Liberal Education* (New York: Teachers College Press, 1986).

place as productive and responsible members of society able to engage in public discourse, to take an active part in political deliberation, and to contribute thereby to the good of the regime. The philosophical school, championed by Socrates (ca. 470–399 BC), Plato (ca. 428–348 BC), and their disciples, principally employs the art of dialectic and is focused on rational inquiry. For the Philosopher, the unfettered pursuit of truth (and a whole-hearted embrace of its consequences) is the ultimate purpose of education. There is a strong emphasis in the philosophical school on knowledge *for its own sake*.

Although the differences between the rhetorical and philosophical schools can obviously be overstated, these schools are nonetheless discernably distinct approaches to education within the Western tradition, approaches that typically avail themselves of different texts and different pedagogies in order to educate their students. Augustine's early training in grammar and rhetoric was decidedly within the rhetorical tradition. His reading of Cicero and other authors of rhetorical treatises as well as the speaking exercises and contests he describes are clear evidence of this. Nevertheless, Augustine's journey as recounted in *Confessions* bears witness that as time passed he became more and more influenced by the philosophical tradition. Thus, we could interpret Augustine's response to reading Cicero's *Hortensius* as an intellectual conversion away from the rhetorical tradition and toward the philosophical.[2]

This interpretation has its merits. There is undoubtedly an intellectual turning (albeit imperfect, as we see in the narrative that follows) involved in Augustine's response to reading the *Hortensius*. Even so, to leave it at that is to overlook significant details of the response itself and, moreover, to fail to consider how this response relates to the immediate context of book 3 and the broader context of *Confessions* as a whole. By examining Augustine's reading of Cicero's *Hortensius* together with its immediate and broader context, we find that this episode reveals the beginnings of a third "way of life" proposed by Augustine, one grounded in an intimate, personal encounter with the triune God who is Truth and Love. In what follows, we will begin by considering the

---

2. Incidentally, Cicero himself does not fit tidily into either the rhetorical or the philosophical tradition. Although he no doubt shares the Orator's concern for cultivating the art of rhetoric for the sake of active, informed statesmanship, he also draws generously from authors from the philosophical tradition—especially Plato and Aristotle, but other Greek philosophers as well. One significant fact about Augustine's reading of Cicero's *Hortensius* is that while the work was written by a man steeped in the Roman tradition of rhetoric aimed at participation in political life, the work itself is an exhortation to philosophy. As we will see below, our purpose in delineating key differences between the rhetorical and philosophical schools is in part to show how Augustine integrates elements of these pedagogies into a larger whole.

first two books of *Confessions*, noting how certain passages prepare us for the nascent pedagogy we see developing in book 3. Second, we will consider the *Hortensius* episode within the context of book 3, revealing the close connection between this episode and what precedes and follows it in that book. Finally, we will consider the third way as a fruitful contribution to effective pedagogy today.

1. Books 1 and 2: Intimations of Presence (and Its Lack)

Given our project, the best place to begin is with the opening lines of *Confessions*:

> Great are you, O Lord, and exceedingly worthy of praise; your power is immense, and your wisdom beyond reckoning. And so we humans, who are a due part of your creation, long to praise you—we who carry our mortality about with us, carry the evidence of our sin and with it the proof that you thwart the proud. Yet these humans, due part of your creation as they are, still do long to praise you. You stir us so that praising you may bring us joy, because you have made us and drawn us to yourself, and our heart is unquiet until it rests in you. (1.1.1)

As has often been pointed out, the entirety of Augustine's *Confessions* is a prayer. For Augustine as well as for the Christian tradition generally, prayer is an intimate encounter between persons. Augustine begins his *Confessions* in the presence of God, directing the first words he writes toward God in full-hearted praise: "Great are you, O Lord, and exceedingly worthy of praise; your power is immense, and your wisdom beyond reckoning." In a way, then, *Confessions* begins at the end. Human beings are created by God to praise him for all eternity in his presence. By employing God's own words—quotations from the Book of Psalms, the "prayer book of the Church"—Augustine subtly establishes the priority and the presence of God, a priority and presence that remains in place throughout *Confessions*, orienting and conditioning everything that follows.

Furthermore, these opening lines tellingly introduce human beings in their relation to (and estrangement from) God: whereas God is great, exceedingly worthy of praise, of immense power and incalculable wisdom, human beings are but "a due part of [His] creation" and they "long to praise [Him]." The language of part and whole is crucial to Augustine's understanding of man's place in the created order, as we will see below. For now, it suffices to note that mankind is presented as a part of the whole of creation, and that the whole of creation is completely dependent upon God as Creator.

In addition, this initial depiction of mankind reminds us of our fallen condition: "we who carry our mortality about with us, carry the evidence of our sin and with it the proof that [God] thwart[s] the proud." Although created to offer praise to God—an activity only possible with a certain sort of nature—we human beings "carry our mortality about with us" as "evidence of our sin." Among other things, this mortality involves estrangement from God—a self-imposed exile from His life-giving presence. Nevertheless, these opening lines end on a note of hope: "You stir us so that praising you may bring us joy, because you have made us and drawn us to yourself, and our heart is unquiet until it rests in you." This paragraph is a microcosm of salvation history. Beginning with God as source and origin of all things, Augustine then introduces "[us] humans," the crown of creation made to praise God and yet fallen into sin in general and pride in particular. At last comes the prospect of reconciliation with and rest in God, who is our greatest desire and ultimate end.

As these opening lines indicate, Augustine seeks to render his own life (and human existence generally) intelligible and complete by re-establishing an intimate, personal relationship with God. Whereas Augustine *the author* begins with this conscious act of placing himself (and us readers) in the presence of God, Augustine *the pilgrim* on the journey begins largely oblivious to this divine presence and only comes to realize it in fits and starts along the way. Even so, Augustine the author continually reminds the reader of God's presence and providence throughout Augustine the pilgrim's journey.

After these opening lines, Augustine the author pleads with God to answer his fundamental, pressing questions (1.1.1): "Grant me to know and understand, Lord, which comes first: to call upon you or to praise you? To know you or to call upon you? Must we know you before we can call upon you?"

Augustine wants to know how to begin the journey. How do we go about returning to God? With the help of Sacred Scripture, Augustine resolves to proceed as follows:

> Let me seek you, then, Lord, even while I am calling upon you, and call upon you even as I believe in you; for to us you have indeed been preached. My faith calls upon you, Lord, this faith which is your gift to me, which you have breathed into me through the humanity of your Son and the ministry of your preacher. (1.1.1)

So Augustine will actively seek God, calling upon Him and believing in Him as he does so. And yet, the entire enterprise is grounded in the divine gift of faith. Once again, God takes the initiative. What is more, we begin to see that God delights in dispensing his gifts through mediators—first and foremost, "through the humanity of [the] Son" but also through "the ministry of [the] preacher." The implication, it would appear, is that there is an unbroken line of mediators running from Jesus Christ, through the Apostles, and then through "generations" of bishops—all the way to Augustine's spiritual father, Bishop Ambrose of Milan, through whose preaching Augustine was finally able to receive the Gospel wholeheartedly.[3]

The theme of divine gift introduced in the first chapter of book 1 is a constant reminder of God's presence throughout the narrative of Augustine's *Confessions*. Three fundamental gifts are emphasized in book 1: existence, life, and experience.[4] In the final chapter of the book, Augustine gives thanks to God for his boyhood. If God had not willed that he should live beyond boyhood, Augustine remarks, "Even then I existed, I lived, and I experienced" (1.20.31).

Augustine then offers a brief recapitulation of his life as a boy and concludes with a prayer in verse, thanking God for these abundant gifts and accusing himself of failing to receive them as such at the time:

> I did not endow myself with [these gifts], but they are good, and together they make me what I am. He who made me is good, and he is my good too; rejoicing, I thank him for all those good gifts which made me what I was, even as a boy. In this lay my sin, that not in him was I seeking pleasures, distinctions and truth, but in myself and the rest of his creatures, and so I fell headlong into pains, confusions and errors. (1.20.31)

---

3. There are other possibilities regarding the identity of the "preacher" (*praediactoris*), the most obvious being Christ himself or the Apostle Paul, whose Epistle to the Romans (esp. 13:13–14) was so instrumental to Augustine's dramatic conversion in the garden in Milan (*conf.* 8.12.29 ff.). Given the way in which Augustine writes his *Confessions*, often intending more than one meaning in any given word or phrase, it is quite possible that he means for the reader to think of all three of these preachers as an unfolding of the Christian faith handed down through faithful preaching of the Gospel.

4. Augustine presents existence and life as gifts of God at 1.6.10. In chapter 7, speaking of God's gifts to himself as an infant (and by extension, to all infants) Augustine prays,

> Your will is that I should praise you, O Lord my God, who gave life and a body to that infant; you will me to praise you who equipped him with faculties, built up his limbs, and adorned him with a distinctive shape. . . . None but yourself, the only God, can bring [these gifts] into existence. From you derives all manner of being, O God most beautiful, who endow all things with their beautiful form and by your governance direct them in their due order. (1.7.12)

He also repeatedly refers to God as his "life" (1.4.4; 1.17.27).

Significantly, Augustine's sin involves a turning away from God, the giver of all good gifts[5], and toward himself and the rest of creation. Casting his own turning away from God (and return to him) in terms of the Parable of the Prodigal Son (Luke 15:11–32), earlier in book 1 Augustine explains:

> Not with our feet or by traversing great distances do we journey away from you or find our way back. That younger son of yours in the gospel did not hire horses or carriages, nor did he board ships, nor take wing in any visible sense nor put one foot before the other when he journeyed to that far country where he could squander at will the wealth you, his gentle father, had given him at his departure. Gentle you were then, but gentler still with him when he returned in his need. No, to be estranged in a spirit of lust, and lost in darkness, that is what it means to be far away from your face. (1.18.28)

Thus Augustine removes himself from God's presence by turning his heart ("in a spirit of lust") and his mind ("lost in darkness") away from God in proud, "self-sufficient" ingratitude.

Throughout books 1 and 2 as he seeks God's presence and providence in the events of his past life, Augustine has many severe things to say regarding human custom in general and his formal education in particular. "Woe, woe to you, you flood of human custom! Who can keep his footing against you? Will you never run dry?" (1.16.25). Augustine presents his education as a significant part of this "flood." When preparing to describe his early schooling, he recalls, "I waded deeper into the stormy world of human life" (1.8.13). At the time, neither Augustine's parents nor his teachers sought anything in his education beyond the attainment of worldly success: "The program for right living presented to me as a boy was that I must obey my mentors, so that I might get on in this world and excel in the skills of the tongue, skills which lead to high repute and deceitful riches" (1.9.14). The young Augustine came to view education in much the same way. When he was lazy or distracted in his studies, Augustine was beaten; nevertheless he finds fault with himself and his fellow students, regardless of the dubious intentions and actions of their parents and teachers: "All the same, we were blameworthy, because we were less assiduous in reading, writing and concentrating on our studies than was expected of us" (1.9.15).

---

5. The theme of God as the source of all good things runs throughout book 1. For instance, in speaking of the gift of milk received from the breasts of his mother and nurses, Augustine says, "It was a bounty for them, and a bounty for me from them; or, rather, not from them but only through them, for in truth all good things are from you, O God. Everything I need for health and salvation flows from my God. This I learned later as you cried the truth aloud to me through all you give me, both within and without" (1.6.7).

Furthermore, although Augustine's education was part and parcel of the turbulent waters ever drawing him away from God, the fundamental content of his education was good; words were certainly abused in many of the school exercises, but such abuse by no means invalidated their proper use: "I am blaming not the words, which are finely-wrought, precious vessels, but the wine of error mixed for us in them by teachers who are drunk themselves" (1.16.26). In fact, though Augustine did not perceive it at the time, God's providential presence was achieving it purposes, in spite of the waywardness of Augustine and his teachers: "I learned only under compulsion, and no one is doing right who acts unwillingly, even if what he does is good in itself. The people who forced me on were not acting well either, but good accrued to me all the same from you, my God" (1.12.19).

In hindsight, Augustine is able to discern the good accomplished through his early education:

> Those early lessons in literacy were unquestionably more profitable because more dependable; by means of them I was gradually being given a power which became mine and still remains with me: the power to read any piece of writing I come across and to write anything I have a mind to myself. (1.13.20)

Augustine's retrospective assessment of his early education is one instance of an attitude toward education that we see expanded and refined in the books that follow. It is not education *as such* that Augustine criticizes; instead, what he finds reprehensible is the misunderstanding and misuse of education that treats it only as an instrument to "get ahead" in this mortal life.

Among the central themes of book 2 are love and friendship, or perhaps more accurately, illicit love and "unfriendly" friendship. In this book, the gap between Augustine the author and Augustine the pilgrim grows ever wider as the prodigal son wanders farther away from his Father and his fatherland. In the opening lines Augustine clarifies his authorial intentions: "Now I want to call to mind the foul deeds I committed, those sins of the flesh that corrupted my soul, not in order to love them, but to love you, my God" (2.1.1). As Augustine points out, his task is fraught with difficulty: "I will try now to give a coherent account of my disintegrated self, for when I turned away from you, the one God, and pursued a multitude of things, I went to pieces" (2.1.1).

How is a coherent account of a being disintegrated by sin possible? Augustine does the best he can by identifying his disordered loves and revealing where they lead him:

> What was it that delighted me? Only loving and being loved. But there was no proper restraint, as in the union of mind with mind, where a bright

boundary regulates friendship. From the mud of my fleshly desires and my erupting puberty belched out murky clouds that obscured and darkened my heart until I could not distinguish the calm light of love from the fog of lust. (2.2.2)

Unable to tell love from lust, Augustine meanders aimlessly as God looks on, apparently in silence: "I was wandering away from you, yet you let me go my way. I was flung hither and thither, I poured myself out, frothed and floundered in the tumultuous sea of my fornications; and you were silent" (2.2.2).

The torrents of human custom continue to have their influence on Augustine the pilgrim, but here in book 2 Augustine the author assigns more and more responsibility for his plight to himself: "I was far too impetuous, poor wretch, so I went with the flood-tide of my nature and abandoned you" (2.2.4). Yes, he tells us, "the frenzy of lust imposed its rule on me," but "I wholeheartedly yielded to it" (2.2.4).

When he was sixteen years old, Augustine's formal studies were interrupted due to his parents' lack of funds. During this period of idleness, the seeds of rebellion planted earlier in Augustine's mind and heart grew unchecked: "The thorn-bushes of my lust shot up higher than my head, and no hand was there to root them out" (2.3.6). As Augustine the author interprets the words and deeds of his parents at the time, neither has a consistent concern for his spiritual well-being. He relates an incident with his father while at the public baths: "When at the baths one day he saw me with unquiet adolescence, my only covering, and noted my ripening sexuality, he began at once to look forward eagerly to grandchildren, and gleefully announced his discovery to my mother" (2.3.6).[6] Augustine interprets his father's response as completely this-worldly: "His glee sprang from that intoxication which has blotted you, our creator, out of this world's memory and led it to love the creature instead, as it drinks the unseen wine of perverse inclination and is dragged down to the depths" (2.3.6). His mother's response, on the other hand, reveals a genuine concern for the state of his soul.

In retrospect, Augustine the author sees in his mother's words of maternal caution a warning from God himself (2.3.7). Even so, when she was made aware of Augustine's sexual sins, she "warned [him] to live chastely, but did not extend her care to restraining [Augustine's behavior] within the bounds of conjugal love . . . even though she judged it to be corrupt already and likely to be dangerous in the future" (2.3.8). In addition, at that time both of Augustine's

---

6. Augustine's "unquiet adolescence" here is no doubt meant to call to mind the "unquiet heart" from the opening lines of book 1.

parents were still insistent that their son make progress in his rhetorical studies for the sake of worldly success—"my father, because he thought next to nothing about you and only vain things about me; and my mother, because she regarded the customary course of studies as no hindrance, and even a considerable help, toward gaining you eventually" (2.3.8). On the whole, then, Augustine was either harmed or at best not helped by his parents in his struggles with various sins.

Whereas the first half of book 2 focuses principally on Augustine's sexual sins, the pear-tree episode in the latter half serves as an occasion for Augustine to reflect upon sin in general.[7] Obviously intended to remind the reader of the account of mankind's fall in Genesis 3, Augustine analyzes his theft of a neighbor's pears with comrades from a number of different vantage points. Along the way, he presents this sin—and *all* sin—as fornication against God, who is the true Lover of our souls:

> A soul that turns away from you therefore lapses into fornication when it seeks apart from you what it can never find in pure and limpid form except by returning to you. All those who wander far away and set themselves up against you are imitating you, but in a perverse way; yet by this very mimicry they proclaim that you are the creator of the whole of nature, and that in consequence there is no place whatever where we can hide from your presence. . . . Was I, in truth a prisoner, trying to simulate a crippled sort of freedom, attempting a shady parody of omnipotence by getting away with something forbidden? How like that servant of yours who fled from his Lord and hid in the shadows! (2.6.14)

Notice yet again the language of presence. Here, all sin is depicted as fornication—an illicit turning toward created things and uniting of oneself to them, which simultaneously involves a turning-away from the soul's one true love, God himself. References and allusions to clouds, shade, and shadows permeate book 2. Although the unfaithful soul attempts to cover itself, thereby ironically obscuring its own vision, nothing hides it from God's penetrating, loving gaze. But whereas the soul cannot truly flee from God's presence, it can nevertheless fracture itself by pouring itself out in disparate, disordered loves. A prisoner of its own unruly desires, the best it can achieve is "a crippled sort of freedom,

---

7. Kim Paffenroth relates the pear-tree episode to Augustine's general disgust at his own education and how he went on to educate others before his conversion. See Kim Paffenroth, "Bad Habits and Bad Company: Education and Evil in the *Confessions*," in Kim Paffenroth and Kevin L. Hughes, eds., *Augustine and Liberal Education* (Lanham, MD: Lexington Books, 2008), 3–14. In what follows, I in no way intend to deny Paffenroth's general thesis; instead, I am simply drawing out the particular aspect of presence.

attempting a shady parody of omnipotence." In doing so, the wandering soul merely repeats the foolish pride of Adam. And insofar as such souls band together in rebellion against God, the greatest unity they can hope to attain is the "unfriendly friendship" of co-conspirators who roam the streets of "Babylon," the biblical symbol of the City of Man devoted to a lust for power. Book 2 ends with another allusion to the Parable of the Prodigal Son: "I slid away from you and wandered away, my God; far from your steadfastness I strayed in adolescence, and I became to myself a land of famine" (2.10.18).

In summary, we find in books I and II the constant loving presence of God and Augustine's ever-increasing attempt to flee from that presence. Although God is the giver of all good gifts, Augustine, rather than turning to him in thanks and praise, turns to himself and other creatures to try to fill the void. A fornicating soul who pours himself out in false loves, he finds that even friendship itself proves unfriendly. Augustine is in shadowy darkness, wandering far from God and becoming ever more miserable and starved for truth and love in the process. Since his revolt involves a turning away of both mind and heart from God, his return must necessarily involve a conversion of mind and heart. This observation prepares us for an examination of book 3.

2. The *Hortensius* Episode and Book 3

For anyone reading book 2 for the first time, the *Hortensius* episode is hardly what one would expect to follow, given the opening lines of the book:

> So I arrived at Carthage, where the din of scandalous love-affairs raged cauldron-like around me. I was not yet in love, but I was enamored with the idea of love, and so deep within me was my need that I hated myself for the sluggishness of my desires. In love with loving, I was casting about for something to love; the security of a way of life free from pitfalls seemed abhorrent to me, because I was inwardly starved of that food which is yourself, O my God. (3.1.1)

As Augustine continues to expand on the theme of illicit loves, at first it appears that book 3 will simply pick up where book 2 left off. There is indeed continuity between books 2 and 3, but in the latter Augustine takes the notion of illicit loves to a higher plane. Rather than dwelling further on disordered bodily loves (as these opening lines might suggest), after the first chapter Augustine proceeds to examine disordered loves related to the soul and its powers.[8] In

---

8. In a way, this move was anticipated in book 2 by Augustine's treatment of disordered friendships. There, however, Augustine's relationships never rise to the level of genuine friend-

addition, he mentions a "way of life free from pitfalls," thereby introducing key questions of the book: What way of life will Augustine choose, and why? He also reminds us of his spiritual hunger mentioned in the final lines of book 2.

Augustine employs the metaphor of inner hunger extensively in book 3; in the passage just quoted, he looks longingly toward his true food, God himself. For the time being, though, his spiritual hunger remains unsatisfied. Strangely, Augustine says, unlike bodily hunger "this inner famine created no pangs of hunger in me. I had no desire for the food that does not perish, not because I had my fill of it, but because the more empty I was, the more I turned from it in revulsion" (3.1.1).

Another theme that comes out in the first chapter is superficiality, often expressed by describing deep, spiritual realities as if they were superficial, bodily ones: "My soul's health was consequently poor. It was covered with sores and flung itself out of doors, longing to soothe its misery by rubbing against sensible things; yet these were soulless, and so could not truly be loved" (3.1.1). Among other things, this flinging of Augustine's own soul "out of doors" involved sexual sin whose only end was to "enjoy a lover's body" (3.1.1); but even these sins of the flesh were rooted in something deeper: "All the while, befouled and disgraced though I was, my boundless vanity made me long to appear elegant and sophisticated" (3.1.1). The Augustine of book 3 lives life on the surface, vainly concerned with appearances and without a care for deeper wounds that keep him in a state of misery. Bearing Augustine's then-current superficiality in mind sheds light on several of the episodes found in this book.

Significantly, the first topic that Augustine addresses in detail is his craving for theatrical shows. "I was spellbound by theatrical shows full of images that mirrored my own wretched plight and further fueled the fire within me" (3.2.2). This introduces another thread running through the book—namely, what one "sees" and the way in which one "sees" it. Augustine soon makes this explicit:

> In the capacity of spectator one welcomes sad feelings; in fact, the sadness itself is the pleasure. What incredible stupidity! The more a person is buffeted by such passions in his own life, the more he is moved by watching similar scenes on stage, although his state of mind is usually called misery when he is undergoing them himself and mercy when he shows compassion for others so afflicted. But how real is the mercy evoked by fictional dramas?

ship. Rather than leading him to higher things, these "friends" left him more deeply bound to worldly cares and preoccupations. For a similar reading of book 3 as moving from bodily loves to something more spiritual, see Todd Breyfogle, "Book Three: 'No Changing Nor Shadow,'" in Kim Paffenroth and Robert P. Kennedy, eds., *A Reader's Companion to Augustine's Confessions* (Louisville, KY: Westminster John Knox Press, 2003), 35–52.

The listener is not moved to offer help, but merely invited to feel sorrow; and the more intensely he feels it the more highly he rates the actor in the play. (3.2.2)

It is easy to misunderstand Augustine's critique here. Some readers are initially inclined to view it as a crotchety condemnation of theater as such. Actually, Augustine's principal concern is with the spectator (the one "looking on") and how he or she responds to the theatrical performance—what one "sees" and the influence it has on one's way of living after the spectacle. The problem is that all too easily, one can view theatrical shows in such a way as to immerse oneself in one's own emotions and to insulate oneself artificially from a real, compassionate response to those truly in misery. By becoming completely and habitually invested as a spectator in such theatrical fictions, "keenly attentive" and bent on "enjoy[ing] a good cry" (3.2.2), one begins to dissociate one's emotions from genuine affective responses to real people in actual need. Although this danger may seem remote and far-fetched, in fact it is not. Now perhaps more than ever, our culture is glutted with various forms of entertainment that provide just such an emotional escape from reality that encourages us to sever our affective responses from real-world suffering.

Augustine explains further,

Even today I am not devoid of merciful sensibility, but at that time it was different; I rejoiced with lovers on the stage who took sinful pleasure in one another, even though their adventures were only imaginary and part of a dramatic presentation, and when they lost each other I grieved with them, ostensibly merciful; yet in both instances I found pleasure in my emotions. Today I feel greater pity for someone who takes delight in a sinful deed than for someone else who seems to suffer grievously at the loss of pernicious pleasure and the passing of a bliss that was in fact nothing but misery. (3.2.3)

The young Augustine's emotional responses to the lovers' situation onstage—first joy, then grief—are of course not directed to anything real. As a spectator, he has no true joy and no true grief (or mercy) for a fictional character undergoing dramatic "pleasure" or "pain." In both cases Augustine turns inward and is preoccupied with his own emotions, not with any proper response to instances of real joy or suffering in the world. Furthermore, insofar as these ersatz emotions arise in Augustine's soul, they are not the appropriate responses to what would have been actually good and actually evil, had the characters been engaged in the joys and sufferings of real life.

Ironically, Augustine continues, "At that time I was truly miserable, for I loved feeling sad and sought whatever could cause me sadness. . . . Such doleful tales being told enabled me superficially to scrape away at my itching self, with the result that these raking nails raised an inflamed swelling and drew stinking discharge from a festering wound" (3.2.4). All the while that Augustine looks upon such spectacles, engrossed in his emotions and yet unaware of his deplorable state of soul, God is looking down upon Augustine with merciful compassion: "Far above me your faithful mercy was hovering" (3.3.5). Thus, at the same time that Augustine looks upon theatrical performances, unable to see his own true suffering yet enamored with a false sense of mercy toward fictional characters, Augustine's heavenly Father mercifully looks upon Augustine in his true misery, ready to come to Augustine's assistance.[9] Nevertheless, Augustine follows the lead of his own "impious curiosity," going so far as to "indulge in carnal desire and conduct" within a church (3.3.5), in the sight of God and his faithful ones.

Having given his emotions free rein, becoming a spectator even of his own experiences and the other persons involved in them, Augustine has no qualms with objectifying another to enjoy her body. "I withdrew further and further from you, loving my own ways and not yours, relishing the freedom of a runaway slave" (3.3.5). He presents himself as a fugitive, on the run from a loving God as well as on the run from a loving comportment toward those persons around him.

The next brief episode mentioned by Augustine is his reaction to the "wreckers"—a group of fellow-students of rhetoric "whose perverse and diabolical nickname is almost a badge of good education" (3.3.6). Augustine's attitude toward them is deeply ambivalent. The passage opens with Augustine accusing himself:

> The prestigious course of studies I was following looked as its goal to the law-courts, in which I was destined to excel and where I would earn a reputation all the higher in the measure that my performance was the more unscrupulous. So blind can people be that they glory even in their blindness! Already I was the ablest student in the school of rhetoric. At this I was elated and vain and swollen with pride. (3.3.6)

9. Book 3 ends with an echo of this divinely illumined perspective by pointing out the way that Augustine's mother, Monica, looks upon her wayward son. Strikingly, Augustine describes his mother as "[regarding him] as dead" (3.11.19). As Monica weeps over her "dead" son, she receives consolation through a dream in which she is told "to take good heed and see that where she stood, there also stood I [Augustine]" (3.11.19). At the end of this book, then, Monica's perspective is presented as an image of the divine perspective, one that will ultimately enable Augustine to see through the vanity of Manichean doctrine and lovingly embrace the truth of the Catholic faith.

Although these fellow-students had a "perverse and diabolical nickname," Augustine—himself "elated and vain and swollen with pride"—"associated with them and sometimes enjoyed friendly contacts" (3.3.6). Even so, he could not bring himself to participate in their acts of torment: "They would chase sensitive freshmen relentlessly, taunting and hounding them on no provocation, simply for their own malicious amusement" (3.3.6). Although Augustine detests their diabolical behavior, he nevertheless fraternizes with them, "ashamed of the sense of shame that held [him] back from being like [them]" (3.3.6).

Comparing the deeds of these ruffians to Augustine's obsession with the theater brings important similarities and differences to light. First, whereas Augustine looks on theatrical shows as a spectator, turned in on himself emotionally and disengaged from real suffering, the wreckers actually act out horrible spectacles, preying upon innocent newcomers and inflicting real pain and suffering upon them. Whereas Augustine is enamored of the fictional portrayal of suffering, the wreckers crave the "malicious amusement" of creating a spectacle involving true suffering. And yet, it is difficult to see how Augustine could part ways with the wreckers on principle. Granted, he is repulsed by their violent behavior; but he is guilty of using others for his own amusement as well. Having turned away from God in his mind and heart, he is incapable of true friendship with other souls.

This brings us to Augustine's encounter with Cicero's *Hortensius*. He introduces the episode by connecting it with the preceding account of the wreckers: "Still young and immature, I began *in the company of these people* to study treatises on eloquence. This was a discipline in which I longed to excel, though my motive was the damnably proud desire to gratify my human vanity" (3.4.7; emphasis added). As it turns out, Augustine is not all that different from the wreckers. He and they share a desire to excel, to dominate others in a lust for power and prestige, to "make a name for themselves" as did the builders of the Tower of Babel (Gen 11:1–9).

Seen from this perspective, the wreckers are quite like Augustine's "unfriendly friends" of book 2. All are roaming the streets of "Babylon," deeply committed to their own worldly advancement and self-glorification. Thus, when Augustine happens upon Cicero's *Hortensius* in the "customary course of study" he does so as one not just caught up in, but actively contributing to the torrent of human custom discussed above. His fundamental allegiance is to the City of Man, "created by self-love reaching the point of contempt for God" and opposed to the City of God, created "by the love of God carried as far as contempt of self."[10]

---

10. Augustine, *City of God*, trans. Henry Bettenson, Penguin Classics (New York: Penguin Books, 2003), 14.28.

In light of our examination of all that precedes Augustine's narration of this episode in *Confessions,* the way in which Augustine describes his response to reading Cicero's *Hortensius* is particularly striking:

> The book changed my way of feeling and the character of my prayers to you, O Lord, for under its influence my petitions and desires altered. All my hollow hopes suddenly seemed worthless, and with unbelievable intensity my heart burned with longing for the immortality that wisdom seemed to promise. I began to rise up, in order to return to you. (3.4.7)

Reading Cicero's *Hortensius* changes Augustine's *feelings* and alters his *desires*; it transforms the character of his *prayers* and *petitions* to God. It deflates his hollow *hopes* and instills in his heart a deep *longing* for wisdom. Clearly, there is more going on here than a dispassionate intellectual conversion. In addition to whatever intellectual turning occurs, Augustine's heart—understood here as the soul's center of affectivity—changes.

What is more, in making these statements about how the reading affected him, Augustine alludes once again to the Parable of the Prodigal Son, this time at the very point of the wayward son's conversion: "I began to rise up, in order to return to you" (cf. Luke 15:20). Without a doubt, Augustine intends for us to interpret this change as a "conversion" of sorts. And yet, the book Augustine has been reading was not religious in character. What exactly is going on here?

The presence of divine providence pervades this episode. Augustine continues to describe what happened:

> How ardently I longed, O my God, how ardently I longed to fly to you away from earthly things! I did not understand then how you were dealing with me. Wisdom resides with you, but love for wisdom is called by the Greek name, 'philosophy,' and this love it was that the book kindled in me. (3.4.8)

Looking back on the episode, Augustine the author confesses that at the time, he did not understand how God was at work in the situation. Nevertheless, he affirms the agency of God in the *Hortensius* episode and establishes a crucial connection between philosophy, the pursuit of wisdom, and Wisdom itself, which comes from God (cf. Prov 2:6; Sir 1:1–7). The pursuit of wisdom puts Augustine on a path (i.e., a "way") toward an encounter with Wisdom itself, ultimately identified in the New Testament with Jesus Christ, "the wisdom of God" (cf. 1 Cor 1:18–25; Col 2:1–8). Furthermore, Augustine describes his reading and response to *Hortensius* as a conversion, for God as a provident Father and heavenly Teacher is actively at work in these events, leading Augustine first to love the truth wholeheartedly so that in time, he can come to love the God who is Truth (John 14:6).[11]

We will return to God as Truth below. For now, let's take a moment to step back and see what is happening from a pedagogical point of view. The pedagogy that Augustine the pilgrim comes to embrace is a leading of the soul that begins with God's initiative as a loving, provident Teacher and continues with the free, loving response of the student. A passage from the Old Testament sheds light on this divine pedagogy: "The Lord will give you the bread you need and the water for which you thirst. No longer will your Teacher hide himself, but with your own eyes you shall see your Teacher. While from behind, a voice shall sound in your ears: 'This is the way; walk in it,' when you would turn to the right or to the left" (Isa 30:20–21). Mindful of our hunger and thirst for truth and love, God as Teacher progressively reveals himself to us, gently and unobtrusively pointing the way to union with himself. When we veer off course, he speaks from behind us, redirecting out steps back to the path. The gentle, unobtrusive direction of the heavenly Teacher that becomes manifest in the *Hortensius* episode is an image of the way in which Augustine the author crafts the *Confessions* as a whole. Following the lead of the divine Teacher, Augustine shows us the way in which God has led him, and simultaneously the author uses this very pedagogical method to lead us readers, as well.[12]

What Augustine says next further reveals the divine pedagogy at work in the *Hortensius* episode, confirming this interpretation:

> There are people who lead others astray under the pretense of philosophy, coloring and masking their errors under that great, fair, honorable name. Nearly all who did so in Cicero's own day are mentioned and shown up in his book; and there too one can almost find an exposition of the salutary warning given by your Spirit through your good, devout servant: *Take care that no one deceives you with philosophy and empty, misleading ideas derived from man-made traditions, centered on the elemental spirits of this world and*

11. Later in book 3, when Augustine the author is describing his years of wandering in the wasteland of Manichaeism, he says, "You [God] were more intimately present to me than my innermost being, and higher than the highest peak of my spirit" (3.6.11). So whereas Augustine the pilgrim becomes ever more estranged from God, God remains intimately present to Augustine—more present to him than he is to himself. Involved in Augustine's journey back to his Heavenly Father, then, is a journey back to himself, as well.

12. For a distinct yet complementary reading of Augustine's pedagogy, see Thomas F. Martin's "Augustine's *Confessions* as Pedagogy: Exercises in Spiritual Transformation," in Paffenroth and Hughes, eds., *Augustine and Liberal Education*, 25–51. Martin's basic thesis is that the *Confessions* amounts to a series of "spiritual exercises" that both employs and transcends pedagogical models common in antiquity.

not on Christ; for in him all the fullness of the Godhead dwells in bodily wise
[Col. 2:8–9]. At the time these words of the apostle were still unknown to
me; but you know, O light of my heart, that there was one thing and one
only that brought me joy in the exhortation to wisdom: that by its call I was
aroused and kindled and set on fire to love and seek and capture and hold
fast and strongly cling not to this or that school, but to wisdom itself, whatever it might be. (3.4.8)

Notice Augustine's concern with defending the "great, fair, honorable
name" of philosophy. Before his account of the episode is over, another name
will be defended, as well—the name of Christ. Although Cicero defends the
name of philosophy in *Hortensius*, "there too one can almost find an exposition of the salutary warning given by your Spirit through your good, devout
servant," the Apostle Paul. In this passage we find an instance of the remark-
able exegesis Augustine will practice at greater length when expounding the
doctrines he discovered in the "books of the Platonists" (see book 7, especially
chapter 9). Instead of quoting the text of Cicero itself, Augustine quotes Sacred
Scripture, words "given by [the Holy] Spirit" to warn against being taken in
by "*empty, misleading ideas derived from man-made traditions, centered on the
elemental spirits of this world and not on Christ.*" Although he had not read this
passage from St. Paul at the time, he is nevertheless illumined by God ("light
of my heart") and "set on fire to love and seek and capture and hold fast and
strongly cling . . . to wisdom itself."

Augustine's imagery of being "set on fire" by what he reads occurs repeatedly hereafter in *Confessions*, but typically this enkindling comes about when
Augustine reads Sacred Scripture (as, for instance, when he meditatively reads
Psalm 4 at Cassiciacum [9.4]). Being "set on fire" is most likely a metaphor for
inspiration by the Holy Spirit, who is often symbolized by fire (see, e.g., Acts
2:3–4). It would seem, then, that Augustine is presenting his reading of Cicero's
Hortensius as in some sense inspired.

Even so, the name of Christ was absent from the Cicero text: "Only one
consideration checked me in my ardent enthusiasm: that the name of Christ
did not occur there" (3.4.8). Why would this matter, seeing that Augustine was
at the time far away from God, spiritually hungry in a land of famine? Given
the superficiality that characterizes Augustine the pilgrim throughout book 3,
one might simply see his preoccupation with the absence of Christ's name as
nothing more than superstition. Clearly at this point in the narrative he does
not know the person signified by the name. Why, then, would the name itself
matter? Perhaps it is just childish fancy. Once again, the answer is God's providential compassion:

> Through your mercy, Lord, my tender little heart had drunk in that name, the name of my Savior and your Son, with my mother's milk, and in my deepest heart I still held on to it. No writing from which that name was missing, even if learned, of literary elegance and truthful, could ever captivate me completely. (3.4.8)

As Augustine tells the story, the name of Christ has incredible power to direct him. So much power, in fact, that the next thing Augustine records is his reading of Sacred Scripture in an attempt to find wisdom and eloquence along with the name of Christ.

Before we examine that episode, we need to take stock of where Augustine stands at this point. What way of life is he choosing, and why? In the introduction, I mentioned two schools of thought and practice as regards the nature and purpose of education in the Western tradition—the way of the Orators, and the way of the Philosophers. Prior to reading Cicero's *Hortensius*, Augustine was clearly more influenced by the rhetorical tradition than the philosophical. In the *Hortensius*, however, Augustine sees these two traditions combined. It is not so much that Augustine turns away from the rhetorical way in favor of the philosophical way; instead, he begins to embrace a way of life that incorporates the greatest insights of both these ways.

Admittedly, Augustine does come to see the priority of wisdom over eloquence: "My interest in the book [*Hortensius*] was not aroused by its usefulness in the honing of my verbal skills. . . ; no, it was not merely as an instrument for sharpening my tongue that I used that book, for it had won me over not by its style but by what it had to say" (3.4.7). Even so, Augustine is not inclined simply to set rhetoric aside and pursue philosophy instead. Rather, he is looking for a way that embraces *both* wisdom *and* eloquence. And as was mentioned above, he also wants the name of Christ to be present. Although Augustine the pilgrim does not see it at the time, Augustine the author is pointing to a synthesis of the way of rhetoric, the way of philosophy, and the way of Christ. The difficulties inherent in trying to reconcile these three ways together with Augustine the pilgrim's deeply entrenched pride are what lead to his disappointing first response when he attempts to read Scripture.

As Augustine begins to describe this initial attempt, he comments on how what he sees in the Scriptures has changed over time:

> What I see in them today is something not accessible to the scrutiny of the proud nor exposed to the gaze of the immature, something lowly as one enters but lofty as one advances further, something veiled in mystery. At that time, though, I was in no state to enter, nor prepared to bow my head and accommodate myself to its ways. My approach then was quite different

from the one I am suggesting now: when I studied the Bible and compared it with Cicero's dignified prose, it seemed to me unworthy. My swollen pride recoiled from its style and my intelligence failed to penetrate to its inner meaning. (3.5.9)

Still swollen with pride, Augustine makes his own mind the measure of wisdom. Without a deeper knowledge of Christ—especially the humility and charity of the Incarnation[13]—he misjudges both the style and the substance of what he reads in Scripture. Augustine still has to learn to become lowly so that he can enter the way of Christ; as he puts it later in book 3, "through loving humility we find our way back to you" (3.8.16). Sadly, he first wanders for nine years among the Manicheans, seeking a means of reconciling these three ways of life without first surrendering himself to Christ and giving the way of loving humility priority. Although his impulse to reconcile the three ways is admirable, Augustine does not yet realize that Christ not only points to the way (as would any good teacher); he *is* the Way (John 14:6).

Later on in the middle of book 5, Augustine comments once again on the divine pedagogy we have been considering. By that point in the narrative, he has made much progress since his reading of Cicero's *Hortensius* and first encounter with Scripture. After recalling his disappointment upon meeting Faustus[14], who was acclaimed as a great teacher and defender of Manichean doctrine, Augustine says,

> For some time, . . . you had been teaching me in wondrous, hidden ways, my God (and I believe what you have taught me because it is true; there is no other teacher of truth except you, though teachers aplenty have made a name for themselves in many a place); so I had learned under your tuition that nothing should be regarded as true because it is eloquently stated, nor false because the words sound clumsy. On the other hand, it is not true for

13. Augustine presents humility and charity as the beginning and end, respectively, of his journey toward happiness in God. In describing the effect of reading the books of the Platonists, Augustine says to God, "You wanted to show me first and foremost how you thwart the proud but give grace to the humble, and with what immense mercy on your part the way of humility was demonstrated to us when your Word was made flesh and dwelt among men and women" (7.9.13). For all the good that reading the books of the Platonists does him by leading him to knowledge of immaterial being, they nevertheless lack charity (7.20.26), without which the happy life cannot be possessed.

14. Debra Romanick Baldwin draws attention to the "contrasting and complementary" teaching styles of Faustus and Ambrose and how these two models influence Augustine's own pedagogy. See Debra Romanick Baldwin, "Models of Teaching and Models of Learning in the *Confessions*," in Paffenroth and Hughes, eds., *Augustine and Liberal Education*, 16–24, especially 18–21.

being expressed in uncouth language either, nor false because couched in splendid words. (5.6.10)

The balance evident in Augustine's more mature assessment of truth and eloquence is a result of his tutelage under the one Teacher of truth, Jesus Christ. His notion of God as the one true teacher resonates with the image of Christ as "Inner Teacher" presented in his dialogue *De magistro* (11.38 ff.). Given that Christ is the one true Teacher, Augustine sees his own efforts as simply serving the real work of teaching that goes on within the soul of the learner: "Therefore, when I'm stating truths, I don't even teach the person who is looking upon these truths. He's taught not by my words but by the things themselves made manifest within when God discloses them" (*De magistro* 12.40). This is Augustine's pedagogy of presence, grounded in an intimate, personal encounter with the God who is Truth and Love.

BOOK 4

Fugitive Beauty

Erika Kidd

"Tempus fugit," Virgil writes. Time flies. It's fleeting, momentary. But the famous version of Virgil's words is something of a misquotation. Virgil's actual line is "fugit irreparabile tempus"; irrecoverable time flies.[1] Time is *fugitive*. It flees, slips through our fingers. Even when Augustine simply tries to talk about time in *Confessions* 11, he finds it passing faster than he can get a handle on it.

And if time flies, the same can be said too of all temporal beings; they pass, slip away, will not stay still. Death—that awful interrupter—reminds us, from time to time, of the impermanence of temporal beings. Our more ordinary experience reminds us too. Blocks of Minnesota snow finally melt. Trilliums bloom, but only for a month. "Nothing gold can stay," a poet wrote, now himself gone too. Time flies, and so do temporal beings.

The topic of this essay is *Confessions* 4, the book known for Augustine's confessional and self-critical account of the death of his friend. Although the book is famous for its lyrical descriptions of grief and tears and friendship, the present essay aims to accent not grief but beauty. Therefore, rather than starting with Augustine's description of his grief, I begin with Augustine's brief mention of a little volume he wrote titled *De pulchro et apto*.

In book 4, Augustine, a self-proclaimed lover of beauty, is confronted with

---

1. Line 284 of book 3 of Virgil's *Georgics*, translation mine. For Virgil's Latin, see R. A. B. Mynors, *P. Vergili Maronis Opera* (Oxford: Oxford University Press, 1969).

many ways beauties tend to slip from his grasp. In the face of that fact, he comes to hope that the passing of created beauties (those he loves) does not signify their meaninglessness. Instead, Augustine proposes that those beauties are words of love from the Creator, and he tries to learn to become more attentive to how the Word of God speaks in and through them.

Augustine's attraction to and preoccupation with beauty is precisely what makes death so painful to him. We readers miss the substance of book 4 if we divorce Augustine's grief from his reflection on how to relate to created beauties.

1. Books on Beauty

At the time he wrote his books on beauty, Augustine was a self-proclaimed lover of beauty (4.13.20). He and his friends liked to ask each other, "Do we love anything save what is beautiful?" It is perhaps an odd remark to make to one's friends, who may or may not be beautiful in body and soul. One might wonder if Augustine and his friends noticed the strangeness of describing their love in such abstract ways. In any case, they believed they knew what they loved, and that was beautiful things. Admittedly they weren't sure what *was* beautiful, or what beauty itself might be, but the topic intrigued them as it attracted them, and Augustine undertook to write a book on the topic.

Why is beauty such a big deal for Augustine? It is important for just the reason he acknowledges: he loves it. It attracts him. Thinking about beauty is, for Augustine, a lens for thinking about his desire, an aspect of himself that is sometimes troublesome. One commentator suggests Augustine writes a book about beauty in order to understand why he is attracted to things considered evil by the Manichees: why, if these things are bad, do they hold any attraction at all?[2] This reading is plausible, for the question of "what is beauty" is immediately followed in *Confessions* 4 by the question "What is it that entices and attracts us in the things we love?" to which Augustine answers, "Surely if beauty and loveliness of form were not present in them, they could not possibly appeal to us" (4.13.20).

The distinction between the beautiful and the fitting (or harmonious) that Augustine introduces in his early books is arguably meant to explain to Augustine himself why he could be attracted to something the Manichaeans said was evil or ugly in itself. An evil or ugly thing—say, sexual relations with his

2. Colin Starnes, *Augustine's Conversion: A Guide to the Argument of Confessions I-IX* (Waterloo, Ontario: Wilfrid Laurier University Press, 1990), 103.

longtime partner—could display a kind of relative attractiveness. Even things not absolutely beautiful might seem fitting or appropriate to a given circumstance or need; that is how they might attract Augustine.

But true beauty on Augustine's account, is a "quality inherent in the whole." It can be distinguished from "a different quality that was seemly in something that was harmoniously adapted to something else, as a part of the body to the whole, or a sandal to the foot, and other similar things" (4.13.20). If no feet existed, sandals would not be particularly beautiful. Apart from the body, an arm has no beauty of its own. As part of a well-functioning body (like the arm of a great baseball pitcher), it can attract us. Both the beautiful and the fitting appeal to us, but only the beautiful is able to do so absolutely and without qualification.

The examples Augustine offers to explain his distinction between the beautiful and the fitting are all material. Thus, he struggles when he turns, in his books on beauty, to the topic of the nature of the soul. In a foreshadowing of book 7, Augustine finds it impossible to think what is incorporeal. "Truth was thrusting itself upon me, staring me in the face, but I averted my trembling thought from incorporeal reality and looked instead toward shapes and colors and distended mass, and, since in the soul I could not see these, concluded that I was not able to see the soul" (4.15.24). When he attempts to think about the soul, Augustine is stymied by his material imagination. The soul must surely be beautiful, but Augustine's experience of beauty is so thoroughly material he cannot even begin to fathom what the beauty of the soul would look like.

What Augustine can see is the appeal of "the peace that accompanied virtue" and the undesirability of the discord that accompanies a vicious life (4.15.24). Accordingly, it occurs to him that unity must be the supreme good. That insight suggests to Augustine a distinction between two parts of the soul: the Monad (a sexless unity) and the Dyad (where he locates anger and self-indulgent cravings and anything else that would rend the soul into pieces). The Dyad is the source of the soul's appetites for carnal pleasures, for crime, and for vice. Presumably beauty is associated with the Monad, and that is where Augustine wants to locate his identity as well, at least to the extent he can, because the Dyad is an ugly but persistent force.

Whereas the youthful Augustine was quite proud of his books, thinking he had discovered some real insights, the older Bishop Augustine explains why the enterprise was destined to come up short. Throughout his early account, Augustine looks to beautiful things, but he examines them as things divorced from their true source. He tries to grasp beauty, but without knowing Beauty itself—the source of those created beauties he desires to understand—he is unable to find what he seeks. As Carl Vaught puts it, "When Augustine writes his first book, he does not understand that the reason things are beautiful is that God has created them."[3] Augustine admits his pursuit of beauty left him grasping at ideas forced into "material shape" by his own "vanity" (4.15.26).

Augustine's speculation about these material images—the clamor of his error—drowns out the "inner melody" of "gentle truth." He admits, "I did not yet see that the whole vast question hinged on your artistry, almighty God, who alone work wonders" (4.15.24). Apart from that recognition of the Author and Source of Beauty, his investigation is doomed to fail.

Interestingly, Augustine spends not much more than few sentences on the apparently crucial distinction of these early books. It looks as though this is not an analysis Augustine is keen to commend any longer. Instead the discussion serves to reveal an inauthenticity in Augustine's supposed love for beauty. Although at least one scholar has proposed that the distinction between the beautiful and the fitting is at the heart of Augustine's aesthetics,[4] Augustine the Bishop arguably has a different focus. He gives little time to clarifying his distinction and considerably more time discussing his reasons for dedicating the book to the Syrian orator, Hierius, who had developed an impressive reputation for Latin oration in Rome. He explains that attracting the attention of a successful and eloquent man would be a professional boon. Augustine also tells us that he loved the man, though his love was sparked by the praise of others, not by the substance of the man, whom Augustine did not in fact know. Had the man been not praised but criticized for the same deeds, Augustine admits that he would have felt no interest. For the ambitious young Augustine, the reputation of Hierius was more important than his substance, and Augustine's affections were beholden to the opinions of others.

In trying to hitch his research to Hierius's star, Augustine finds that his soul is "tossed and turned, whirled and spun, by every breath of opinion from the mouths of those who think they know, its light obscured by clouds" (4.14.23). Thus the enterprise that purported to be about gaining real insight into the substance of the beautiful is framed by Augustine's desire to receive admiration, as though outside appreciation would confirm and legitimate both Augustine's insight and his very person. As James Wetzel observes, "He was after his ideal

3. Carl Vaught, *The Journey Toward God in Augustine's Confessions: Books I–VI* (Albany, NY: State University of New York Press, 2003), 109.

4. David Lyle Jeffrey argues that the distinction is at the heart of Augustine's aesthetics, though he naturally has to go well beyond these few lines to show this is so. See his "The Beauty of the Cross in Augustine's Aesthetics," *Nova et Vetera* 12, no. 3 (2014), 769–789.

self, whose beauty would be confirmed or denied for him in a word from an important man."[5]

Augustine's reflections on the beautiful serve less to memorialize his youthful insight than to confirm the great distance between his supposed commitment to beauty and truth, on the one hand, and the substance of his engagement with those realities, on the other. Though superficially attracted to them, Augustine was arguably less of a lover of beauty (and truth) than he purported to be.

Perhaps the most important feature of these books is that Augustine lost them. Though he was quite proud of his books, he cannot even remember whether there were two or three of them. Worse yet, he no longer knows where they are. In noting this detail, Augustine signals to the reader that his attempt to get a grasp on beauty—even just conceptually—was a failure. His book on beauty slips through his fingers—and that is just the last in a string of beauties that slip away in book 4. Augustine's friend passes, all created beauties on earth are passing, and the unnamed woman introduced in book 4 will be forced to pass from Augustine's life too.

Arguably Augustine's basic insight in book 4 is that beauties are fugitive. They slip-slide away, refusing to stay in place. Augustine's theoretical reflection at the end of book 4 records his last youthful stab at trying to get a grip on them. As Vaught puts it, in writing his books on beauty, Augustine turns

> away from the place where the loss of beautiful things occurs to a domain where he can cover over the existential anxiety that continues to pervade his life with a theoretical veneer. This drives a wedge between experience and reflection, allowing the philosopher to shift his attention from the flux of experience to the reflective level where he can try to bring stability to it.[6]

Any philosopher worth her salt has tried this strategy before: use theory to bring stability to what threatens to slip away. This impulse might be detected too in Augustine's book 4 reflections on astrology, for knowledge of the stars promises to lend intelligibility and thus a certain stability to human experience. When the young Augustine's experience reveals the passing of the beauty that attracts him and the shocking fragility of what he loves, he casts about for consolations. The key question—for both readers and for Augustine himself—is whether the fragility of created beauty and its inevitable passing are problems to be solved.

5. James Wetzel, "Trappings of Woe: Augustine's Confession of Grief," in *Parting Knowledge* (Eugene, OR: Cascade Books, 2013), 76.
6. Vaught, *The Journey Toward God*, 107.

2. A Friend's Passing

To answer that question, we need to return to the scenes of love and loss that come earlier in book 4. These are the experiences of beauty the young Augustine tried to whip into theoretical shape in his books on the subject.

At the age of twenty-one, Augustine returned to his hometown of Thagaste to teach. There he reconnected with a schoolyard acquaintance and their relationship quickly blossomed into a friendship. It was, to be sure, not a perfect friendship; the two young men were not bound together by the Holy Spirit (4.4.7). Yet the young man was "exceedingly dear" to Augustine, who reports that his "soul could not bear to be without him" (4.4.7).

Augustine does not describe his friend as *pulcher*, but his strong attraction to him makes clear he saw beauty there. The union was sweet at the time, sweeter than any friendship Augustine had known.

Augustine, freshly returned from Carthage and a new Manichaean hearer, was eager to share his urban sophistication with his new friend. He quickly lured the friend from the faith of their childhood and toward "the superstitious and baneful fables" over which Monica grieved: the Manichaean religion (4.4.7). The Bishop Augustine admits to God that the two men were "your fugitives," (*fugitivorum tuorum*) running from the truth, with God close at their backs. His retrospective view is that their friendship was, more or less, rooted in affection and error.

They were astray together, and Augustine explains that their "similarity of outlook lent warmth" to their friendship (4.4.7). In this friendship, unity was the watchword. Augustine writes, "It was well said that a friend is half one's own soul. I felt that my soul and his had been but one soul in two bodies" (4.6.11). Though Augustine distances himself from this overwrought statement in his *Retractationes*,[7] it does seem to reflect the attitude of the younger man. If several years later (in his volumes on beauty), Augustine would describe unity as the supreme good, arguably here we see him living out that belief. Yet unity suggests union or wholeness, and that is not quite what Augustine enjoyed with his friend. It is more accurate to call "identity" or "sameness" the true watchword of the friendship. For as soon as the first hint of difference enters the relationship (in the form of a substantial disagreement), darkness follows and the friendship disintegrates.

About a year into the friendship, the friend unexpectedly is taken ill. Feverish, unconscious, and with dwindling hope for recovery, he is baptized. Up

---

7. See Augustine, *Retractationes*, CCSL 57 (Turnholt, Belgium: Brepols, 1984), 2.6.2.

until that point, Augustine had kept constant vigil—"for I did not leave him," he writes, "so closely were we dependent on each other" (4.4.8).

When the friend rallies and grows stronger, post-baptism, Augustine begins to joke with him about the unconscious baptism. Augustine is confident that there is no way some rite performed on the friend's unconscious body could be stronger than Augustine's influence over his friend's mind. Yet the friend recoils with what Augustine calls "amazing, new-found independence" (4.4.8). He warns Augustine that if their friendship is going to survive, Augustine must cut out such talk.

At that point, Augustine decides to give his friend some space, thinking that they could take up the matter again once the friend was fully restored to health. At that later point, Augustine thinks to himself, "I would be able to do what I liked with him" (4.4.8). Yet Augustine's temporary separation from his friend—in body and in soul—is made permanent when the friend takes a sudden turn for the worse and dies in Augustine's absence (4.4.8).

Augustine's sorrow plunges him into darkness. "Black grief closed over my heart," he writes, "and wherever I looked I saw only death" (4.4.9). Every place reminds him of the time they shared. Everything they had once enjoyed together now brings him "hideous anguish." None of the pleasures of the senses—time outdoors, songs and shows, feasts, the "pleasures of couch or bed," reading, and so on—could give him a moment's relief from his sorrow (4.7.12). Augustine summarizes, "everything that was not what he was seemed to me offensive and hateful, except for mourning and tears, in which alone I found some slight relief" (4.7.12). Crushed under the burden of his misery, his very heart longed to flee from itself. Only escape from himself could bring him escape from his grief, so deeply was his friend grafted into his heart.

Unable to escape himself, Augustine escapes Thagaste and finds relief in Carthage—not in consolation, but in distraction. "Time does not stand still, nor are the rolling seasons useless to us," (4.8.13) he observes. The passage of time grants Augustine memories and new hopes as he enjoys the company of friends: talking and laughing together, deferring to one another, reading together, and only rarely disagreeing with one another.

Regarding these new, replacement friends, Augustine writes, "our minds were fused inseparably, out of many becoming one" (4.8.13). Both the dead friend and the fresh new friends remain unnamed, suggesting an absence of particularity. The friends are, in time, more or less interchangeable. Moreover, the form of friendship Augustine is seeking—fusion or a kind of one-soul identity—tends to occlude the particularity of the participants. Distraction by replacement hardly seems a satisfying resolution to grief.

Yet distraction can be the only cure for Augustine's grief, precisely because his Manichaean beliefs offer such scant consolation. In the midst of his grief, Augustine says, he feels he has become a great enigma to himself; he wonders why he is so dispirited and sorrowful following the death of his friend. Contemporary readers might see no mystery here; he is sad because his friend died. Yet Augustine is perplexed by his grief because his religious beliefs ought to put that grief to flight. When he tells himself to "trust in God," his soul disobeys, "for the man it had held so dear and lost was more real and more lovable than the fantasy in which it was bidden to trust" (4.4.9). The friend seems more real than the (Manichaean) God.

Manichaean theology promises liberation for whatever light existed within the individual. Yet it is hard to connect that promise with Augustine's sense of what was lost with the friend's death. Augustine enjoyed spending time with his friend, enjoyed their spirited conversations and their happy pastimes. His friend's presence—concrete, tangible, even changeable—was what Augustine was connected to. Colin Starnes writes,

> When he died, Augustine, who believed what the Manichees said, could not think that his friend was still somehow "there" in God. In theory they intended to preserve the individual; in practice they destroyed him—for the individual could only be "saved" by being dissolved into the contraries which were all that he really was.[8]

It surely felt to Augustine as though the Manichean God had neither memory nor affection for the man Augustine had loved and called a friend.

Augustine's grief is more or less the only way to keep the friend alive; it is the only way to keep a grip on the beauty of his friend and of their friendship. Without his grieving memory, those goods threaten to vanish altogether.[9] And yet Augustine is troubled by his grief; it is not merely an innocent

---

8. Starnes, *Augustine's Conversion*, 95–96.

9. Current research reveals novel, technological ways mourners try to keep the deceased "alive" in his or her particularity and specificity, when the consolations offered by religion or other forms of culture are inadequate. Some contemporary mourners, left cold by funeral rites and burial, look to social media engagement with others and with the deceased's social media presence to keep the deceased alive in memory. "One participant noted, '[the] funeral is your last glimpse of them in person, but social media will forever remind you of who that person was.' . . . Mourners compared traditional grief to grieving via SNS as the means to immortality. 'Cemeteries mean death to me. Online means you live on and you will continue to live on.'" Jensen Moore, Sara Magee, Ellada Gamreklidze, and Jennifer Kowalewski, "Social Media Mourning: Using Grounded Theory to Explore How People Grieve on Social Networking Sites," *OMEGA—Journal of Death and Dying*, 79, no. 3 (2019), 250.

memorializing of what had been lost. He finds it overwrought, arguably theatrical.[10] In a moment of damning self-criticism, Augustine admits that weeping itself replaced his friend as the "only comfort" of his soul (4.4.9). Something about his grief is problematic, even sinful, on his telling. As more than one commentator has noted, Augustine makes a *confession* of his grief. For those of us accustomed to thinking of grief as a normal, healthy reaction to loss, this may sound odd. Augustine's grief seems appropriate, even needful. So why does he confess it?

3. Confessing Grief

One take on Augustine's confession is that his grief reveals his sin of loving what will only disappoint. Nicholas Wolterstorff sees Augustine as standing at the origin of a long tradition of Christian piety which tells us that grief signifies a problem of bad attachment and a love of the wrong things. Here's a representative line from Wolterstorff's essay "Suffering Love": "[Augustine's] reason for exposing his grief [in *Confessions* 4] was to share with his readers his confession to God of the senselessness and sinfulness of a love so intense for a being so fragile that its destruction could cause such grief."[11] If what we love can bring us to grief, then Wolterstorff's Augustine would tell us we have chosen the wrong object of love. If we love fragile, passing beauties, we must not be surprised if our hearts break. More importantly, we should try not to make the same mistake in the future.

Wolterstorff does not pull his interpretation out of thin air. Augustine does make comments that can be taken as a loose justification for such a reading. In the context of discussing his turn to new friends, Augustine laments, "for how had that sorrow been able so easily to pierce my inmost being, if not because I had poured out my soul into the sand by loving a man doomed to death as though he were never to die?" (4.8.13). The new friends brought consolation, but it is hardly permanent. They will die too. Love of mortal beings can't but end in grief. Wolterstorff glosses the passage as follows: "The cure is to detach one's love from such objects and to attach it to something immutable and indestructible."[12] The beauties we love are fleeting and fragile, and so we grieve.

10. The performance of grief today has a much larger stage across social media where those with little connection to the deceased sometimes pretend to be more connected or more bereft than they truly are. See "Social Media Mourning," 246.

11. Nicholas Wolterstorff, "Suffering Love," in *Augustine's Confessions: Critical Essays*, ed. William E. Mann (Lanham, MD: Rowman and Littlefield Publishers, 2006), 107.

12. Wolterstorff, "Suffering Love," 110.

The cure for grief is to love what is not fragile, what will never pass. On such an account, God is clearly the only worthy and stable object of our love. Grief is a sign that one has failed appropriately to contract the sphere of one's love.

Wolterstorff's Augustine confesses a struggle to discipline his heart. He knows what he should love (God alone, not mortal beauties), but he continues to be seduced by those beauties in which his heart can find no rest: "Though we may *know* that only in loving God is abiding happiness to be found, yet the beauties of the world sink their talons so deep into our souls that only by the grace of God and the most agonizing of struggles can we break loose."[13] Wolterstorff casts the beauties of the world (including friends and those we love) as raptors, birds of prey that snatch up our souls, preventing them from resting in God and knowing true happiness. This image (which is, to my knowledge, Wolterstorff's, not Augustine's) reproduces a tired trope about created beauties: they are dangerous, they seduce, they prevent us from knowing and loving God.

The only object of grief for which Wolterstorff can find Augustinian justification is grief over our misplaced love of what changes and decays. Our converted, God-focused self will never get over its backward glance towards created beauties—not in this life, at least. Thus, in an extended reading of several passages from Augustine's *City of God*, Wolterstorff argues that the proper object of grief is sin and the state of the sinful soul, which still wants to attach itself where it should not. Grief *must* be present in this life because of human beings' continued imperfection. But the ideal life, on Wolterstorff's reading of *City of God*, is that of the Stoic sage: "An ethic of the perfect sage is not an ethic for the imperfect lover of God."[14]

What must not be grieved is anything worldly, any fragile beauties, according to Wolterstorff's reading of book 4:

> In the presence of all those griefs which ensue from the destruction of that which we love, Augustine pronounces a "No" to the attachments rather than a "No" to the destruction—not a "No" to death but a "No" to love of what is subject to death. Thereby he also pronounces a "Not much" concerning the worth of the things loved. Nothing in this world has worth enough to merit an attachment which carries the potential of grief—nothing except the religious state of souls. The state of my child's soul is worth suffering love; the child's company is not.[15]

13. Wolterstorff, "Suffering Love," 110, emphasis original.
14. Wolterstorff, "Suffering Love," 115.
15. Wolterstorff, "Suffering Love," 137.

Augustine was wrong to grieve his friend's passing, because he was wrong to love and be attached to a mortal man at all—at least on Wolterstorff's telling.

Unsurprisingly, Wolterstorff, who was himself deprived of the company of his child (his beloved twenty-five-year-old son Eric, who died in a mountain-climbing accident), cannot abide the Augustinian picture he has painted. Honestly, few of us could. Wolterstorff loves created beings. In one's love, he explains, one says "yes" to the worth of persons or things; one's suffering grief is a refusal of their destruction.[16] In the preface to *Lament for a Son*, a journal of grief Wolterstorff published in the aftermath of his son's untimely death, he comments about Eric, "If he was worth loving, he is worth grieving over. Grief is existential testimony to the worth of the one loved. That worth abides."[17] He challenges the view he attributes to Augustine: that we must only care for or be attached to God. We must not only love God, Wolterstorff explains; we should also love what God loves.[18] On his view, Augustine confesses that he has loved "too much," or, more accurately, that he loved the wrong thing. But Wolterstorff's deep dissatisfaction with that view does nothing to blunt his confidence that he has accurately represented Augustine's views and explained Augustine's self-criticism over his grief.

In an interview about his book, *Lament for a Son*, he observes, "My grief wasn't about grief. It was about Eric."[19] He was not interested in grief; he was interested in his son. He explains that never managed to read more than a handful of pages from any "grief" book. He didn't want to think about his grief in the abstract, his experience of grieving, or—worst of all—grief in general. He was grieving his son, Eric, and the details of what that loss meant for Eric himself and for the family left behind. That crucial difference (between preoccupation with grief and preoccupation with what is lost) is not a difference Wolterstorff chooses to highlight in Augustine's story. Yet it is a difference that can be discerned in *Confessions* 4. It is, I think, a difference of which Augustine was keenly aware.

If "every lament is a love song," as Wolterstorff rightly opines,[20] then those who fail to love truly cannot grieve truly. This is the heart of Augustine's

---

16. Wolterstorff, "Suffering Love," 138.

17. Nicholas Wolterstorff, *Lament for a Son* (Grand Rapids, MI: Wm. B. Eerdmans Publishing Co., 1987).

18. Wolterstorff, "Suffering Love," 138.

19. Nicholas Wolterstorff, "Lament for a Son: Nicholas Wolterstorff on Grief and Suffering," at *The Table* (October 8, 2018), at https://cct.biola.edu/lament-for-a-son-nicholas -wolterstorff-grief-suffering/.

20. Wolterstorff, *Lament for a Son*, 6.

problem. Augustine confesses his grief because it reflects his failure to love his friend truly, to love him "in God." What the young Augustine wants is a creature of his own desires, including his desire to have control over another. Augustine tries to hold on to his friend in life (by initiating him into Manichaeism) and in death (by clinging to his mourning). Yet in both cases, the attempt to hold on to his friend fails. The friend is not captured but lost through the process.

Augustine's grief may mask a worry that he never really loved his friend at all. For his grief seems to be less about the individual who died (not even named) and more about Augustine's experience of loss and grief. Even as Augustine ostensibly grieves his friend, he finds himself running again and again into himself or simulacra of himself: his grief, his tears, his preoccupation with not dying, his inability to escape himself—to escape his very heart (4.4.9–4.7.12). Yet nothing in Augustine's grief prompts him to return to himself.

In book 4, Augustine gives us a window into what Wetzel calls Augustine's "inclination to use beauty as a venue for self-exit."[21] Augustine confesses his grief not because he means to confess he has loved "too much," but because he has loved badly.

Augustine's explicit self-criticism is twofold: (1) that he had poured out his "soul into the sand by loving a man doomed to death as though he were never to die" (4.8.13) and (2) that he had failed to love his friend in God (4.9.14). Undoubtedly these two admissions can be tricky to fit together. Wolterstorff takes the first as a requirement that one pare down one's sense of what is really worthy of love and attention (God and His Beauty) and discipline one's attention and affections toward what is stable and eternal and will never bring one to grief. Yet the second possibility Augustine raises—that it might be possible to love what we love well, even though it be mortal—stands as a direct challenge to Wolterstorff. What does it mean to love friends well? Is there some legitimate way to love any created beauty?

Midway through book 4, Augustine puts in theoretical terms the difficulty he has been describing in existential terms. We might put it like this: we rivet ourselves (*figitur*) to things beautiful, but they flee (*fugiunt*). When we try to cling to beauties apart from God, we cling only to sorrow: "for wheresoever a human soul turns, it can but cling to what brings sorrow unless it turns to you, cling though it may to beautiful things outside you and outside itself" (4.10.15). "Yet," Augustine continues, "were these beautiful things not from you, none of them would be at all." With this remark, Augustine challenges the notion that the fragility of beauty is meant to serve as a divine warning. The problem is not

21. Wetzel, "Trappings of Woe," 76.

the beauty, nor the fragility and passing. The problem is the way we cling to things, trying to make them lasting and eternal and *ours*. That clinging divorces the beauty from its source—and its true meaning. The temporal loss of created beauties is inevitable; the clinging gets us nowhere. So what are we to make of the inevitable passing?

4. Words and the Word

Augustine does affirm created beauties can be legitimate objects of love, but it is a hard-won insight. He comes to see that God's heart shares his best and truest affections, and he comes to that recognition by reflecting on how God has communicated with him. In book 4, drawing an analogy between the passing of created beauties and the passing of syllables, Augustine offers his readers a way of thinking about created beauties not just as instruments in a divinely meaningful plan but as expressive of God's love (for them and for Augustine).

As he turns from the record of his grief to his theoretical reflection, Augustine explains that temporal passing does not result in ultimate loss. He acknowledges the transience of created beauties; they grow toward perfection, but also grow old (most of them) and perish (4.10.15). In their passing away and succession, created beauties "form a whole, of which the several creatures are parts" (4.10.15). Our carnal perception, Augustine warns, tempts us to think that the passing is absolute, drawing everything into permanent loss. That perception misleads, leaving us sighing in longing for the part, when instead we should long to know the whole. "Were your carnal perception able to grasp the whole, were it not, for your punishment, confined to its due part of the whole, you would long for whatever exists only in the present to pass away, so that you might find greater joy in the totality" (4.11.17). If we could see the whole, we would no longer cling to the part.

This part-whole language may strike us as a little odd or strained. Starnes reads this passage as expressive of a certain form of Platonism, where love for the whole trumps attachment to the parts. (Starnes thinks Augustine finds this Platonic view inadequate.) Once the whole is in view, the passing of the parts may seem a little trifling, and love of the whole can serve as satisfactory replacement for love of the particular.[22] This is of course a form of Wolterstorff's reading: that we ought *not* to love the parts (creatures), but only love the whole (God). It is also worth noting that generic part-whole language could, with minimal adjustment, be made to fit with the Manichaean promise that the bits of light

22. Starnes, *Augustine's Conversion*, 99–100.

and goodness within the individual are set free and subsumed into light itself. The parts long to reconnect with the whole, where they find their true meaning and satisfaction. Yet the language of parts and wholes seems to degrade the value of the individual life, and it certainly does little to respond to and capture the human sense of grief and loss—if only temporarily—of what is held dear.

Augustine uses the language of part and whole, but he does not do so loosely. He qualifies it in an essential and specific way, by introducing an analogy between creatures and syllables. Just as individual creatures form a whole, so too individual words are spoken and die away in order to give rise to a "whole utterance." Although the soul seeks to rest in what it loves, those creatures which are destined to go, there can be no rest in what is transient. Nor can the passing of creatures be halted: "who can seize them, even near at hand?" (4.10.15). Nor do we even want to halt that passing; when we listen to speech, we desire that each syllable might fly on its way, making room for others, so that we might hear the whole (4.11.17).

There is a potential misreading or two lurking in this analogy. First, readers might think Augustine has simply landed on a flowery way of assuring us nothing is lost. Yes, a word fades from hearing, but it is preserved in the sentence or paragraph in which it finds its ultimate home. It would be silly to fixate too much on one word—or worse, one syllable!—when the word's true value or meaning is only revealed once it has taken its place with the others. Second, readers might think Augustine simply means to assure us there is meaning in loss. We will not have any way—for now—of knowing what that bigger picture and ultimate meaning might be, but we can rest assured that God does; we can be confident that our loss is justified. We might suppose the analogy offers consolation along the lines of "to make an omelet, you've got to break a few eggs." Or, mutatis mutandis: "To get a meaningful sentence, a few words need to pass on. Don't worry; you won't miss them. Or at least you won't once you see a vision of the meaningful whole."

Augustine's question cuts much closer to the bone. He does not want merely to be assured that God can bring meaning out of loss. Even the Manichaean God can do that. It is worth remembering where this essay started: with Augustine's love of beauties. Beauty attracts Augustine. He is not only concerned with the question of whether beautiful creatures are completely lost, or whether some abstract meaning can be found in the passing, or if there is a way of making sense of death and loss in some divine scheme. As a great lover of beauty, facing the loss of beautiful creatures, Augustine needs to know: do such creatures hold any place in God's heart? He is trying to figure out if God loves what he loves. Augustine is attracted to beauty, and it is perhaps not too much of a stretch to say he wonders if God is too. The question of Augustine's relationship to God is at the very heart of his reflection here. It would not be enough (for Augustine) to be assured that God will preserve the things He made out of some sense of economy or duty. He seems to want to know whether God loves his friend in any way that could be meaningful to him, or anyone who has lost what they love.

Augustine's analogy is much richer than it may initially appear and offers answers to the very questions with which the author must have been wrestling. It may be tempting to think of words as units of meaning that are assembled into greater wholes within which "meaning" arises. But language introduces intimacy to the question of meaning, because utterances are for people. The bookends of Augustine's analogy are the speakers in the exchange. The first bookend is, at minimum, Augustine's words. "So is it with our speaking [*sermo noster*] as it proceeds by audible signs" (4.10.15). Augustine does not specify who makes up the "our" (him and God, him and anyone with whom he speaks), but he does make clear that the speech he has in mind (with his analogy) is not pure monologue, but dialogue—some kind of speaking *with*. In fact, he turns immediately to prayer, to conversation with God ("Let my soul use these things to praise you, O God, creator of them all"), a prayer which recounts the passing of created beauties and Augustine's thwarted desire to rest in those beauties: "they rend my soul with death-dealing desires, for it too longs to be, and loves to rest in what it loves. But in them it finds no place to rest, because they do not stand firm; they are transient" (4.10.15).

If the first bookend of the analogy is Augustine's word, the second is God's Word. Augustine ends his prayer with an acknowledgement that created beings were created through God's Word (4.10.15). By saying all creatures are held in the Word because created through that Word, Augustine introduces further complexity to the analogy: creatures are analogous to the syllables or words he utters, but they are also expressions of the very Word of God. That is to say, they are how God speaks with his creatures. By implying that these created beauties are God's utterance, Augustine suggests they are the way by which God loves us and calls us to himself. The passing creatures in which Augustine desires to rest (but cannot) are created in God's Word. That Word calls to him, calling him back and calling him to listen (4.11.16).

If Augustine and God are speaking with one another, then Augustine's language analogy offers another important caveat to the part-whole picture: no speaker speaks in a vacuum. Each speaks with another, and what meaning there is, is jointly constituted. In language, as Augustine demonstrates in his early dialogue *The Teacher*, meaning is shared; it is not just something one speaker gets to assign or invent and then impose on others.[23] There can be no grand, explanatory one-sided narratives that fail to account for the affections and concerns of the other interlocutor. Any simple part-whole solution (whether it be Manichaean or Neoplatonic) guaranteeing divine "meaning" in the death of beloved beauties would likely leave the griever cold rather than consoled. Wolterstorff famously comments that he does not believe in grand philosophical or theological explanations for the death of his son. Although he has a deep and abiding faith in God, he refuses "answers" or solutions to the problem of evil and the death of his child.[24] Such explanations seems too far removed from Eric, his son. Here again, I suspect there is an unacknowledged kinship between Wolterstorff's view and Augustine's. Whatever meaning might come out of a particular loss must be joint (Augustine's and God's), arising from a joint recognition of the beauty of the creature that has passed. Both bereaved men seem less concerned with offering assurances that "God has a plan" and more concerned with speaking *to* and *with* God. In this context of mutual exchange, they might be able to work out with God what it means both to love and (temporarily) lose what they love. They might also, apart from grand narratives, learn to see what kind of love God has for his creatures. This kind of exchange would of course require trust, a trust that thrives in a mutual understanding of the real value of the created order: "Entrust to Truth whatever of truth is in you, and you will lose nothing" (4.11.16).

Here is how such an exchange (between Augustine and God) unfolds in book 4: Augustine professes to be a lover of beauty. Experience reveals he is and is not. His clear-eyed assessment is that his God-bereft heart was less faithful to beauty (and beauties) than he would have hoped. Augustine loved his beautiful friend. Yet when he fails in that love, his heart breaks over his failure to apprehend the true beauty of what he thought he loved. He learns for himself that "anything that comes from him [God] will justly turn bitter if it is unjustly loved by people who forsake him" (4.12.18). God reminds Augustine that loving apart from God must always end badly. That is so not because God is a jealous God who does not want his creatures to notice the beauty of what he has made. Instead, it is because love of beauty that is separated from love of God, who is

---

23. See Erika Kidd, "Making Sense of Virgil in De Magistro," *Augustinian Studies* 46, no. 2 (2015): 211–224.

24. "I believe in God the Father Almighty, maker of heaven and earth and resurrecter [sic] of Jesus Christ. I also believe that my son's life was cut off in its prime. I cannot fit these pieces together. I am at a loss. I have read the theodicies produced to justify the ways of God to man. I find them unconvincing. To the most agonized question I have ever asked I do not know the answer." Wolterstorff, *Lament for a Son*, 68.

Beauty itself, will always come up short. It will always devolve into bad forms of self-love. When we love created beauties apart from God, we inevitably cling to them, trying to make them *ours* and trying to guarantee their permanence. But these beauties are made to flee. On the one hand, Augustine's love of beauty is a constant liability because it cannot survive apart from love of God and quickly devolves into a grasping, imperfect love. On the other hand, Augustine's love of beauty draws him towards salvation.

Book 10 gives us a portrait of Augustine, as a more and less imperfect lover of beauty. When the author laments his headlong rush "upon the shapely things" God had made, he acknowledges that his attraction to creatures held him back from God (10.27.38). Augustine was not crazy to notice the beauty of what God had made, but he confesses his failure to hear how God was speaking to him through that beauty, trying to draw him into deeper and truer loves. God helps him make the connection between his attraction to beauty and his restless longing for God. In an earlier book 10 passage, Augustine's attentive spirit questions the created order: what do I love when I love my God? The creatures reply with their beauty, and it is, finally, the beauty of creatures that gives Augustine a vision of who God is (10.6.9). The beauty of creatures is not a trap nor a distraction; it is a revelation. And though Augustine's truest and deepest love of Beauty comes late, God offers Augustine forgiveness as he encourages Augustine in deeper faithfulness to that love.

The great consolation of book 4 is this: God does love his creatures, even more wholeheartedly than Augustine yet does. Augustine enjoins his readers: "Let us love him [God], for he made these things and he is not far off, for he did not make them and then go away: they are from him but also in him" (4.12.18). God remains close to what he made. His creatures are from him and in him, even as they pass in time. God is "most intimately present to the human heart" though "the heart has strayed from him" (4.12.18). Augustine's heart is attracted to beauty, though he frequently fails in his faithfulness to that attraction. In response to that failure, God invites him to know and understand the true beauty of what he loves—and shows him how to love it well. What passes is not only not lost—it is loved. For Augustine, lover of beauty, that is a blessed assurance.

This is what it means to love souls in God: to know that they, like every created beauty, cannot support the absolute affections of our restless hearts, and to know as well that they are created by Him and can be loved in Him when He is acknowledged as their loving Author and Source. "If kinship with other souls appeals to you, let them be loved in God, because they too are changeable and gain stability only when fixed in him; otherwise they would go their way and be lost" (4.12.18). When we try to grasp the beauties we love and hold them "apart from God," we lose the very beauty we seek to make stable. When we entrust what we love to God's keeping, we are told we will lose nothing. His heart holds our own.

5. Christological Conclusion

"It is generally easy, when reading Augustine, to turn God and the created world into competing objects of desire," notes Wetzel, before terming such an approach a "disastrous misreading."[25] The "craving for an absolute antithesis between God and humanity" is put to rest, Wetzel explains, by a turn to the incarnation.[26] The passing of created beauties does not signal their lack of value. Far from it. God himself, in the person of Christ, also dies and passes. He races through his passing, "impatient of delay." He withdraws from us, yet his passing signals not abandonment nor a devaluation of the created order, for he could never abandon what he had made. He withdraws from us in order that he might draw us to himself, and he withdraws to the place he never left—as Creator of all that is (4.12.19). If we want to understand how to love created beauties well, we can do no better than looking to Christ, the Word through whom they were made. Christ's passing is an invitation to life and an affirmation of his love for what remains, still temporally passing.

Augustine's love of beauties and love of Beauty is a thread that runs throughout the *Confessions*. The whole of the text is arguably a story of Augustine's attraction to and flight from beauty. Yet the beauty he seeks to grasp eludes him and slips through his fingers, inasmuch as he tries to grasp it while fleeing from God. Augustine reminds us, his readers, that it is precisely our disposition to resist the passing of created beauties, our desire to try to hold them and secure them in our own hands, that threatens to deform (or causes us to lose) the beauty of what we love.

It is hard not to grasp after what one loves, to make it secure and hope for its stability in this life. Yet Augustine reminds us that to cling to a created beauty is to make it into an idol, something apart from God that one clings to and finds security in. For those of us who make our way now as temporal beings, created beauties are meant to be fugitive, but that need not mean they are lost, or that we have failed to find adequate ways to preserve them. They are held in Christ and in the very love of God, even as they pass from our sight. For Augustine, this is cause for praise.

25. Wetzel, "Trappings of Woe," 78.
26. Wetzel, "Trappings of Woe," 78.

BOOK 5

Narrating Radical Inclusivity and Dysmorphic Identities

Christopher Thompson

> "But if man is two-fold, he is also one; and this mystery, far from destroying, is the very basis of his individual existence—that of a being who has to integrate that which is already one."
>
> JEAN MOUROUX[1]

Every conversion story is comprised of at least two features: change and continuity. What changes are aspects or features of a person's sense of themselves and their experience—from a profligate to reformed; the sinner to saint; the crapulous to the sober.

What endures is a "character," here serving the dual purpose as an enduring protagonist through a narrative sequence and the enduring identity of a moral agent through change and, presumably, growth. (This forms the basis for the field known as "narrative ethics.") It is precisely this feature of narrative continuity at the heart of conversion stories that is the focus of this reflection.

Conversion constitutes the turning away from, or renunciation of some portion of one's identity and the embrace of some putatively more integral and integrating aspect of one's experience, the "truer I" or "more authentic I." This latter "I" claims narrative authority over and emerging from those elements of one's personal history that now, in retrospective reflection, appear alien, or at least dissonant from the deeper, more enduring, more preferred character or identity.

---

1. Jean Mouroux, *The Meaning of Man* (London: Sheed and Ward, 1948), 268.

In clinical psychology, "ego syntonic" and "ego dystonic" are terms often employed to identity aspects of an enduring identity, a single character within a drama of change and conversion. Desires and choices which are closer to one's primary aspiration are considered "syntonic" and those that one experiences as being at odds with one's deepest aspirations are "dystonic." Syntonic elements identify those components of personal identity which comprise authentic or true self, whereas "dystonic" names those portions of one's identity which constitute alien or destructive or disruptive elements of one's identity. As Richard Joelson explains,

> Ego-syntonic refers to instincts or ideas that are acceptable to the self; that are compatible with one's values and ways of thinking. They are consistent with one's fundamental personality and beliefs.
>
> Ego-dystonic refers to thoughts, impulses, and behaviors that are felt to be repugnant, distressing, unacceptable or inconsistent with one's self-concept.[2]

Syntonic and dystonic integration pertains to more than simply those occasional episodes of indecision and deliberation. Rather, this pairing of elements is meant to identify deeper, constitutive features of one's personal identity and its fractured components. Thus, a posture of choice-worthiness concerning the meaning of one's self emerges in this dialectic. In engaging in these types of integration, the individual seeks to make decisions beyond what pertains to this or that occasional episode—decisions that rather pertain to the kind of character he or she wishes to be. Through these decisions, a kind of fundamental conviction is established about the person we seek to claim.

All of us have syntonic components to our personal stories, elements of our personal history that, when reported in a narrative of personal identity, constitute the substance of our enduring values and experiences and give shape to our convictions and aspirations about ourselves. Perhaps we identify as Catholic, as faithful, as honest, as heterosexual, as healthy.

At the same time, we all have dystonic elements as well—that is, portions of our experience, perhaps ongoing and enduring, which seem counter, or alien, or dissonant from that story of our identity which we prefer, or find solace and due pride. Dystonic aspirations or inclinations, to alcohol, promiscuity, pornography, or power, for example, constitute those features of ourselves that are incongruent with our idealized, flourishing self, the self fully integrated as

---

2. Richard Joelson, "Syntonic and Dystonic," at https://richardbjoelsondsw.com/articles/syntonic-dystonic/.

an emotional, rational and embodied agent of moral worth and appropriation. Presuming none of us to be saints—that is, fully actualized in our capacity for total flourishing—it is safe to assume that ego-dystonic elements to our personal narrative still persist and, notwithstanding our intentions to act otherwise, are likely to perdure during the span of our lives.

Typically, in the sacrament of reconciliation, for example, our ego-syntonic self is sufficiently aware so as to provide an account, however bitter, of those ego-dystonic elements of our selves or actions and narrate them in such a way that they are identified, appropriated, and at the same time repudiated concerning our future personal narrative. "To sin no more and avoid the near occasion of sin" is the typical rallying cry of the ego-syntonic, contrite heart.

How one begins to consider syntonic and dystonic aspects of a single person over time constitutes an essential question for Christian personal identity and points out the essential work of the *Confessions* of St. Augustine. For the *Confessions* does more than simply narrate the experience of a single person over time through various syntonic and dystonic moments. Rather, the *Confessions* is fundamentally an argument, as opposed to a simply personal telling, for a particular vision of personal identity precisely in light of the competing components.

This paper will examine various models of narrative identity that comprise syntonic and dystonic elements and then suggest normative criteria for evaluating those models drawn from what I take to be the argument of the *Confessions*. Critical to the normative evaluation of competing versions of personal identity is the recognition that first-person accounts are especially vulnerable to selective preference and prejudice and it is for this reason that they alone cannot constitute a normative description for Christian identity. Instead, it will be the Church's theology of creation that provides the normative principle that allows St. Augustine (and us) to reject certain narrative identities and adopt a particular narrative posture. That stance, it turns out, will become the normative stance for Christian identity for centuries to come and it is its particular success as the norm for Christian identity that speaks to the genius of St. Augustine.

1. Agonistic Identity

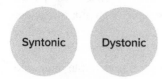

The first model for narrative identity is what I would identify as the Agonistic Model. In this narrative sequence the protagonist, or enduring "I," in fact names an amalgam of rival principles, each competing for dominance in the field of identity. Manichaeism, with its promotion of a thoroughgoing materialist cosmos, offers a narrative of dualist identities in an enduring struggle (agony) for control. In this narrative sequencing, the protagonist is loosely identified with ego-syntonic aspirations, but is, on a regular basis overruled by dystonic, rival principles for motivation. "I still thought it was not ourselves who sin," Augustine says in book 5, "but some other nature within us that is responsible [*sed nescio quam aliam in nobis peccare naturam*]. My pride was gratified at being exculpated by this theory," he says (5.10.18). In other words, my narrative of personal identity allowed me to draw upon a cosmology which rendered those uncomfortable portions of character to be sufficiently sequestered off as "dystonic," that is, alien to the truer notion of who I am. "When I had done something wrong," he continues, "it was pleasant [i.e., I found it to be a beneficial strategy for confronting cognitive dissonance] to avoid having to confess that I had done it" (5.10.18).

The Agonistic Self is something of a microcosm of the larger cosmic conflagration of good and evil. The Good Principle is victim to attacks by the Evil Principle and, in that sense, shares in the dystonic struggle of various creatures, both human and otherwise. Here the subject of narrative identity draws upon a kind of sympathy with the divine who is also subject to dystonic experiences in otherwise integral identity. The self, being the microcosm of a macrocosmic struggle, participates in a galactic agony of good and evil.

Because Manichaean psychology is so inextricably linked with bizarre cosmogonic elements, it is tempting to dismiss its proposed narrative of personal identity as fantastic and largely absurd. But this would be to ignore the compelling features it apparently offered to its worldwide followers, including Augustine. In this landscape of macrocosmic agony, the self with its dystonic features is easily recognized and, in some ways, comforted by acknowledging an affinity and empathy with more pervasive, global, or cosmic suffering. The Manichees were known for their austere asceticism, in part motivated by what some may call their exaggerated empathy with all living creatures—who similarly share in the cosmic agony.

The encounter with Faustus the Manichee will prove disappointing, however, as he appears to Augustine as woefully underprepared to address Augustine's most compelling concerns. Impressed by Faustus' rhetorical skills and personal humility, Augustine will nonetheless become increasingly disenchanted with the sect (largely on cosmological grounds, later on psychological terms) and begin to disentangle himself from the utter confusion surrounding a plausible narrative of personal experience. "Thus it came about that this Faustus, who was a death-trap for many, unwittingly and without intending it began to spring the trap in which I was caught, for thanks to your hidden providence, O my God, your hands did not let go of my soul" (5.13).

Through events detailed in the subsequent books, Augustine will begin to disentangle himself from a net of false propositions, each of which served to construct a narrative of personal identity that proved utterly absurd. Against the notion that there is a kind of correspondence between cosmic forces and rival, internal ambitions, for example, he will narrate the very ordinary experience of multiple and conflicting motivations for actions (8.13). The materialist schema seems to buckle under the strain of lived experience, Augustine argues, if we ascribe to our motives external substances of varying degrees of influence. An honest assessment of our everyday actions betrays a myriad of motivations entangled with each other—some good, some evil, none of which could be said to give witness to a singular dominant cosmic principle. In the world of cosmically driven impulses, "the soul is torn apart in its distress" (8.10.24). The agonistic narrative, in other words, does not seem to bear up under the stress of actual experience.

Through his brief stint with the Academics and a more sustained encounter with Neoplatonism, Augustine begins to wean himself off of the notion of Evil as a substantive entity and thereby comes to see that the very notion of an "evil substance" is philosophically implausible. For my purposes, it is important to note that the shift in narrative identity follows as a result in a shift in a theology of created being. This transition in cosmology will set the stage for the psychological conversion to follow in book 8, as it is along this axis of cosmology that a narrative identity of a Christian sort will begin to emerge. Augustine will begin to recover and see in the Church's theology of creation not simply a rival vision of the cosmos but a rival vision of self as an enduring protagonist within that cosmic drama. Evil impulses (dystonic elements) within a narrative of personal identity will not betray some large-scale cosmic conflagration, but the oscillating weakness of a single soul (*totam eram*) weighed down by customs and habits—all of which find their origins in the choices of the singular protagonist over time, a self of enduring substance through a narrative of sin and conversion.

The Agonistic Self will collapse, then, under its own weight both for its inability to sustain a plausible account of the multiple motivations within a single identity and for its dependence upon incorrect notions of such foundational matters of substance, evil, goodness, creation, and God. The self is not a microcosm of agonistic struggle, for the "dystonic" elements are not rooted in any kind of rival substance of material sources. The "I," then, narrated in a story of personal identity, cannot be sufficiently described as a victim of rival forces. The self that emerges in the story of Augustine is a singular substance whose origins are entirely good, surrounded by a myriad of objects in a cosmos of supreme goodness. Syntonic and dystonic elements do not identify rival substances, rather, they identify rival features of a single substance, an enduring self within a drama of sin and healing.

2. Political Identity

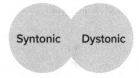

Remnants of this agonistic identity find some parallels in contemporary communities. Alcoholics Anonymous literature speaks repeatedly of recognizing the powerlessness one experiences, not so much in terms of a cosmically oriented entity but rather as a particular weakness, namely, alcohol. "We know that little good can come to any alcoholic who joins A.A.," their literature states, "unless he has first accepted his devastating weakness and all its consequences."[3] Indeed, the very first and crucial step in this program of recovery is admitting "that we were powerless over alcohol—that our lives had become completely unmanageable."[4] In this case, it seems the dystonic elements of a personal narrative are accounted for in language that is largely passive before a power that overwhelms and supersedes otherwise self-directed activity. In some ways, A.A. describes the alcoholic who denies this fact in a manner

3. *Twelve Steps and Twelve Traditions* (New York, NY: Alcoholics Anonymous World Services, 1981), 21.

4. *Twelve Steps and Twelve Traditions*, 21.

similar to that of Manichaean literature. If there is a gnosis associated with a path toward liberation in the more contemporary A.A. literature, it is the acknowledgement that before alcohol the person stands as a victim of forces beyond his or her capacity for self-control.

3. Political Identity in Alcoholics Anonymous

A.A., however, is not entirely agonistic in its narrative structure, for while the rhetoric of powerlessness dominates the descriptions of the alcoholic before the deadly liquor, they do maintain a significant degree of syntonic aspirations or self-directedness. The second crucial step in the famous twelve-step program calls upon the individual to "come to believe that a Power greater than ourselves could restore us to sanity."[5]

With this step, a not-insignificant element of self-directedness begins to emerge, for it is from the personal resources of the individual protagonist that the recognition of a higher power is made possible. Unlike the Manichaean schema, A.A. does not ask individuals to assume a globally passive stance before the narrative events of one's life. Rather, inasmuch as the person is a passive victim, his or her victimization takes place in a much more localized manner, namely, in the presence of alcohol. And this is key: it is from that position of authentic self-awareness that the person begins to consider other resources available for his or her assistance.

Step Three in the twelve-step program further underscores the self-directed decision-making capacities at the center of the A.A. narrative. In this step, individuals are encouraged to make "a decision to turn our will and our lives over to the care of God as we understand him."[6] More will be said about this latter qualification. For now, I wish to point out that in this narrative structure, the individual protagonist adopts a more authentically self-directing posture in the overall schema. Although a certain weakness predominates in some portions of the individual's life, the individual maintains enough of a first-person capacity to identify, claim, admit, denounce, or otherwise engage the dystonic. More

5. *Twelve Steps and Twelve Traditions,* 25.
6. *Twelve Steps and Twelve Traditions,* 34.

specifically, the person identifies himself or herself as both a subject under the (presumably) provident Power and as one who is enabled to invoke assistance in containing and, perhaps overcoming, the dystonic elements.

In this political identity, then, an individual exercises a certain self-directing choice for one's overall condition and, invoking another subject with significantly higher resources (the higher power), begins to broker an arrangement in which the newly formed life story is no longer vulnerable to the devastating attacks of alcohol and its allures. Note that the agreement does not eliminate the threat from those dystonic portions but instead seeks containment and control, much like a majority political party in the face of strong and persistent but now (hopefully) minority voices. One is never cured of alcoholism, A.A. maintains; one is simply recovering from its consequences and achieving, with the assistance of a higher power, one's overall syntonic aspirations and identity.

4. Concerning the Political Self

One might raise a similar criticism against the Political Self as that which was brought forward against the agonistic narrative. Though one might applaud, I think, the notion that there is a dominant protagonist who essentially makes the decisions at the center of the political narrative, this notion still grants a quasi-substantive agency to alcohol itself, a kind of granting of significant power and standing over and against the individual and his or her syntonic wishes. Although this may ring true experientially, Augustine would surely want to challenge investing alcohol with too much determining authority.

Most importantly, it seems, Augustine would challenge the notion of the higher power being entirely subject to the individual's own construal—"as one understands Him." Although it makes little sense to invoke a higher power one does not understand, the absence of a revelatory doctrine or community to provide normative content to the notion of a higher power seems perilous. (The two classic pieces of A.A. literature, the "Big Book" [*Alcoholics Anonymous*][7] and *Twelve Steps and Twelve Traditions*, certainly allude to traditional Christian elements of providence: care and well-being for the subject of divine affection, but A.A. literature repeatedly argues against any sort of doctrinal affiliation in its literature despite the clearly Christian bias in its tone).

---

7. See *Alcoholics Anonymous* (New York, NY: Alcoholics Anonymous World Services, 2001).

Against the political narrative of personal identity, Augustine will assert that the conception of God as the supremely good Creator is not merely the subjective preference of a Christian in search of a personal equilibrium, but the received doctrinal tradition to which a Christian must submit. In affirming the Church's theology of creation, one indirectly assumes the structure of personal identity that now must follow from it.

These normative elements of Augustine's newly discovered Christian faith are well documented throughout the scholarly literature and need not be repeated here. For our purposes it is enough to highlight a few central features.

5. Cosmology and Conversion

Augustine comes to see that the God of the Christian faith is the one, supremely good Creator of all that exists. All things in this cosmogonic theology participate in the divine goodness by the sheer fact of their existence. Any instance of evil in the universe is understood, then, not as the product of some direct, creative action on the part of God, but as a diminution of a good that is already present. Evil is not a substance with its own ontic independence, but instead names a lack or privation of being, which diminishes the creature.

Our experience of morally dystonic events, then, is not due to an encounter with a rival substance or alien character, but the lived experience of singularly good self, suffering a kind of diminishment due to the lingering effects of original sin and the habitual distortion of the will. Agonistic theories of personal identity fail, then, along a trajectory that is theological, not therapeutic. For the failure is due to its inadequate notions of evil and goodness as such. Augustine will argue that the dystonic features of one's personal experience will be due to some kind of an "internal" diminishment of an enduring self, and not the agony of a creature caught in a galactic drama of good and evil principles.

Finally, the content of the theology of creation will extend beyond a consideration of the mere goodness of existence, extending rather to the goodness of the unfolding of the universe, whether in its parts or in its entirety. There is a telic structure to the unfolding of things, in other words, and it is precisely the "natures of things," that will form the normative structure for ongoing discernment of the dystonic elements.

What makes a feature of the Christian self authentically dystonic, in other words, will not be the fact that it makes one's self uncomfortable, embarrassed, powerless, or ashamed, but that the dystonic behavior is out of sorts with the structural integrity of the human person as occupying an ordered cosmos. Over time, the feelings of dystonia will have to be trained according to this telic structure. One must learn what precisely ought to be an occasion for dystonic or cognitive dissonance.

6. Anomic Christianity

Over time, the axis of integration shifts from an egocentric equilibrium to that of a single character within a cosmic (or theological) axis. What constitutes those "disordered" portions of the self, then, will not be some kind of internal evaluation, but an objective evaluation. The integrated self will be coordinated with the cosmos and its telic structures established by God, not the personal or affective states of an isolated individual. That is why the *Confessions* ends with an extended meditation on the structure of the cosmos and its theological significance. The "I" becomes integrated not with its own horizons of concern but with the design and ordering of the universe at large.

This shift toward "objective disordering" of the dystonic narrative elements is critical in the development of a Christian personality, whereby the axis of integration shifts from an exclusively subjective axis to an objective axis of nature and cosmos. In the absence of an objective ordering context, the search for equilibrium can become entirely anomic.

It is precisely the abandonment of the ordered cosmos that has led to the emergence of what I would identify as the anomic Christian.

7. Anomic Identity: "Coming Out"

LGBT narratives of "coming out," at least from the perspective of traditional Christian narrative identity, seem to have accomplished this abandonment of the ordered cosmos. Over and against communities of narrative identity that traditionally have described non-telic sexual inclinations as a dystonic facet of one's personal identity, LGBT rhetoric (broadly conceived) argues that it is certain traditionally dystonic elements that now must be reimagined as syntonic, that is, consonant with one's overall aspirations and values.

In this newer schema, one's narrative identity seems to no longer include sexually dystonic elements but is, instead, repositioned as consonant with the newly reconstituted self. Interestingly, this reconstitution of narrative identity is often accompanied by a newly articulated "creation narrative" of sorts. The "at one time held to be dystonic" elements are redescribed as a feature of one's identity present from the very origins of consciousness, the original setting in which an identity unfolds. Dystonic elements of one's narrative are now simply admitted as a constitutive given, and not a matter of choosing, and thus not candidate to be evaluated from the syntonic side of things.

And so it seems that when asked to re-describe sexual preference as a dystonic feature capable of being confronted from the vantage of one's syntonic aspirations, one is met with a declaration of refusal, the dystonic now embraced and re-identified as syntonic. Because one no longer accounts for one's self as a person with dystonic, homosexual inclination, but instead as a gay person, any framing of non-telic sexual praxis as dystonic is rejected. In this scenario, the call to chastity is received as an invitation to self-loathing.

8. Character, Conversion, and Cosmos

Authentic Christian identity cannot be derived from such subjective conditions alone, I will argue, and thus stands in stark contrast to this modern narrative milieu.

Ironically, one might thank the Manichaean tradition for introducing into the West through Augustine the strong corollary between objective, cosmic circumstances and psychic distress. Augustine will eventually abandon Manichaean gnostic cosmology and replace it with critically important new elements: a supremely good Creator who creates out of sheer love and generosity, a Creator of all things that are substantially good, a Creator incapable of producing an evil substance. But Augustine will retain the fundamental convictions that ego identity is a product of cosmic convictions, and that the self is not a Cartesian consumer who merely shops among a set of rival versions of personal identity and adopts various postures as convenience permits. Instead, "I" am an enduring substance in a created universe, willed into existence from nothingness by a God who is supremely good and intensely interested in my authentic well-being; a Creator who empathizes with the creaturely existence and provides a strategy for healing, renewal, restoration—not control, conquest, domination, or destruction.

The progression from Christian cosmos to Christian character also provides an objective, normative standard for authentically identifying syntonic and dystonic features of one's narrative identity. Dystonic elements become more than simply self-referential obstacles or interference, they become sin—a willful distortion of one's fundamental, objective, telic trajectory toward eternal friendship with the Divine.

For Augustine, the breakthrough regarding his conversion narrative was less about embracing the dystonic features of his psyche and more about discovering the implications of the Church's theology of God and creation and its implications for personal identity. Through his discovery of the Christian God as Creator and Redeemer, Augustine discovers himself as an enduring agent through conversion and change, a character made whole by a God who is the supremely Good Creator of all that exists. Evil cannot connote the presence of a substantive agency, and so cannot be a "character" in the story of conversion and redemption. As a privation, it lacks the qualifications of personified agency.

The goodness of God as the Creator of all that exists, and the source of the telic structure of the cosmos newly discovered, allows Augustine to find himself by no longer seeking himself, for the search for happiness is not satisfied within the horizon of an ego-syntonic axis alone. Against the modern Anomic Self, Augustine proposes a broader context of discernment, beyond the ego-enclosed world of self-satisfaction and equilibrium and within a theology of creation and redemption, a relationship to a wholly other, the Creator and Redeemer of all that is good.

In fact, the Church does not privilege any ego-syntonic narratives, in that the Church is not immediately concerned about the status quo of any psyche. Holiness is achieved through intimacy with God, not personal equilibrium. Boors and blockheads are all candidates for the kingdom; for it is divine intimacy, not psychic adroitness or managed equilibrium, in which fulfilling happiness is found.

9. Christian Identity

The modern obsession with self-acceptance, personal equilibrium, and the endless quest to overcoming cognitive dissonance in the pursuit of psychic integrity is in some ways the fruit of the collapse of a normative ordering of creation of the material order as given. Set adrift in a cosmos of an indifferent biology, the modern self is left to its own self-enclosed horizon of therapeutic feelings, condemned to seek an equilibrium among diminishing returns, subject to an endless list of ever evolving demands, which are framed not through a tradition-guided inquiry but rather through virtual mob rule.

The very framing of sexual integrity along personal identities shows how far from a normative ordering of material creation we have traveled. In fact, the Church has no teaching against homosexuality any more than she has a teaching against stealing twenty-dollar bills. Just as it is entirely *per accidens* that the amount stolen is in twenty-dollar notes, so, too, it is *per accidens* that one's non-telic sexual activity is expressive of so-described homosexual inclinations. No matter what the interests of the parties involved, sodomy, fellatio, masturbation and the like are condemned in their very objective structure. This is the foundation of the much-hated expression "objectively disordered" acts. They are objectively evil, not because one's personal dignity is to be maligned, but because one's private inclination is not particularly relevant in establishing the moral norm. Personal inclination is something of a null set, irrelevant to the negative moral evaluation of the sexual action involved. For this reason, too, one can sometimes risk a kind of Catholic Cartesianism at work when appeals to the "body/soul" composite are invoked against a hyper-subjectivism without a sufficient affirmation that the body/soul composite names an organic substance at work in an objectively ordered cosmos.

Human nature must be understood on the basis of the unity of body and soul, far removed from any sort of physicalism or naturalism, we are told. But this runs counter to the core affirmation of Augustine's efforts, for it was precisely in coming to affirm the goodness of material creation that he was able to more fully grasp what it would mean to be a self, a soul united to a material body. That union would be more than a mere accidental occasion of interaction; it would be an ontically rich union that carries with it normative implications. Certain feelings and thoughts would become dystonic, Augustine would learn, not because of any conflict with any equally compelling sentiment but rather because they were in conflict with the biological structure of his body to which he was substantially united. The lodestar would shift from a zero point of personal equilibrium to a still point of truth outside the self, in the created order of a loving Creator. In the realist world of created goodness, I am less concerned about interior conflicts and more concerned with stepping out of tune with being itself. The goal, if that is the way to put it, is to unite in my experience that which is already integral.

The goodness of God is manifest in the telic structure of the cosmos, the telic structure of the body, the creation of the substantial soul, and the plan for its healing and restoration. In this fundamental framework, "I" am an enduring character over time, one subject, created by God. Any dystonic elements (which are not in accord with the telic structure of the universe and its creatures) are due to my own decision-making, my own habits, and thus are of my own making.

I am, nonetheless, neither destroyed nor defeated by these dystonic forces, save by my own choosing, and in confronting these elements through the process of reform and conversion, enter more deeply into the fundamental order of things, the prevailing grace of a good God, who is *the* enduring protagonist in the drama of all stories of sin and redemption.

Augustine comes to see, through reflecting deeply on the implications of the Church's theology of creation, that it is truer to one's self to narrate a story of a prodigal son reconciled to a loving Father than to settle for a broken self in a cosmic fracture, or manage a brokered détente with rival forces utterly beyond one's power, or entertain a dramatic fantasy of imaginative integrity. Turning to the goodness and beauty of things, he casts himself on the care of a loving Creator and Redeemer, and in so doing discovers himself as a complete person, loved into existence by God and called from eternity into an enduring friendship of love.

10. Epilogue

Whether through the primitive cosmologies of the ancient world or the more sophisticated narratives of the modern self, one can only look upon the human condition with profound compassion and see in its perennial struggle the inescapable burden of confronting its woundedness and seeking a path toward a remedy.

The Church, as it moves forward in pastoral care in the contemporary landscape, may wish to put forward a greater effort in renewing confidence in the presence of the good Creator. By reflecting more deeply on the goodness of creation and its structures, it may enable the seeker to come to see that the aim of Christian living is not to achieve personal equilibrium but rather to attain greater attunement with the objective ordering of creation in the Logos/ Christ, whose wisdom is our norm, whose promise of redemption is our only ground for hope.

It is the singular intention of this essay inspired by Augustine to propose to the contemporary reader the total Christ, to see in the Logos of all things and the Redeemer of all sin, the One who comes forward to meet us in our quest for a resolution. Only in the encounter with the total Christ may the human person's total self be understood, a self that is sustained by love, fractured by sin, attracted by grace. Only in the face of the total Christ are the deepest aspirations of the human heart fulfilled—to be transformed by a truth made love, to be affirmed through a recognition made acceptance, to be freed through a confession made the occasion of lasting joy.

BOOK 6

Augustine's Anxiety and Ours

Andrew Hofer, OP

In the Prolegomena to his unparalleled commentary on the *Confessions*, James J. O'Donnell focuses on Augustine's "powerful and evident anxieties— evident on every page."[1] O'Donnell speaks of the Bishop of Hippo's urgent concern with the right use of language, "for to use language wrongly is to find oneself praising a god who is not God."[2] For O'Donnell, Augustine's anxiety is intensified because of a loss of privacy: he cannot hide from God. "Anxiety so pervades the *Confessions*," O'Donnell claims, "that even the implicit narrative structure is undermined."[3] One might expect that "the text will move from restlessness to rest, from anxiety to tranquility."[4] In some ways that is true, O'Donnell continues, but in other ways we find Augustine still anxious in books 10–13, after he tells us of his baptism and his peace in book 9. Shouldn't the bishop by now be enjoying more repose in the wake of all his troubles? Instead, he deems human beings opaque to themselves, and must always submit to God in order to know the truth of who they are. Augustine's God, on the other hand as O'Donnell reminds us, is utterly without anxiety.

1. James J. O'Donnell, *Augustine: Confessions*, vol. 1, *Introduction and Text* (Oxford: Clarendon Press, 1992), xvii. This three-volume work is publicly available in electronic form at www .stoa.org/hippo/comm.html.

2. O'Donnell, *Augustine: Confessions*, vol. 1, xvii.

3. O'Donnell, *Augustine: Confessions*, vol. 1, xviii.

4. O'Donnell, *Augustine: Confessions*, vol. 1, xviii.

From that focus on Augustine's anxiety, O'Donnell turns to give one of the greatest lines of Augustinian scholarship in the past fifty years: "All of us who read Augustine fail him in many ways."[5] He summarizes no less than seven ways of failing Augustine. In this list, we can notice, perhaps, O'Donnell's own anxiety in offering his brilliant commentary on one of the world's literary masterpieces—a work that he finds riddled with anxiety. Although O'Donnell does not define what he means by anxiety, we can ponder how we use the term and reflect upon the prevalence of anxiety today.

Rollo May's *The Meaning of Anxiety* is considered a classic study of the topic. In the revised edition, he writes, "It is agreed by students of anxiety—[Sigmund] Freud, [Kurt] Goldstein, [Karen] Horney, to mention only three—that anxiety is a diffuse apprehension, and that the central difference between fear and anxiety is that fear is a reaction to a specific danger while anxiety is unspecific, 'vague,' 'objectless.'"[6] May continues, "The special characteristics of anxiety are the feelings of *uncertainty* and *helplessness* in the face of the danger" (emphases in original).[7] Anxiety draws attention to the core of our being, our very awareness of existence, in an inner conflict. May gives this definition: "*Anxiety is the apprehension cued off by a threat to some value that the individual holds essential to his existence as a personality*" (emphasis in original).[8] In anxiety, our existence could be threatened by many perceived evils—death, the loss of freedom, meaninglessness, or the separation from someone or something that defines us.

Anxiety sounds awful, but it varies considerably and always affirms to protect our existence when we perceive ourselves to be vulnerable or under attack. When anxiety is healthy, it enables us to be alert for a possible danger, just as healthy people should have fears about certain objective dangers. Normal anxiety can and should be used for the betterment of life. In his review of cases of those with anxiety, Rollo May finds that people who score highly on intelligence and creativity tests are more apt to be anxious.[9] It is true that if we are not aware, not engaged with the complexities of the world, we will not be anxious. It is also true that if we have certainty and feel helped in the face of problems, we will not be anxious—no matter how terrible things are.

More recently than the revised edition of May's classic work, the National

---

5. O'Donnell, *Augustine: Confessions*, vol. 1, xix.

6. Rollo May, *The Meaning of Anxiety*, rev. ed. (New York: Norton, 1977), 205.

7. May, *The Meaning of Anxiety*, 205.

8. May, *The Meaning of Anxiety*, 205.

9. May, *The Meaning of Anxiety*, 384–89.

Institute of Mental Health distinguishes between occasional anxiety and anxiety disorders. It states:

> Occasional anxiety is an expected part of life. You might feel anxious when faced with a problem at work, before taking a test, or before making an important decision. But anxiety disorders involve more than temporary worry or fear. For a person with an anxiety disorder, the anxiety does not go away and can get worse over time. The symptoms can interfere with daily activities such as job performance, schoolwork, and relationships.[10]

Anxiety disorders appear in several forms, including generalized anxiety disorder, panic disorder, and sundry phobias. Let us concentrate on the first. Generalized anxiety disorder is manifest over most days for at least a six-month period. Its symptoms, according to the National Institute of Mental Health, include:

- Feeling restless, wound-up, or on-edge
- Being easily fatigued
- Having difficulty concentrating; mind going blank
- Being irritable
- Having muscle tension
- Difficulty controlling feelings of worry
- Having sleep problems, such as difficulty falling or staying asleep, restlessness, or unsatisfying sleep.

Because of its significance and prevalence, we can look at anxiety in many ways that could be combined—psychological, physical, medical, social, and spiritual. Each of these ways could be further subdivided and then considered by approaches that differ markedly from each other. No single approach of ours could possibly make all anxieties understood or, more importantly, disappear. For example, a saint who accepts abundant spiritual blessing could have a chemical imbalance that makes him or her prone to a certain kind of anxiety. Nevertheless, we can believe that the God who heard Augustine's *Confessions* wants us to receive his certainty and his help about what is most important in life.

This chapter contributes to the project of interpreting Augustine's *Confessions* in tandem with our contemporary culture by focusing on book 6 through the lenses of Augustine's anxiety and ours. This dual approach may give us insight into this literary masterpiece and our anxiety-ridden culture. I will first

---

10. National Institute of Mental Health, "Anxiety Disorders," at www.nimh.nih.gov/health/topics/anxiety-disorders/index.shtml.

review Augustine's anxiety narrated in book 6. After that, I will position those findings of Augustine's anxiety as a mirror to help us see something of our own anxious state. In doing so, we should ask ourselves questions to think through how our culture can stand to benefit from this reflection. The chapter concludes with Augustine's preaching on the Pauline passage, "The Lord is very near; do not be anxious about anything" (Phil 4:5–6). By seeing book 6 as a mirror of anxieties for a bishop's audience, we can find something of ourselves in this work and be led to the rest that only knowing God's merciful presence can give.

1. Anxiety in Book 6

Book 6 begins with a series of questions indicating that Augustine has become wayward from God, even though God created him to be "wiser than the birds in the sky" (Job 35:11). He confesses to God: "Yet I was walking a dark and slippery path, searching for you outside myself I had sunk to the depth of the sea. I lost all faith and despaired of every finding the truth" (6.1.1).[11] We thus immediately find anxious questioning, meandering, utter faithlessness, and complete despair. Augustine, it seems, wants us to read the rest of the book from that perspective.

He first offers two models for his life: Monica and Ambrose (6.1.1–5.8). Next, Augustine concentrates on the anxieties regarding extremes found in the world: himself at the imperial court and the drunken beggar (6.6.9–10). Then, still in the world, but of greater nobility, are his friendships with Alypius and Nebridius and the anxieties that beset them (6.7.11–10.17). These friendships bear upon how Augustine considers things even more intimate. Augustine turns inward to his life, reviewing his past and his sexual loves regarding the mother of his son, a prospective girl for marriage, and a mistress—all left unnamed, unlike Alypius and Nebridius (6.11.18–15.25). Finally, he turns in his heart up to God in the context of discussions with friends to consider the shortness of his life and God's judgment (6.16.26). We begin with the two models of right faith for Augustine: his mother and his spiritual father.

Monica and Ambrose: Models of Catholic Faith for an Anxious Heart
A common fear in classical and late antique literature appears in descriptions of a sea voyage, and Augustine uses that *topos* to emphasize his mother's peace

---

11. In her translation, Sister Maria Boulding omits a phrase immediately after "searching for you outside myself." Augustine writes there: *et non inveniebam Deum cordis mei* ("and I was not finding the God of my heart").

in contrast to his own sorry state. He turns immediately from how he had sunk into the depth of the sea of iniquity to his mother's journey from North Africa across the sea to rescue him in Italy. Whereas it would be expected that Monica would show anxiety on the sea, she is instead shown to be steadfast in her fidelity and full of trust in God. When her ship encountered dangers, she encouraged the sailors because she knew from a dream of God's assurance (6.1.1).

Monica reached Augustine and found him in despair of ever discovering the truth. She, in contrast, was confident in the Lord. Back in book 3, Augustine wrote that Monica had an inspired dream, which "gave her comfort in her present anxiety." In the dream, she saw him standing with her on the wooden ruler of faith (3.11.20). An unnamed North African bishop then confirmed to her that "a son of tears" would not be lost (3.12.21). In book 6, Monica's crying, rather than showing anxiety, bespeaks faith in Christ, who would answer the widow's grief by raising her son from the dead and returning him, speaking, back to his mother (cf. Luke 7:11-17). She knew that God would make Augustine a faithful Catholic before she departed from this life. Monica's trust in God led her in Italy to hang on the words of another bishop, this time Ambrose of Milan. This illustrates that she found her faith in the Catholic Church and gladly submitted to the Church's bishop. In fact, when she was corrected for continuing a North African practice of bringing bread and wine to the martyr's tombs, she immediately abandoned her custom in favor of Ambrose's judgment. Later, in book 9, we will learn that many years earlier Monica herself had become addicted to wine. It is therefore significant that here Augustine upholds her as "not enslaved to any habit of wine-bibbing" (6.2.2). An anxious heart at times turns to alcohol for soothing, but Monica turned to God—through the preacher Ambrose.

In narrating this time in Milan, Augustine thinks it unlikely that Monica would have acted so virtuously if the bishop had been anyone other than Ambrose, whom she so revered. She trusted him primarily because of her hope in Augustine's salvation, and thought his preaching flowed with the waters of eternal life. When Ambrose praised her to Augustine, Augustine felt that the bishop did not really know what kind of a son she had. He writes, "I was full of doubts about all these things and scarcely believed it possible to find the way of life" (6.2.2). Augustine was not even yet praying to God, and he was "restlessly eager for argument" (6.3.3). Ambrose, who served as a model of the faith for Monica's perseverance, appears ready to assist for Augustine's conversion—even when Augustine does not want to reach up to God.

Augustine admits that, seeing his bishop at the time, he could not have guessed what was going inside of Ambrose's heart: the hope he had, the struggles against temptations to his high office, the encouragement he received, and the delights of the Word of God he savored. These, presumably, were exactly what was going on within the heart of Augustine the bishop as author of the *Confessions*. Ambrose seemed almost always busy in service to others. Although he would occasionally refresh himself, such as in his silent reading, Augustine never found the bishop available to answer his private questions, which were arising from his inner turmoil as it came to a feverish pitch. In lieu of private conversation, Ambrose's public preaching assisted Augustine to think through his heart's concerns. It prompted him to wonder what it meant to be made to the image of God. By listening to Ambrose's sermons, Augustine came to be free of the carnal imagination that he entertained as a Manichean of God's materiality. God's image in us is not found in our bodily form.

Augustine was gradually learning from the Church's preaching this new way of thinking and living, but only gradually. "The anxiety which gnawed at my inner self to determine what I could hold onto as certain," Augustine comments, "was the more intense in proportion to my shame at remembering how long I had been deluded and beguiled by assurances that falsehoods were certain, and had in my headstrong, childish error babbled about such very dubious things as though they were proven" (6.4.5). In other words, Augustine was understanding how for many years he had been certain about things erroneous. He came also to reject the hypocrisy of the academics who rigidly claim that no certainty exists. Instead, he was being moved by Ambrose's preaching toward the surety of Scripture. He found himself wanting to believe, and he began to prefer the Catholic faith—but he still wavered. Augustine closes this section of the models of Catholic faith with the admission of his anxiety and the Lord's faithfulness to him:

> All the while, Lord, as I pondered these things you stood by me; I sighed and you heard me; I was tossed to and fro and you steered me aright. I wandered down the wide road of the world, but you did not desert me. (6.5.8)

The Anxieties of the Imperial Court and the Drunk Beggar: The World's Extremes

After depicting Monica and Ambrose as models of the faith, Augustine turns to two extremes found in the world: himself at the imperial court and a drunken beggar on a street. Augustine came to Milan because of his promotion to be the Emperor's orator. He realized his misery before giving a speech of praise (full of lies) for the Emperor, the most powerful man in the world. Augustine looks back on himself and laments, "My heart was panting with anxiety and seething with feverish, corruptive thoughts" (6.6.9). His pride was a weight too heavy to bear. He wanted happiness but could not find it in his sinful profession of lies. Instead, he noticed a drunk beggar, and compared that man's life on the streets with his own.

The beggar did not enjoy true happiness, but at least as drunk he had a temporal happiness that eluded Augustine, who remarks, "He was carefree, I apprehensive" (6.6.9). Augustine considers how he would have responded if someone had asked him at the time if he should want to be like that beggar: "I would have chosen to be myself, laden with anxieties and fears" (6.6.9).

Augustine laments that his own life was so much worse than the drunken beggar's. The beggar would sleep off his intoxication, but Augustine in his pride was drunk with a pursuit of worldly glory every morning. The beggar had a sort of merriment; Augustine was miserable. The beggar received some coins after he wished passers-by a good day, something he truly meant, but Augustine received his money by lying in the imperial court. In this depiction, the beggar seems to have no anxiety—and is a more honest man than Augustine, who was not turning to God in humility for help.

Augustine gives a concluding reflection to this scene by recounting how he would converse with his friends about this parallel. It is now to these conversations that we turn and note how anxieties are there described.

Alypius and Nebridius: Friendship and Anxieties

Augustine begins this section by repeating how he discussed what he narrated with his friends, this time naming Alypius and Nebridius. One way of reading the long digression of recounting Alypius's life is to consider how book 6 features Alypius for the reader's anxious heart. Alypius is not a model parental figure (as Monica and Ambrose are), but is a longtime student of Augustine's, one who becomes a close friend. Like Augustine, he was trapped in the anxieties of the world, but he was always guided by our provident God. Augustine and Alypius thus share a common story. In the *Confessions*, Augustine describes himself so often with friends and in terms of his friends. We will later encounter Alypius in Augustine's conversion in the garden (8.11.30). That moment is understood to be *their* conversion, leading to *their* baptism (9.6.14). Augustine's example for his readers, always present to him in his prayer to God that constitutes the *Confessions*, comes after (and through) his example for his friends in the narrative.

Alypius and Augustine hailed from the same town (Thagaste, Numidia), where Augustine first taught Alypius. After Augustine moved back to Carthage, he taught Alypius there as well. Alypius had a fine nobility of character, but Augustine became disturbed by Alypius's addiction to the immoral Carthaginian circus games. Augustine writes, "I was extremely anxious because he seemed to me bent on wasting his excellent promise" (6.7.11). Augustine recounts how one day he was speaking to his students against the immorality of those shows, not thinking of Alypius at all; Alypius was eagerly listening. The result was that God used the unwitting Augustine's heart and tongue to cauterize Alypius's promising mind. Alypius was healed of that affliction, but he became caught in the snare of Manicheanism that was entrapping Augustine. Looking back at the Manichean way of life, Augustine describes it as offering only the appearance of virtue, for it was all a sham.

After this time, Alypius left for Rome to pursue worldly gain in law and arrived there before Augustine. One day a group of friends convinced Alypius to go to the stadium for gladiatorial entertainments; Alypius protested that he would not even look at the show. Rather than trusting in God, Alypius trusted in his own power not to be swayed. The roar of the crowd made him open his eyes to see the bloodshed, and he was caught: "He watched, he shouted, he grew hot with excitement, he carried away with him a madness that lured him back again not only in the company of those by whom he had initially been dragged along but even before them, dragging others" (6.8.13). Augustine comments that God, much later, rescued Alypius from this plight.

As Augustine narrates, Alypius would indeed learn his lesson from this addiction, and from an episode about his earlier study days in Carthage when he was accused of theft. There as a youth, Alypius had heard a commotion, seen another youth run away, and picked up the dropped axe that had been used during the course of the crime. Suddenly, men came and caught Alypius red-handed, or so it seemed. God protected Alypius, and through a providential encounter with an architect responsible for the public buildings, relieved him of the impending corporal punishment or imprisonment. Augustine comments, "The man who would one day be the dispenser of your word and the judge of many a case in your Church departed more experienced and better informed" (6.9.15). In these vignettes from Alypius's life, Augustine shows us how God's hand is at work—even when it cannot be seen at the time. This is one of the most important lessons for the anxious heart: God provides. His help is certain. God provided through Augustine's words, even though the speaker was unaware of it, and he provided through the architect. In a sense, God was building the house of Alypius, for without God all labors are in vain.

In the last descriptions of this section featuring Alypius we find him in Milan, where he came with Augustine. Alypius rose to a high position as Assessor to the Chancellor of the Italian Treasury. Although not yet a Catholic model of faith, Alypius becomes more markedly an example of natural virtues. Alypius laughs at bribes and spurns threats. Nothing, it seems, can deter him—well, almost. He eventually overcame a temptation to use his position's privilege to acquire copied books at a low price. Whereas Augustine begins recounting his friend's life by describing himself as "extremely anxious" for Alypius, he concludes it by showing his fine character as a friend wanting to discuss the most important things about how to live.

Along those lines, we see Nebridius, whom Augustine called his sweet friend (e.g., 9.3.6). Nebridius shares in the aspirations of Augustine and Alypius. As such, Augustine relates that he was "tossed to and fro along with us" (6.10.17). Nebridius had left his parents' wealthy estate near Carthage to live with Augustine. *His* mother, Augustine reports, did not try to follow him. Augustine depicts his group of friends anxiously asking amidst their dissatisfaction and unease with their lives (6.10.17), "How long are we to go on like this?" Augustine concludes this section by commenting, "We were perpetually asking this question, but even as we asked it, we made no attempt to change our ways, because we had no light to see what we should grasp instead, if we were to let go of them" (6.10.17). Their lives were certainly not all bad, but their lives were collectively anxious.

The Anxieties of Life, Marriage, and Loss: Intimate Struggles of the Heart
Augustine begins the next section by reviewing his life:

> For my own part I was reflecting with anxiety and some perplexity how much time had elapsed since my nineteenth year, when I had first been fired with passion for the pursuit of wisdom, resolving that once I had found it I would leave behind all empty hopes and vain desires and the follies that deluded me. (6.11.18)

What follows is a fascinating collision of memories, as Augustine lets his readers hear snippets of conversations and thoughts from the years since he read Cicero's *Hortensius* at the age of 18. He describes this dialogue with himself as wind blowing from this way and that, "hurling my heart hither and thither" (6.11.20). From here, we now enter into Augustine's accounts of the woman he loved, an underaged girl, and a convenient mistress for his uncontrolled sexual appetite.

Whereas Alypius had an awkwardly bad sexual encounter earlier and suffered from some temptations to fascination about sexual pleasure (but not greatly from sexual temptation itself), Augustine could not imagine his life without sex. Augustine had become a teenage father to Adeodatus, and he remained faithful to Adeodatus's mother for all the years since their teenage union. Monica had plans for Augustine to have a proper marriage with a woman of class before his baptism. Arrangements were made for the thirty-one-year-old imperial orator to have a young girl prepared to be his wife. At this time, Augustine and several friends dallied with the idea to form an intentional community, but when they realized that their wives or potential wives might not consent to this arrangement, they abandoned the idea. Augustine's own common-law wife of many years was torn from his side for the sake of his worldly career. She returned to Africa with a vow never to be with another man. Since Augustine could not wait a couple of years for the betrothed girl to be available for marriage, he showed himself a slave to lust and got himself another woman. His decisions for intimacy did not result in relief for his anxious heart, but "the pain became a cold despair" (6.15.25).

Anxiety for Death: God at the End (and All Along the Way)

Book 6's concluding section turns to Augustine's praise of God in the present moment and the recollection of his friends' conversation at that time about life and its judgment. Augustine in some ways favored Epicurean philosophy but knew that it could not be right, as Epicurus refused to believe in the life of the soul after bodily death. In the midst of his miseries, Augustine loved his friends and their conversing with him. In a telling phrase that shows for some today true love, but for the bishop Augustine grave distortion, he writes, "I loved these friends for their own sake, and felt myself loved by them for mine" (6.16.26). Only God is to be loved for his own sake in an everlasting embrace, and all other persons are to be enjoyed only in the Lord. Augustine teaches that in his *On Christian Doctrine* book 1, written about the same time as the *Confessions*. It shows how the first commandment of love, whereby we are to love God with our *whole* heart, *whole* soul, and *whole* mind, has within it space for another commandment of loving, where we are to love our neighbor as ourselves (Matt 22:34–40). Yet as a thirty-one-year-old, Augustine did not accept that.

Augustine concludes book 6 by speaking of his ways as tortuous. He describes his lack of rest in the language of insomnia: "Toss and turn as we may, now on our back, now side, now belly—our bed is hard at every point, for you alone are our rest" (6.16.26). Whereas Augustine's younger self in book 6 does not yet pray, Augustine as the bishop-writer hears how God rescues him from his wretched meanderings: "Run: I will carry you, I will lead you and I will bring you home" (6.16.26). The certainty and the help needed to overcome anxiety are available; Augustine has only by grace to accept. From that review of book 6, we turn to examine our own lives.

2. Augustine's Anxiety in Book 6 as a Mirror for Our Anxiety

How can we relate in some way to the anxiety of book 6? Many people find themselves or their loved ones anxious. An admirer of Augustine's *Confessions*, W. H. Auden published his long reflective poem titled "The Age of Anxiety" in 1947.[12] Some take the titular expression to be apt to characterize the mid-twentieth century.[13] Our society has become, unfortunately, only more anxious since that time.

Various lists of what has made people anxious over the past seventy years or so could be drawn up. Consider the threat of nuclear war during the decades of the Cold War; the increasing rates of marriage and family separation; the digital boom with social media promising instant knowledge and gratification (but often yielding anxiety); employment volatility; and various crises said to threaten the Church, civilization, and the planet.

Most recently at this writing, the Centers for Disease Control and Prevention reported that the coronavirus pandemic has dramatically raised anxiety in the United States.[14] This anxiety has been especially afflicting the young, which may mean that they will develop patterns of anxiety throughout their lives if not healed.

One way of addressing our anxiety is to read the *Confessions* as a mirror for our lives. As with many other writers of antiquity and late antiquity, Augustine used the image of a mirror for his readers' reflection. He considered Sacred Scripture to be a privileged mirror. In fact, as an old bishop he compiled scriptural passages useful for living the Christian life and called his compilation *Speculum*, i.e., The Mirror. In a homily on Psalm 103, Augustine preaches on self-knowledge in order to receive the love of the Lord in beauty: "Your first duty is therefore to see clearly what you are; that will deter you from going in your ugliness to receive the kisses of the beautiful bridegroom. 'But where shall I look, to see myself?' you ask."[15] Augustine continues:

---

12. For a study of Auden's Augustinianism, see Stephen J. Schuler, "Augustinian Auden: The Influence of Augustine on W. H. Auden," Ph.D. diss. Baylor University, 2008. Schuler later published *The Augustinian Theology of W. H. Auden* (Columbia, SC: University of South Carolina Press, 2013).

13. May, *The Meaning of Anxiety*, 4–8.

14. Mark É. Czeisler, et al, "Mental Health, Substance Use, and Suicidal Ideation During the COVID-19 Pandemic—United States, June 24–30, 2020," *MMWR Morbidity and Mortal Weekly Report* 69, no. 32 (2020): 1049–1057, at 1053.

15. Exposition 1 of Psalm 103.4, in *Expositions of the Psalms, 99–120*, trans. Maria Boulding, OSB, WOSA vol. III/19 (Hyde Park, NY: New City Press, 2003), 110.

He has provided his scriptures as a mirror for you, and there you are told, *Blessed are the pure of heart, for they shall see God* (Matt 5:8). In that text a mirror is held out to you. See whether you are one of the pure-hearted it mentions, and grieve if you are not yet like that; grieve in order to become so. The mirror will reflect your face to you. You will not find the mirror flattering you, and neither must you beguile yourself. The reality that is yourself, that is what the mirror shows forth. Look at what you are, and if what you see disgusts you, seek to become otherwise. If in your ugly condition you find yourself repulsive, you are already pleasing to your beautiful bridegroom.[16]

Augustine does not think, however, that only Scripture serves as a mirror. His own works can be mirrors. Augustine writes a letter on the virtuous life for Boniface, an exceedingly high-ranking layman in the imperial government of North Africa, which he concludes by calling the letter a mirror for Boniface.[17] Whatever Boniface finds in that letter or in Sacred Scripture that he still lacks, he is encouraged to acquire it by action and prayer. Similarly, the *Rule of Augustine* concludes by bidding its readers, "Examine yourselves in this little book as in a mirror."[18] We now take book 6 of the *Confessions* as a mirror, using the book's division given above.

Models of Catholic Faith for an Anxious Heart

As a bishop-writer, Augustine does not wallow in the anxiety that he experienced soon after arriving in Milan, but rather instructs his readers through their anxiety. One way of coping with anxiety is to have models of faith in our lives. Monica and Ambrose are, in different ways, ideal models. Because of her faith, Monica could calm even anxious sailors in her voyage to be with her son, and she calmly trusted Bishop Ambrose, who appears in book 6 as the exemplary pastoral leader.

We need parental figures who can model faithful stability when we experience what seems to be an endlessly stormy sea. Some are blessed with a parent or two parents exemplary in the faith. It is significant that the Church wants those baptized to have sponsors, commonly called godparents, who profess the faith for us and with us. Religious are called to be spiritually fruitful in offering

---

16. Exposition 1 of Psalm 103.4, in *Expositions of the Psalms 99–120*, 110–111.

17. Epistle 189.8, in *Letters 156–210*, trans. Roland Teske, SJ, WOSA vol. III/3 (Hyde Park, NY: New City Press, 2004), 262.

18. *Rule of St. Augustine*, chap. 8. For my study, see Andrew Hofer, OP, "Looking in the Mirror of Augustine's Rule," *New Blackfriars* 93 (2012): 263–75.

their lives for the salvation of souls. Clergy can exercise spiritual paternity, and it is common to call a priest "Father" to signify that. In various ways, people can become parental figures by providing solid examples of faith for those who feel at sea.

Who are our faith models in life? Augustine actually must have spent very little private time with the busy Ambrose. Augustine benefited from Ambrose's public preaching. Augustine was gradually being released from certain anxieties because of clarifications of the Catholic faith occurring within the public liturgy. If we feel that we cannot be helped by preachers around us, what about reading great spiritual classics and especially the lives of the saints? Monica can be our spiritual mother; Ambrose can be our spiritual father. Many religious, such as Dominicans, call Augustine "holy father Augustine" because of his Rule that they profess to follow. Personally, I am very grateful for Augustine's paternal care for my community and me.

Moreover, we can be models of faith for others, even when we may have some anxiety still lurking in our heart. We can help others especially through our persistent prayer and in our talk about God. Our tears for our loved ones can be like faithful Monica's. Ambrose cleared away some of Augustine's anxious problems by allowing him to know what the Catholic faith taught about the image of God and how to read the Bible. Ambrose was communicating a new template to interpret reality, a new worldview on all things by giving him a God's-eye view. We can do the same for others. We all need certainty, and the anxious do not have it. It is important not to give them a false certainty. People, after all, could be certain about what is, in fact, not true. As models for others, we can distinguish what is unknown or doubtful and what is most certain because of the Word of God. In this way, God may make us a Monica or an Ambrose for the young Augustines around us.

The World's Extremes

After we see Monica and Ambrose in the mirror of book 6, we find Augustine the successful orator and the drunken beggar on the street. This can reflect for us two extremes in badly coping with anxiety today: the busy workaholic and the non-working alcoholic. Many of us know at least one of these types all too well.

In a recent study of 16,426 working Norwegians, those who could be called "workaholic," according to the Bergen Work Addiction scale, had significantly higher rates of psychiatric illness than those who were not addicted to work. Of the different kinds of illness studied, anxiety was most prominent. About one-third of workaholics met anxiety criteria, whereas (only) about 12 percent of non-workaholics had anxiety.[19] The connection between work addiction and anxiety could be reciprocal, as anxiety leads some to excessive work and excessive work makes some people more anxious.

With regard to the other extreme, although some alcoholics can also be workaholics, we are thinking of non-working alcoholics, especially those who are homeless. Alcohol can lead some to lose their home, and those who are already homeless may turn to alcohol or another substance in addiction to try to cope with the vast problems of their lives. Well over a half a million people were estimated to be homeless in the United States in 2017. Those most adversely affected by addiction are the young. We read such statistics as "71 percent of missing, runaway, throwaway, or abducted children reported a substance abuse."[20]

Neither the workaholic nor the alcoholic may grasp how divine providence can steer an anxious heart away from presumption and despair. Whereas successful workaholics master, control, and produce according to their own efforts by presumption, defeated alcoholics have given up their own worth and the usefulness of their efforts in despair. Sometimes people alternate in their anxieties between presumption and despair. The ends touch, as the saying goes. Since neither one of these approaches is guided by truth, neither can ultimately satisfy the anxious heart. The heart can be deadened by all sorts of things opposite to each other but can be satisfied by only One.

Of the two extremes mirrored in book 6, our attention in Augustine's narration falls more to the one of worldly success, young Augustine the proud lying orator, who comes to see how he is like the drunken beggar—and worse than him. Can we see something of ourselves in Augustine at the imperial court? Do we have a way of living that has something of a lie at its core? Many people pretend, act, or downright lie not just for a job, but also for their relationships.

With Augustine, we now turn to those relationships that are friendships.

19. These statistics are from C. S. Andreassen, M. D. Griffiths, et al., "The Prevalence of Workaholism: A Survey Study in a Nationally Representative Sample of Norwegian Employees," PLoS ONE 9.8 (2014), as summarized in Mark D. Griffiths, "Workaholism and Psychiatric Disorders," at Psychology Today (December 1, 2016), at www.psychologytoday.com/us/blog/in-excess/201612/workaholism-and-psychiatric-disorders. After anxiety, the most prevalent pathology was ADHD (attention deficit, hyperactivity disorder), which was higher than OCD (obsessive-compulsive disorder).

20. Addiction Center, "The Connection Between Homelessness and Addiction," at www.addictioncenter.com/addiction/homelessness/.

Friendships and Anxieties

Augustine features how God assists Alypius through others who are not even aware of God's presence. Augustine admits that he was not even thinking of Alypius or of God when he taught against addiction to games, and we have no evidence that the unnamed architect in Carthage had in mind the Divine Architect who was designing Alypius's life. In describing his friends, Augustine wants us to know God's hidden hand helping other people's lives. Do we believe that God is at work in those around us?

We may think of friends merely in terms of how they are related to our heart's need and how they construct relationships for the need of their hearts. What I do and what they do may align more or less in ways that form or weaken friendships. This may play out in social media's user statistics. Users may want to gain lots of "friends" or "followers" and may measure how often others "like" their posts. Yet, increased rates of social media, rather than relieving anxiety, are accompanied by increased anxiety. Consider this conclusion of a professor of psychology specializing in digital dependence:

> Several recent articles have suggested that social media use is associated with anxiety and this anxiety comes in many forms–all of which are problematic for the person's wellbeing. More than this association, it seems that social media, at least in part, feeds off the anxieties that it generates— subverting the social and psychological tendencies, that most of us have, to fuel its usage.[21]

We do not see social media in book 6, but we do find attention given to friendship and what will satisfy Augustine and his friends. Ultimately, Augustine shows that even fine people drawn together as friends are left wanting something more than what they can give to each other. They need to accept the one who says, "I no longer call you slaves, for a slave does not know what his master is doing. I have called you friends, because I have told you everything I have heard from my Father" (John 15:15).

We also must learn to accept that friendship on the Lord's terms for our anxious heart. By doing so, we in faith will know of the Lord's presence not only in our own lives, but also in the lives of those around us. Even when they do not realize his presence, we can, in friendship with the Lord, be assured of his assistance.

---

21. Phil Reed, "Anxiety and Social Media Usage: Does Anxiety Drive Excessive Usage?" at Psychology Today (February 3, 2020), at www.psychologytoday.com/us/blog/digital-world-real-world/202002/anxiety-and-social-media-use.

Intimate Struggles of the Heart

After Augustine reviews many years of his life through a whirlwind of past thoughts, he lets us see something of his intimate struggles regarding three nameless females: the common-law wife, the girl who enters an arrangement for future marriage, and the convenient mistress. When the first of these three was removed from his life, Augustine described it in terms of his heart being torn out of his body and trailing blood (6.15.25). We know that he writes this account as a celibate bishop, still under suspicion (by others and himself) regarding sexual sins. What do we see in this mirror regarding our own temptations and sins?

In their November 2015 pastoral letter *Create in Me a Clean Heart: A Pastoral Response to Pornography*, the U.S. Bishops conclude with this assurance:

> As we close, we assure all who are struggling with the sin of pornography and striving to cultivate chastity that you are not alone in your struggle. Jesus is with you, and the Church offers you love and support. Trust in and be led by the Holy Spirit. The Lord's mercy and forgiveness are abundant! "As far as the east is from the west, so far has he removed our sins from us" (Ps 103:12). God's grace and concrete help are always available. Healing is always possible.

"Jesus is with you." That is the message of comfort for those struggling with unchastity, and indeed it is what Jesus wanted all to know. On the night before he died, Jesus says, "Do not let your hearts be troubled. You have faith in God; have faith also in me" (John 14:1). He did not leave us orphaned. He promised that he would send another Advocate, the Holy Spirit. In Matthew's account of the Gospel, the risen Lord about to ascend to heaven promises, "I am with you always, until the end of the age" (Matt 28:20).

God at the End (and All Along the Way)

In the brief last section of book 6, Augustine considers God's judgment. He writes, "As I grew more and more miserable, you were drawing nearer. Already your right hand was ready to seize me and pull me out of the filth, yet I did not know it" (6.16.26). Augustine continues, "The only thing that restrained me from being sucked still deeper into the whirlpool of carnal lusts was the fear of death and of your future judgment, which throughout all the swings of opinion had never been dislodged from my heart" (6.16.26). Can we see something about ourselves in this mirror? Can we find that an anxious dissatisfaction with the things of this world may turn us from this passing world to its Creator?

Fear of future judgment can be a salutary remedy for many, but Augustine wants us to see something more than that. He wants us to know of God's presence now, even if we do not feel that presence. We may feel like a restless insomniac, but Augustine wants us to know how God is drawing closer and closer to us in our own restless misery. God stands ready and shouts to us, as he did to Augustine at the close of book 6: "Run: I will carry you, I will lead you and I will bring you home" (6.16.26).

3. Conclusion: From Anxiety to Joy

St. Paul says in the Letter to the Philippians, "The Lord is very near; do not be anxious about anything" (Phil 4:5–6). The Apostle signals a causal relationship. Because of the Lord's nearness, our anxiety can be removed. That is perhaps why book 6, which shares Augustine's anxieties, ends with God's closeness to Augustine.

God's present Word removes anxiety and does something greater. After all, some people look to remove anxiety through mental techniques, excessive work, sleep, pornographic fantasies, volunteering to help others, heavy intoxication, medication, drugs, or even death. Some efforts to remove anxiety are virtuous; others are vicious. In any case, all our efforts, if done without God's grace, are inadequate for what we most need. We need something more than the absence of anxiety, and God gives that. The divine presence not only removes anxiety, it also gives joy. For St. Paul says in this passage to the Philippians, "Rejoice in the Lord always. Again, I say it: rejoice" (Phil 4:4).

We began this chapter with James J. O'Donnell's observations of Augustine's anxiety in the *Confessions* and considerations of anxiety's meaning and prevalence for our contemporary culture. To conclude this chapter on Augustine's anxiety and ours, we listen to some of the preaching of Augustine the bishop on Phil 4:4–6.[22] He preaches not only for his audience about 1600 years ago in North Africa; he preaches for us.

Paul commands his listeners to rejoice in the Lord, and Augustine does not want his people to rejoice in the world. Augustine then imagines an objection, "I'm in the world; obviously, if I rejoice, I rejoice where I am."[23] Here he returns

---

22. Sermon 171, on Phil 4:4–6, in *Sermons (148–183) on the New Testament*, trans. Edmund Hill, OP, WOSA vol. III/5 (Hyde Park, NY: New City Press, 1992), 247–50. All quotations are taken from that translation, with minor adjustments.

23. Sermon 171.1 in *Sermons (148–183)*, 247.

to Paul's own preaching in Athens where we hear, "In him we live, and move, and are" (Acts 17:28). Augustine preaches:

> Seeing that he is everywhere, after all, is there anywhere he isn't? Wasn't he urging precisely this point upon us, for our encouragement? *The Lord is very near; do not be anxious about anything* (Phil 4:5-6). This is something tremendous, that he ascended above all the heavens, and is very near to those who dwell anywhere on earth. Who can this be that is both far away and near at hand, but the one who became our near neighbor out of mercy?[24]

In his mercy, the Lord, who is eternally just and immortal, came close to us, unjust and mortal. He did not become a sinner, but he did become mortal while remaining just. Augustine says, "By taking on your punishment, while not taking on your fault, he canceled both fault and punishment. So, *the Lord is very near, do not be anxious about anything* (Phil 4:5-6)."[25] Augustine explains, "Even if he has ascended above all the heavens in his body, he has not withdrawn in his greatness. He is present everywhere, seeing that he made everything."[26] In fact, God has made us sons and daughters. Augustine asks, "How do we prove this?"[27] He continues:

> The only Son died for us, in order not to remain the only one. He did not want to be the only one, though he died as the only one. The only Son of God made many sons and daughters of God. He bought himself brothers and sisters with his blood, he accepted us though rejected himself, he redeemed us though sold himself, he did us honor though dishonored himself, he gave us life though slain himself. Can you doubt that he will give you good things, seeing that he did not decline to take upon himself your bad things?[28]

Those who are anxious need certainty and help in the face of danger or threat to personal existence. Augustine came to accept the great certainty and help of God, heard in his Word made present in the Church. Through the rest of his life, he continued to accept that help in the face of whatever anxiety that threatened his heart and to offer that divine help to others through his ministry. By God's grace, we can accept Augustine's words, communicating the very Word of God, in newfound joy. Augustine concludes for his original audience and for us:

---

24. Sermon 171.1 in *Sermons (148–183)*, 247.
25. Sermon 171.3 in *Sermons (148–183)*, 249.
26. Sermon 171.3 in *Sermons (148–183)*, 249.
27. Sermon 171.5 in *Sermons (148–183)*, 250.
28. Sermon 171.5 in *Sermons (148–183)*, 250.

So then, brothers and sisters, *rejoice in the Lord,* not in the world; that is, rejoice in the truth, not in iniquity; rejoice in the hope of eternity, not in the brief flower of vanity. Rejoice like that, and wherever and as long as ever you are here; *The Lord is very near; do not be anxious about anything.* (Phil 4:5–6)[29]

29. Sermon 171.5 in *Sermons (148–183),* 250. I am grateful to Fr. James P. Flint, OSB, and Abbot Austin G. Murphy, OSB, for their help in this essay and in my life.

The Liminality of Vision

Gerald P. Boersma

A theology of the spiritual senses and their operations is a rich vein running through Augustine's writings. Just as the *homo exterior* is equipped with diverse senses that enable him to discern sensible reality, so the *homo interior* is furnished with interior senses to perceive God and his presence in the world. However, it quickly becomes evident that, for Augustine, interior sight predominates among the spiritual senses. Augustine readily avails himself of language such as *acies mentis, aspectus, oculus cordis, oculus mentis, uisio,* etc. to describe this interior vision of the heart.

Sight has a particularly pronounced place in *Confessions* 7. This essay will ask what sight delivers to Augustine in that book, but also how sight fails. I will argue that in book 7, the liminality of Augustine's state of conversion is expressed in the language of unconsummated vision. I will demonstrate that the overwhelming question of that book, namely, how to understand the nature of the divine substance, is described as a deficient quest to see. With the aid of divine illumination through the mystical vision(s) at Milan, Augustine does receive intellectual clarity about the divine substance. As such, the ecstasy of book 7 highlights the restored sense of spiritual sight. Nevertheless, the vision of Milan is short-lived; Augustine is left dissatisfied, underscoring the liminal character of book 7 and the inability of sight to deliver, at least in this life, a vision of God.

Of all the senses, maintains Augustine in his *De Trinitate* (*trin.*), sight is "the most excellent" as having the greatest affinity to spiritual vision.[1] Corpo-

---

1. *trin.* 11.1.1.

real and spiritual sight are superior to all other senses on account of their unitive power. In *Soliloquies* 1.6.12–7.13, Augustine offers an analogy between the operation of physical vision, which requires the illumination of the sun in order for the eyes to see, and the operation of interior vision, which requires divine light for reason's gaze to understand. The close relation that he posits between physical sight and interior vision is unsurprising given classical understandings of the operation of sight. As Margaret Miles explains,

> For the classical people who originated the metaphor, sight was an accurate and fruitful metaphor for knowledge because they relied on the physics of vision, subscribed to by Plato and many others, that a ray of light, energized and projected by the mind toward an object, actually touches its object, thereby connecting viewer and object. By the vehicle of the visual ray, the object is not only "touched" by the viewer, but also the object is "printed" on the soul of the viewer. The ray theory of vision specifically insisted on the connection and essential continuity of viewer and object in the act of vision.[2]

Undoubtedly, Augustine's use of the language of sight as a controlling metaphor to express the relation between God and the soul draws on the broader Platonic worldview he inhabits. One immediately perceives the valence ancient ophthalmology has to Augustine as the conceptual infrastructure of his spirituality. First, the will and desire of the viewer must be engaged. Vision, for Augustine, is not a passive exercise. And, second, vision results in a union between the viewer and the object beheld.

The necessary intention, direction, and weight (*pondus*) of vision, in Augustine's understanding, suggest a triangular relation between vision, knowledge, and love. The mind, for Augustine, "joins itself to these images with such extravagant love that it even comes to think itself something of the same sort. . . . It gets conformed to them."[3] The soul, we might say, is molded and formed according to the image to which it looks with affection. Or, in the words of Plotinus, "We are what we desire and look at."[4] Finally, vision is the crowning spiritual sense because, already now, it proleptically leans into the eschatological union between God and the soul that obtains in the beatific vision.

---

2. Margaret Miles, "Vision: The Eye of the Body and the Eye of the Mind in Saint Augustine's '*De trinitate*' and '*Confessions*,'" *The Journal of Religion* 63 (1983): 125–142, at 127.

3. *trin.* 10.6.8.

4. *Enn.* 4.3.8.

1. The Liminality of *Confessions* 7

After the profusion of sputtering questions about the nature of divine presence in the opening paragraphs of the *Confessions*, Augustine advances a definition of God's simultaneous, total, and immaterial presence with the formula *ubique totus*. In many ways, the rest of the *Confessions* tells the story of the circuitous route Augustine took to find the intelligibility of this definition. His time as a student in Carthage, his early encounter with Cicero's *Hortensius*, reading Aristotle's *Categories*, becoming trapped in the Manichean quagmire, and hearing Ambrose preach, all lead up to the dramatic encounter with the "books of the Platonists" in Milan. There, as described in book 7, vision finds its paradigmatic expression, culminating in an enraptured mystical experience. In one flash of light (an *ictus*), Augustine sees all things in light of immutable being and "rests" (if but for a moment) in the sight of the simultaneous, eternal presence of being itself.[5] This divine reality, which is *ubique totus*, is the ground in which all contingent being has its intelligibility and existence.

But, of course, this is not the whole story. The experiences described in book 7 are abortive. The mind's eye does not continue to "rest" in immutable being. The ascent is short-lived. Augustine crashes down, unable to sustain the vision of being itself. He is rebuffed (*reuerberasti*). Nevertheless, the experiences of book 7 offer substantive cognitive payoff. Augustine becomes intellectually certain (*certus*) of the faith he received from Monica and Ambrose, and his quest to understand the nature of the divine substance and the origins of evil finds a degree of resolution. At this point, we still await the momentous moral conversion of book 8 and Augustine's entry into the sacramental life of the Catholic Church in book 9, such that the apogee of his autobiography occurs at Ostia with his mother, Monica. As such, the narrative of *Confessions* presents the vision of Milan as *penultimate* rather than ultimate. *Confessions* 7 has a liminal place in Augustine's conversion.

Liminality, a word derived from the Latin word *limen* meaning "a threshold," marks the theological aura of book 7;[6] this sense of "being-in-between"

---

5. Augustine presents this moment of ecstasy with the word *ictus* (a blow or strike). He uses *ictus* elsewhere either to describe a sudden blow or a mystical experience that feels like a sudden blow. Cf. *conf.* 7.1.1;7.17.23; 9.8.18. Andrew Louth writes, "This ecstasy is sudden and fleeting, and draws out the whole force of the soul (*toto ictu cordis*) with, it would seem, a certain violence." *The Origins of the Christian Mystical Tradition: From Plato to Denys* (Oxford: Oxford University Press, 2007), 137.

6. Liminality is a significant field in social anthropology. The French anthropologist Arnold van Gennep (1873–1957) first developed the idea in *Les Rites de passage* (1909). For Van Gennep, liminality describes the middle stage of a communal rite of passage in which a

two worlds characterizes the book. Augustine is on the cusp of a major moral conversion and stands on the threshold of sacramental participation in the life of the Catholic Church. He compares his intellectual anguish to birth pangs.[7] Although Augustine believes, he wants to see for himself with interior clarity that which he believes. James O'Donnell captures Augustine's state of liminality:

> Augustine was always a master of capturing in his words what many of his readers have had trouble retaining or expressing, the tension of the middle time between redemption and resurrection, between conversion and beatific vision. The middle time is the time of paradox, and many of the perplexities to which Augustine gives voice, and to which he does not give satisfactory monovalent solutions ... are themselves reflections of this time of paradox in which Augustine saw himself living.[8]

In book 7, Augustine sees, but in a manner that is incomplete and unsustained. The perspective of faith governs his outlook, but it is a faith that, by his own admission, is as yet unformed. His vision needs to be healed and strengthened, and that is the journey of book 7. The lifelong quest to discern the nature of the divine substance and presence comes to a head in this book. Augustine has the "textbook" answer to this theological challenge. The confluence of his philosophic readings, Ambrose's preaching, and the faith in which he grew up provide the contours to the answer. And yet, Augustine remains unsatisfied with this resolution. He wants to be more certain. (The word *certus* appears seven times in this book.) We could say he wants to see for himself.

The verbs that express the action of book 7 relate principally to vision. (The first person singular, *uidi*, appears six times in the book.) The struggle to discern the nature of the divine substance as well as his subsequent mystical vision, which serves to resolve this intellectual challenge, are expressed with the language of sight. A triadic structure resounds throughout the book: (1)

person transitions from one identity, phase of life, or community to enter a new way of life. Liminality expresses this "betwixt and between" stage of transition, in which a person stands on the threshold between two worlds. According to Van Gennep, this state is marked by ambiguity and disorientation. Arnold Van Gennep, *The Rites of Passage*, trans. Monika B. Vizedom and Gabrielle L. Caffee (New York: Routledge, 2013; originally published 1960). The British anthropologist Victor Turner (1920–1983) popularized the term liminality in *The Forest of Symbols: Aspects of Ndembu Ritual* (Ithaca: Cornell University Press, 1967).

7. Cf. *conf.* 7.7.8: "What agonizing birth-pangs [*tormenta parturientis*] tore my heart, what groans [*gemitus*] it uttered, O my God! ... I labored hard in my silent search."

8. Cf. James O'Donnell, *Augustine: Confessions*, vol. 3, *Commentary on Books 8–13* (Oxford: Clarendon Press, 1992), 391–392.

Augustine "strains" (*intendere*) to see an answer to the mystery;[9] (2) he struggles to keep the "gaze of his mind" (*aciem mentis*) fixed and fails to perceive the reality in question; and, (3) with divine illumination, he comes at last to see the intelligibility of that which he already confesses.

2. The Quest to See the Divine Substance

The bedrock of Augustine's confession of the supreme, sole, and true God (*summum et solum et uerum deum*) is that God is immutable (*incommutabilis*). From the marrow of his bones Augustine believes God to be *incorruptibilis*, *inuiolabilis*, and *incommutabilis* (7.1.1). At this time, these alpha privatives serve principally to evince the apophatic character of his confession:

> I did not understand why or how this could be, I saw [*uidebam*] quite plainly and with full conviction that anything perishable is inferior to what is imperishable, and I unhesitatingly recognized the inviolable higher than anything subject to violation, and what is constant and unchanging better than what can be changed. (7.1.1)

Book 7 charts Augustine's growth in coming to see these realities for himself, and this involves cultivating a new way of seeing—an interior vision of that which he confesses.[10]

Augustine's use of the metaphor of vision for grasping the divine substance is ironic: (physical) vision is precisely the problem in his failure to understand (intellectually).[11] Augustine needs first to purge *material* conceptions of sight. The realities he seeks to apprehend are not seen by corporeal eyes or imagined

---

9. Forms of the verb *intendere* (hold out, stretch, strain, exert) appear five times in book 7. The sense of the word is a straining to see or an exertion of one's visual attention. Augustine uses *intendere* to express the spiritual activity of *attention* whereby the eyes of the heart fix their gaze on the object of desire. Jean Rohmer notes, "L'intentionnalité est donc un acte spirituel qui remonte les avenues des sens et se projette au dehors, soudant un processus matériel qu'elle informe à l'object même d'où il procède." Jean Rohmer, "L'Intentionnalité des sensations chez saint Augustin," *Augustinus Magister* 1 (1954): 491–498, at 496. Simone Weil famously remarks, "Prayer consists of attention." *Waiting for God* (New York: Putnam, 1951), 105.

10. Cf. O'Donnell, *Augustine*, 396.

11. The language of vision is an inescapable (and usually unreflective) metaphor for most discussion of understanding. One could give many examples of phrases such as "shedding light on the matter" or "I *see* what you are saying," which prioritize terminology of sight for understanding. Augustine notes this linguistic admission regarding the primacy of sight in *conf.* 10.35.54. An excellent analysis of this is Hans Blumenberg, *Paradigms for a Metaphorology* (Ithaca, NY: Cornell University Press, 2010). Cf. Constance Classen, *Worlds of Sense: Exploring the Senses in History and Across Cultures* (London: Routledge, 1993), 58–59.

with the mind. In the very first paragraph of book 7, Augustine programmatically lays out the challenge of sight that animates the book:

> By now my misspent, impious, adolescence was dead, and I was entering the period of youth [*iuuentutem*], but as I advanced in age I sank ignobly into foolishness, for I was unable to grasp the idea [*cogitare*] of substance except as something we can see with our bodily eyes [*quale per hos oculos uideri solet*]. I was no longer representing [*cogitabam*] you to myself in the shape of a human body, O God, for since beginning to acquire some inkling of philosophy I always shunned this illusion, and now I was rejoicing to find a differing view in the belief of our spiritual mother, your Catholic Church. Yet no alternative way of thinking [*cogitarem*] about you had occurred to me; and here was I, a mere human, and a sinful one at that, striving to comprehend [*cogitare*] you, the supreme, sole, true God. (7.1.1)

Augustine weaves together language of cognition and vision. Although this is unsurprising and even natural, it also exposes precisely the problem of book 7, namely, an idolatrous immanence that attempts to grasp the divine substance according to categories of human perception and intellection.

At the outset of the book, we find Augustine frustrated, as he is continually batting away "phantom shapes [*phantasmata*] that thronged my imagination." He is intellectually convinced that God is not a body, but he has no other way of conceiving God. Materialist conceptions of God swarm about him like flies; no sooner has he swatted one away than another lands on him:

> I strove with this single weapon to beat way from the gaze of my mind [*acie mentis*] the cloud of filth that hovered around, but hardly had I got rid of it than in another twinkling of an eye [*ictu oculi*] it was back again, clotted together [*conglobata*], invading and clogging my vison [*aspectum*]. (7.1.1)

Augustine's attempts to see spiritual reality aright are continually hampered, as he sees only with the eyes of the flesh. His interior vision (*acies mentis*) is dim; he cannot positively make out what he knows to be true about divine realities (7.1.1).[12] He lapses into corporeal (*corporeus*) conceptions of

---

12. The *acies mentis* refers to the highest type of vision, the gaze of the mind, which is at work when the soul sees immaterial truth. Corresponding terms that Augustine uses include *oculus mentis*, *acies animi*, *acies cordis*, and *intellectus*. Classical sources with which Augustine was likely familiar include Plato (rep. 7.533d), Cicero (*de or.* 2.160; *Tusc.* 1.73; *leg. Man.* 4.368), and Plotinus (*Enn.* 1.6.7–9). For Augustine, the soul's vision can be trained (*exercitatio animae*) to cultivate the ability of this spiritual faculty to see divine realities (cf. *an. quant.* 30.61; 33.76). Augustine speaks personally about seeing eternal truth through the *acies mentis* in his ecstatic experiences at Milan (*conf.* 7.10.16–7.17.23) and Ostia (*conf.* 9.10.23–26). It is a term that Augustine continues to use in his mature writings. The soul that has purified

the divine substance, imagining it to be a presence "spread out in space" (*per spatia locorum*), either "infused in the world" (*infusum mundo*) or diffused in the infinity of space beyond the world. Yet he knows that such lapses into material-picture-thinking about the divine presence conflict with his philosophic certainty that God is immutable. However, at this point in his life, Augustine admits, he could perceive immutability only as the *negation* of anything contained in space—as an absolute nothingness (*prorsus nihil*).

A positive articulation of the divine substance predicated on an interior vision of God belongs to the pure of heart. Now, Augustine describes himself at this stage as "gross of heart" (*incrassatus corde*; 7.1.2).[13] He is unaware even of himself, because material conceptions "clotted together" (*conglobata*) obstruct his spiritual vision. He writes,

> For as my eyes were accustomed to roam among material forms, so did my mind among the images of them, yet I could not see that this very act of perception [*intentionem*], whereby I formed those images, was different from them in kind. Yet my mind would never have been able to form them unless it was itself a reality and a great one. (7.1.2)

Existentially, rich knowledge of the divine presence and his own self—to know God and the soul—was, as yet, beyond Augustine. The sad irony, he later realizes, is that the very mechanics of vision whereby he can focus his sight (*intentionem*) to conjure up images in his mind should have disclosed the reality of an immaterial substance (i.e., the soul) necessary to see anything at all. "If we would only look carefully at the very mind we are using to imagine material things," remarks Phillip Cary regarding this passage, "we would have the clue to what is not itself a material thing, something that is not spread out in space but is not just nothing either. It is indeed something very great, but not large in

the *acies mentis*, maintains Augustine in *De Trinitate*, can behold God through faith in this life and directly in the life to come (*trin.* 15.21–23). Cf. Frederick van Fleteren, "acies mentis," in *Augustine through the Ages*, ed. Allan Fitzgerald (Grand Rapids: Eerdmans, 1999). Denys Turner writes, "Where time intersects with eternity, the mind's most intimate interiority is also its 'highest' point, a point which Augustine calls the *acies mentis*, the 'cutting edge' of the mind, the place 'in' it which overlaps with the eternal Light it is in. It is the point at which the mind can most truly contemplate the Trinity and in which the Trinity dwells by participating image." *The Darkness of God: Negativity in Christian Mysticism* (Cambridge: Cambridge University Press, 1998), 99.

13. Augustine's medical description of *epicardial fat* (*incrassatus corde*) derives from Jesus's explanation of why he speaks in parables (Matt 13:15) and the Apostle Paul's explanation of why many fail to believe (Acts 28:27). Both passages are quotations from Isaiah 6:10 (LXX).

bulk or in physically measurable terms. It is the greatness of our own souls."[14] Again, we see how, for Augustine, knowledge of God and the soul are thoroughly interwoven.

Augustine cannot yet bridge the ontological chasm separating the mutable from the immutable. He wrongly imagines God's presence as "spread through space in every direction," such that "all things were full of you" (7.1.2). With an arresting metaphor, Augustine describes his failure to apprehend God's being, which radically transcends that of his creatures:

> I imagined you, Lord, who are infinite in every possible respect, surrounding and penetrating it in every part, like a sea extending in all directions through immense space, a single unlimited sea which held within itself a sponge as vast as one could imagine but still finite, and the sponge soaked in every fibre of itself by the boundless sea. (7.5.7)

The analogy of God as sea suffusing a sponge limps precisely in its materialism, and it is this materialism that Augustine would later come to see as problematic, both in the Manichaeans and in his own youthful understanding of God. At this stage there is no resolution to Augustine's perplexion. He cannot yet properly see an answer to the problem of the divine substance. He remarks tellingly, "You had not yet illumined my darkness" (*sed nondum inluminaueras tenebras meas*; 7.1.2).

If Augustine confesses the reality of the divine substance as immutable, although struggling to hold this truth before his mind's eye, a parallel situation obtains in his attempt to apprehend the *causa mali*. He is philosophically certain that God is not vulnerable to change, but he struggles, therefore, to perceive how evil comes into existence.

> I strained [*intendebam*] to see for myself the truth of an explanation I heard: that the cause of evil is the free decision of our will, in consequence of which we act wrongly and suffer your righteous judgment; but I could not see it clearly [*liquidam cernere*]. I struggled to raise my mental gaze [*aciem mentis*] from the depths, but sank back again; I strove repeatedly, but again and again sank back. I was as sure of having a will as I was of being alive, and this it was that lifted me into your light [*subleuabat me in lucem tuam*]. (7.3.5)

The structure of this struggle is identical to Augustine's description of his struggle to perceive the nature of the divine substance: (1) he "strains"

---

14. Phillip Cary, "Inner Vision as the Goal of Augustine's Life," in *A Reader's Companion to Augustine's Confessions*, ed. Kim Paffenroth and Robert P. Kennedy (London: Westminster John Knox, 2003), 111.

(*intendere*) to see an answer to the challenge of the origins of evil; (2) he fails to keep the "gaze of his mind" (*aciem mentis*) fixed on the resolution; and (3) it is only with the gift of divine light (*lucem tuam*) that he finds intelligibility to what he already confesses.

As with respect to the challenge of correctly perceiving the divine substance, Augustine is already intellectually convinced of Ambrose's (and the Platonic) teaching regarding evil as privation. Evil has its root not in something positive but in lack of something, namely, a lack of a rightly ordered will. Augustine articulates his search as a quest to see, a "straining" for an interior perception (*creui*) and confirmation of that which he already knows to be true.

3. *Confessions* 7.10.16

A resolution to the theological *aporia* regarding the nature of the divine substance and the origin of evil comes to Augustine through a revelation. At one point, a light dawned on Augustine's intellect, a light that transcended him. As such, *Confessions* seeks to underscore that the new insight into the problems that so vexed him is emphatically a gift. The in-breaking of divine light discloses a new cognitive grasp and a new possibility of intellectual vision. In *Confessions* 7.10.16, Augustine relates the first of two descriptions of the ecstatic experience:

> Warned by these writings that I must return [*redire*] to myself, I entered under your guidance the innermost places of my being [*intraui in intima mea*]; but only because you had become my helper was I able to do so, I entered [*intraui*], then, and with the vision of my spirit [*oculo animae*], such as it was, I saw [*uidi*] the incommutable light [*lucem incommutabilem*] far above my spiritual ken [*supra eundem oculum animae*], transcending my mind [*supra mentem meam*]: not this common light which every carnal eye can see, nor any light of the same order but greater, as though this common light was shining much more powerfully, far more brightly, and so extensively as to fill the universe. The light I saw was not this common light at all, but something different, utterly different, from all these things. Nor was it higher than my mind in the sense that oil floats on water or the sky is above the earth; it was exalted because this very light made me [*ipsa fecit me*], and I was below it because by it I was made. (7.10.16)

We have here a vivid description of an experience of interior vision occasioned by the impress of a transcendent spiritual light. Augustine follows a path of spiritual illumination and ascent by the way of interiority proposed by

Plotinus.[15] The site of transcendence to which Augustine is urged to return is *intima mea*.[16] Augustine now sees (*uidi*) immutable light. The preceding extensive quotations from the prologue of John (7.9.13–15) inform us how Augustine wants his readers to think about this light. It is the *lumen uerum* that enlightens every man.[17]

Augustine fuses Plotinian mysticism with Johannine theology to articulate the character of this transcendent light.[18] The immutable light is of an order "wholly other" than all finite existence. Indeed, this light is the cause of all existence, which, Augustine confesses, includes him (*ipsa fecit me*). Augustine's mystical experience reveals that this immutable light is both the epistemological ground in which all things are intelligible and the ontological cause in whom all things have their being. Incidentally, this is, according to Augustine, also the central teaching of both the Johannine prologue and the *libri platonicorum*.

---

15. Cf. Plotinus, *Enn.* 1.6.9.

16. In *ep.* 10 to Nebridius, Augustine describes this site as the "sanctuary of the mind" where the soul can adore God (*mentis penetralibus adorat Deum*); the place where the mind's eye can behold unchanging truth.

17. A helpful analogue is Augustine's *Homilies on the Gospel of John*, in which he compares the healing effect of physical light on the eyes to the healing effect of spiritual light on the eyes of the soul. The spiritual light that restores the eyes of the soul is the eternal Word in whose immutable light we see light (cf. Ps 35:10).

> Thus, in seeing this bodily light, these eyes of ours are restored, and a material thing is seen by bodily eyes. Many who remained too long in the darkness find their vision weakened, as if by fasting from light. When the eyes are cheated of their food (of course, they feed on the light), they are tired out by such fasting and weakened, such that they cannot look at the light they are restored by; and if the light is lacking too long, the eyes go out and the sharpness of light, as it were, dies in them. So what follows, then? Because so many eyes feed on this light every day, does it grow any less? The truth is both that they are restored and renewed and that the light remains whole and entire. If God has been able to bestow this benefit of on bodily eyes with bodily light, will he not bestow on the clean of heart that light which is tireless, remains whole, does not fail at all? (*Jo. eu. tr.* 13.5)

It is to this divine light that Augustine prays for illumination at the outset of the *Soliloquies*: "God, intelligible light, in whom and by whom and through whom all things which give off intelligible light have intelligible light." *sol.* 1.1.3.

18. Unfortunately, Cary opposes what Augustine presents as integrated, namely the philosophic insight of the *libri platonicorum* and the truth of Scripture: "What we find in the books of Plotinus is of more direct relevance to the intellectual problems of book 7 than anything in the Scripture passages Augustine quotes. For it was not the doctrine of the Trinity that solved his problems about the nature of God, but the Platonist notions of incorporeality, incorruptibility, unchangeability, and omnipresence, which are worked out by Plotinus with an intellectual depth and poetic beauty that Augustine would never have encountered before." "Inner Vision," 113.

Augustine highlights the radical dependence of finite being and knowing on the immutable Being and Truth of God:

> Anyone who knows truth knows it, and whoever knows it knows eternity. Love knows it [*caritas nouit eam*]. O eternal Truth, true Love, and beloved Eternity [*O aeterna ueritas et uera caritas et cara aeternitas!*], you are my God, and for you I sigh day and night. As I first began to know you you lifted me up [*adsumpsisti me*] and showed me that while that which I might see exists indeed, I was not yet capable of seeing it. Your rays beamed intensely upon me, beating back [*reverberasti*] my feeble gaze [*aspectus*], and I trembled with love and dread. I knew myself to be far away from you in a region of unlikeness [*regione dissimilitudinis*], and I seemed to hear your voice from on high: "I am the food of the mature; grow then, and you will eat me. You will not change me into yourself like bodily food: you will be changed into me." (7.10.16)

The epistemic power of love in this experience is often overlooked. *Caritas nouit eam.* Love is the key that unlocks the door, granting a vision of a reality that had heretofore been denied him. The mystery that love knows is the Holy Trinity. Augustine's phrasing aims to express the circular, interpenetrating dynamism of his Trinitarian vision: *O aeterna ueritas et uera caritas et cara aeternitas!* Note that the noun used for one divine person becomes the adjective to describe the divine person in the next clause. This cascading phraseology in which each clause takes up the preceding one has the rhetorical effect of linguistically enacting Augustine's Trinitarian theology.[19]

Vision in this experience is in the first instance passive. God lifts Augustine up (*adsumpsisti me*) and reveals divine light to his inner eye. In this light he catches sight of divine infinity and immutability and, at the same time, realizes profoundly his own finitude and mutability. He trembles with love and dread (*contremui amore et horrore*).[20] John Kenney captures the emotional force of the passage: "Inner contemplation shocks the soul, first with the force of this recognition of transcendence, then, by the sense of its own ontological poverty and dependence, and finally by the love that has drawn it into this state of deep

---

19. *Veritas, caritas,* and *aeternitas* form a recurring triadic structure in Augustine's Trinitarian theology. Cf. *Gn. litt.* 8.25.47; *trin.* 4.21.30; *ep.* 169.1.4; *ciu. Dei* 11.28. Pierre Blanchard has noted the significance of this triad for Augustine's mysticism in the *Confessions*: "Connaissance religieuse et connaissance mystique chez saint Augustin dans les 'Confessions', Veritas-Caritas-Aeternitas," *Recherches augustiniennes et patristiques* 2 (1962): 311–330.

20. The phrase "trembling with love" (*contremui amore*) is redolent of Plotinus (*Enn.* 1.6.7) and Ambrose (*De Isaac* 8.78).

cognition."[21] *Amor* and *horror* are the emotions the experience evokes: a love of the fullness of Being seen clearly (if briefly) for the first time and terror at one's own contrasting existential nakedness and abject ontological poverty.

From Pierre Courcelle onward, much scholarship on book 7 has debated whether or not Augustine's ascent is a "success." Courcelle himself offers a negative verdict, describing it as a failed Plotinian attempt to grasp a vision of the divine. His verdict: "vaines tentatives d'extases plotiniennes."[22] In my view, the question itself of whether the experiences are a "success" or a "failure" fails to do justice to the liminal character of book 7.[23] We can affirm that Augustine had an intellectual breakthrough in which he was given a vision of divine immutability as the ground of all being and knowing; this experience constituted a shocking cognitive *nouum*. In this respect, at least, the ascent was a "success." In his mystical vision he "saw" the resolution to the questions that vexed him. Although the first half of book 7 portrays Augustine straining (*intendere*) to keep his mind's eye (*acies mentis*) on a resolution only to be rebuffed by the lack of divine light, here he sees (albeit briefly). Admittedly, Augustine remains incapable of sustaining the vision. He is thrown back (*reuerberasti*); his mind's eye is still weak and sick (*infirmitas aspectus*), unable to keep his vision fixed.[24] When Augustine's vision ceases, he falls back into his ordinary way of being and finds himself in the *regio dissimilitudinis*.[25] In this sense, the experience was not a "success" but is congruent with his earlier unsuccessful attempts to form an *intellectus fidei* regarding his theological conundrums.

21. John Kenney, "Mystic and Monk: Augustine and the Spiritual Life," in *A Companion to Augustine*, ed. Mark Vessey (Oxford: Wiley Blackwell, 2012), 289.

22. Pierre Courcelle, *Recherches sur les Confessions de saint Augustin*, Nouvelle éd. augmentée et illustrée (Paris: E. de Boccard, 1968), 165. Courcelle continues, "L'expérience a donc commencé par une réussite; elle se termine sur un douloureux échec."

23. I share Brian Dobell's critique of Courcelle's evaluation of the ascent at Milan: *Augustine's Intellectual Conversion: The Journey from Platonism to Christianity* (Cambridge: Cambridge University Press, 2009), 132–133.

24. Olivier du Roy writes, "Cet éblouissement [*reuerberasti*] semble être une donnée permanente de l'expérience mystique d'Augustin. Chaque récit qu'il a donné d'une expérience analogue et même la simple description de tout essai de fixer le lumière intérieure, se terminent toujours par cet éblouissement qui force le regard à se détourner." *L'Intelligence de la foi en la Trinité selon Saint Augustin: genèse de sa théologie trinitaire jusqu'en 391* (Paris: Études augustiniennes, 1966), 77.

25. It has been frequently noted that the phrase *regio dissimilitudinis* derives from Plotinus (*Enn.* 1.8.13) and Plato before him (*Statesman* 273d6–e1), but it is likely also informed by the story of the Prodigal, who finds himself in *regionem longinquam et ibi dissipauit substantiam suam* (Luke 15:13). Cf. Leo Ferrari, "The Theme of the Prodigal Son in Augustine's Confessions," *Recherches augustiniennes et patristiques* 12 (1977): 105–118; Robert O'Connell, *Soundings in St. Augustine's Imagination* (New York: Fordham University Press, 1994), 69–94.

The cognitive payoff of Augustine's vision was a newfound awareness about the divine substance as immutable, incorruptible, and omnipresent. This is clear in the coda to the experience of *Confessions* 7.10.16: "I said, 'Is truth then a nothing, simply because it is not spread out through space either finite or infinite?' Then from afar you cried to me, 'By no means, for *I am who am*'" (7.10.16). Cary rightly notes that prior to this breakthrough, Augustine "had no ontology to explain how a being or substance can be unchangeable, and therefore his conception of God's incorruptibility was as inadequate and ill-grounded as his conception of God's omnipresence and bodilessness."[26] The ecstatic experience, which gave existential weight to Augustine's encounter with the *platonicorum libri* and the Johannine prologue, led him to see the insufficiency of materialist conceptions of the divine nature.

As Augustine returns to the two issues that so perplexed him—the nature of the divine substance and the questions involved in the problem of evil—he now recognizes them as intertwined. They are, in fact, variant expressions of the same problem. His ecstatic vision reveals that the only reality that exists of itself, in a non-contingent manner, is the divine substance. All mutable being participates in this immutable being through an ordered hierarchy. But mutable being is, precisely as such, liable to corruption. It is created good, but not indefectible.[27] Creatures do not have being in the fullest (immutable) sense.[28] Augustine articulates this newfound understanding with the language of sight:

> Contemplating [*inspexi*] other things below you, I saw [*uidi*] that they do not in the fullest sense exist, nor are they completely non-beings; they are real because they are from you, but unreal inasmuch as they are not what you are. For that alone truly is, which abides unchangingly. (7.11.17)

---

26. Cary, "Inner Vision," 110.

27. Cf. *en.* Ps. 121.5: "For everything that is constantly changing does not truly exist, because it does not abide—not that it is entirely nonexistent, but it does not exist in the highest sense." Commenting on this passage, Lewis Ayres remarks, "Immutability is the true mark of divine existence and that which marks God as the source and end of all that exists." Lewis Ayres, *Augustine and the Trinity* (Cambridge: Cambridge University Press, 2010), 203.

28. Creation does not contain within itself the cause of its existence. To be human is to have a distinct awareness of existing without possessing existence. Joshua Nunziato puts this paradox well: "Creation does not bear within itself the principle of divine creativity. Only God does. And yet God bears creation within himself. Therefore, creation bears within itself nothing but the creativity that bears it. Creation bears the immaterial within its own materiality. And that is what it means to be created." Joshua Nunziato, "Created to Confess: St. Augustine on Being Material," *Modern Theology* 32 (2016): 367.

The participatory metaphysic that constitutes the theological consequence of Augustine's mystical experience discloses a hierarchy of being. God alone has being in the full sense; all others participate in his being to varying degrees.[29] Augustine can now see the created order (cf. Rom. 1:20) within this hierarchical and participatory framework. Evil is unintelligible except as privation of the good: "it can do harm only by diminishing the good" (*nisi bonum minueret, non noceret*; 7.12.18). The quest to discover the origin of evil is itself wrongheaded: "Everything that exists is good then; and so evil, the source of which I was seeking, cannot be a substance" (7.12.18). Evil is secondary, always parasitical to the good. Only the good has reality, ontological density. Again, Augustine uses the decisive term *uidere* for his newfound understanding: "I saw (*uidi*) for it was made clear to me (*manifestatum*), that you have made all good things, and that there are absolutely no substances that you have not made. I saw too that you have not made all things equal" (7.12.18). Creaturely good, that which holds its borrowed being tenuously, is liable to corruption and defection.[30]

Looking back on the intellectual journey he has traversed, Augustine recalls the idolatrous Manichean conception of divine presence he held prior to his encounter with the Platonic literature: "It had made for itself a god extended through infinite space, all-pervasive [*per infinita spatia locorum*]" (7.14.20). God's healing touch, however, restored *sanitas*, healing his inner vision:

> [You] . . . closed my eyes to the sight of vain things [*uiderent uanitatem*] so that I could absent me from myself awhile, and my unwholesome madness

---

29. In *Confessions* 12.6.6, Augustine also describes the "borrowed" character of created existence, describing it as a "nothing something" (*nihil aliquid*). Even in the creative moment— in the movement from "nothing" to "something"—the "nothing" remains, so to speak, woven into the very DNA of the "something." Jean-Luc Marion eloquently describes this reality: "Nothingness [*Le néant*], in the figure of *de nihilo*, does not hold merely the place of starting point for the created (as that from which it would have exited); it also holds the place of its material (as that of which it will always remain woven). The created does not emerge from nothing except by assuming it again at the heart of its very beingness. It should, then, be said, in a transitive sense, that the created is its nothingness and that it is so because God gives it to it." Jean-Luc Marion, *In the Self's Place: The Approach of St. Augustine*, trans. Jeffrey L. Kosky (Stanford CA: Stanford University Press, 2012), 246. Cf. Nunziato, "Created to Confess," 12; Natale Joseph Torchia, *Creatio ex nihilo and the Theology of St. Augustine: The Anti-Manichaean Polemic and Beyond* (New York: Peter Lang, 1999), 98.

30. The identity of being and goodness as well as the privative character of evil was something Augustine could have read in Plotinus (*Enn.* 3.2.5.25–32). The reference in *ciu.* 10.14 to this text demonstrates that Augustine knew this passage (at least when he wrote *ciu.* 10). However, he could equally have heard these metaphysical truths in Ambrose's preaching in Milan (cf. *De Isaac* 7.60). Other early attestations to Augustine's account of evil as *priuatio boni* include *lib. arb.* 3.13.36 and *nat. b.* 3 and 23.

was lulled to sleep, then I awoke in you and saw you to be infinite [*uidi te infinitum*]; but in a different sense, and that vision [*uisus*] in no way derived from the flesh. (7.14.20)[31]

Having his eyes purged of false phantasms of the divine substance, Augustine was now also able to perceive creaturely existence in a new light:

> I turned my gaze [*respexi*] to other things and saw [*uidi*] that they owe their being to you and that all of them are by you defined, but in a particular sense: not as though contained in a place [*loco*], but because you hold all things in your Truth as though in your hand [*omnitenens manu Veritate*]. (7.14.20)

The participatory metaphysic that constitutes the drumbeat of his ecstatic experience equally offered Augustine a new perspective of creaturely being. Creatures are not autonomous. They do not contain within themselves the cause of their existence. The profound truth of Acts 17:28 (quoted in 7.9.15 to describe the metaphysical import of the *libri platonicorum*) was brought home to Augustine with poignant new clarity: creatures live, move, and have their being in and from the hand of eternal Truth (*manu Veritate*). The mystical experience of *Confessions* 7.10.16 involves the divine gift of spiritual vision, so that Augustine sees this reality for himself.

4. *Confessions* 7.17.23

Confessions 7.17.23 contains the second description of mystical ascent in book 7. In many ways the second ascent mirrors the first. In fact, some commentators suggest that the two accounts comprise the same experience related in two ways.[32] However, in the second description, Augustine's ascent is prefaced by the confession that he now loves God's "very self" and not some "figment of imagination" (*phantasma*). The challenge, Augustine admits, is retaining the attention (*intendere*) of his mind's eye (*acies mentis*), to "continue steadily in the enjoyment of my God" (*stabam frui deo meo*). Augustine acknowledges a spiritual tension in that the weight of his love seems to pull in opposing

---

31. Robert O'Connell has made much of these lines, suggesting that behind them lies the influence of Plotinus's twin treatises on the omnipresence of being (*Ennead* 6.4–5). Robert O'Connell, "Ennead, IV, 4 and 5 in the Works of Saint Augustine," *Revue d'études augustiniennes et patristiques* 9 (1963): 1–39.

32. Some interpret the second experience (*conf.* 7.17.23) as an elaboration on the first experience (*conf.* 7.10.16). For example, du Roy remarks, "Ce qui pouvait sembler un nouveau récit de 'tentative d'extase', n'est donc qu'un rappel de sa situation, tout naturellement amené par le contexte. C'est ainsi que compose Augustin." *L'Intelligence de la foi*, 85.

directions. He is both drawn to God's beauty and dragged down by the weight (*pondus*) of his carnal habit. Nevertheless the "memory" (*memoria*) of what he experienced after reading the *libri platonicorum* (*Confessions* 7.10.16) remains with him, leaving him "no doubt whatever whom I ought to cling to" (7.17.23).

The ascent in *Confessions* 7.17.23 is initiated with Augustine contemplating the human act of judgment. The mind judges that mutable things *ought* to be this way or that. This suggests an eternal and immutable principle upon which the mind bases such judgments: "I realized that above my changeable mind soared the real, unchangeable truth, which is eternal" (7.17.23). *Veritatis aeternitas* is the standard of immutable truth, to which the mutable mind adverts when rendering judgment. Augustine writes,

> Thus I pursued my inquiry by stages [*gradatim*], from material things to the soul that perceives them through the body, from there to that inner power [*interiorem vim*] of the soul to which the body's senses report external impressions. . . . I proceeded further and came to the power of discursive reasoning [*ratiocinantem*], to which the data of our senses are referred for judgment. (7.17.23)

For Augustine, the soul is not static; he intimates that the soul itself is a dynamic entity, intelligible by an upward *motio* that points beyond itself. The *interior uis*, by which the soul receives sense impressions from the body, is an interior force that humans have in common with all sensible creatures endowed with the power of perception. Yet the human soul soars beyond this. His is a reasoning (*ratiocinans*) soul, capable of deliberating and rendering judgment about sense experiences, i.e., "Was this sense experience just, good, noble, etc.?" Augustine describes this reasoning power of judgment as a type of interior vision.[33] Further, the power of reason points beyond itself. Although reasoning is itself mutable, it stretches "upward to the source of its own intelligence" (7.17.23), namely, the unchanging light that enables interior vision to see in the first place:

> It strove to discover what this light was that bedewed it when it cried out unhesitatingly that the Unchangeable is better than anything liable to change; it sought the font whence flowed its concept of the Unchangeable— for unless it had in some fashion recognized Immutability, it could never with such certainty have judged it superior to things that change. (7.17.23)

---

33. Cf. Bernard Lonergan, *Insight: A Study of Human Understanding*, vol. 3 of *Collected Works of Bernard Lonergan* (Toronto: University of Toronto Press, 1992), chap. 9.

The power of human reason and judgment—the soul's insight—is itself flooded by light.[34] Augustine describes the ascent from the corporeal body with its sense perception to the incorporeal soul that sees and renders judgment on what the bodily senses deliver according to its participation in eternal light. This leads him to a confirmation of the metaphysical truths discovered in the wake of the experience of *Confessions* 7.10.16 regarding God's immutable substance:

> And then my mind attained to *That Which Is*, in the flash of one tremulous glance [*ictu trepidantis aspectus*]. Then indeed did I perceive [*conspexi*] your invisible reality through created things, but to keep my gaze [*aciem*] there was beyond my strength. I was forced back [*repercussa*] through weakness [*infirmitate*] and returned to my familiar surroundings, bearing with me only a loving memory, one that yearned for something of which I had caught the fragrance, but could not yet feast upon. (7.17.23)

The similarities with the first account of ascent (7.10.16) are striking—the most conspicuous being the ubiquity of the language of vision to articulate the experience. In a flash of light, Augustine catches sight (*aspectus* in both cases) of immutable being. Again, he is awed and terrified. But once again he is beaten back (*repercussa* here and *reuerberasti* in 7.10.16). In both cases, he attributes the failure to sustain the vision to *infirmitates*. However, two things set this account off from that of 7.10.16. First, here Romans 1:20 features prominently. He now sees creation aright: a participatory ontology frames his thinking. He is able to see all mutable being existing in God (*omnitenens manu Veritate*) and translucent to the divine presence in which it lives, moves, and has its being. Created things are now attestations to God's "invisible reality" (cf. Rom 1:20). Second, memory is mentioned twice in 7.17.23. Memory is, for *Confessions*, the locus of the soul's ascent to God. Augustine now retains a loving memory (*amantem memoriam*), the fragrance (*olefacta*) of his mystical experiences, which inform his thinking on the theologically vexed problems at play in book 7.

---

34. An analogous passage is trin. 8.4.9, in which Augustine considers with what we love when we love a "just man." What the mind sees and is drawn towards in the just man is "the inner truth present to the mind (*ueritas est interior praesens animo*), which is capable of beholding it." Not all are capable of this vision, maintains Augustine, but those that are, do so "by cleaving to that same form which they behold, in order to be formed by it and become just minds." Augustine proposes a certain conformity of the soul to the eternal realities seen.

5. Conclusion

Confessions 7 has a liminal place in Augustine's autobiography. At this point, Augustine has abandoned the quagmire of pernicious Manichean heresy and has renounced the futility and vanity of careerism (*ambitio saeculi*). From intelligent Christians in Milan (especially Bishop Ambrose), he has gained new appreciation for Scripture and Catholic teaching. Indeed, he has come to confess the faith in which he was raised. Now he wants to be more certain (*certus*). Intellectually, he wants to see this truth for himself. However, the heart-wrenching moral conversion of book 8 and the joyous entry in the sacramental life of the Catholic Church in book 9 have not yet occurred. In *Confessions* 7, Augustine stands on the threshold; he presents himself as "being-in-between" two worlds. It is perhaps for this reason that sight predominates in *Confessions* 7.

Vision, in Augustine's Platonic worldview, entails, in the first place, union. Sight is a movement of intention, direction, and will (*pondus*) towards the object of affection. What is seen is always seen with affection and what is looked at with love is given birth in the soul in an immaterial form.[35] Augustine's desire to see—his longing for intellectual and spiritual union with truth—suffuses book 7. The persistent place of sight in *Confessions* 7 veraciously captures the liminal character of this book. Augustine wants to see the truth about the nature of the divine substance (as *ubique totus*) and the related challenge concerning the origins of evil. But, try as he might, his vision is stymied. The problem is an inadequate spiritual vision; Augustine is incapable of transcending materialist conceptions of reality. It is only the gift of Augustine's mystical experiences—the in-breaking of divine light—that enables him to see for himself the truth he knows. It is in this light that he comes to see how the divine substance exists as immutable, incorruptible, and omnipresent and how all contingent being participates in this divine substance in an ordered hierarchy. Further, he sees how the human power of reason is an interior vision that judges contingent reality according to its participating in unchanging light. Despite the power of his mystical vision, the penetrating clarity of sight obtained, and a pulsating experience of union with truth, a certain melancholy pervades book 7. The vision is not sustained; Augustine utters a despondent sigh of unfulfilled desire.[36] His vision retains a longing for completion.

---

35. Cf. *trin.* 9.3–5.

36. Augustine makes much of the verb *suspirare* in *Confessions*. See 6.5.8; 6.10.17; 7.10.16; 9.7.16; 9.10.24; and 9.10.25. See also Courcelle, *Recherches*, 124–125 and O'Donnell, *Augustine*, 130.

BOOK 8

Conversion and the Transformational Journey from the Dissociative Self to the True Self

Paul Ruff

Book 7 of Augustine's *Confessions* ends with this cliffhanger: "in awe-inspiring ways these truths were striking deep roots within me as I read the least of your apostles; I had contemplated your works and was filled with dread" (7.21.7). Compare this to the experience of a 50-year-old male client of therapist Diana Fosha, whose work we will be drawing on for this paper: "Even when I tell you that it is 'searing,' I feel like I am standing on the edge of something that I can only look at sideways [the self I was meant to be] . . . I feel afraid of what comes next—a bunch of stuff is going to happen to me and I am afraid of it."[1]

  Both Augustine and the client find themselves in the fraught and alluring dilemma of transformation from a familiar but compromised self into their truer self. This typifies where we find Augustine in book 8 and will be the frame of this paper's investigation. Rather than the more incremental and orderly operations of will and intellect in processes of growth, the type of conversion or transformation we will be examining has the qualities of being intense, rapid, out of control, and often experienced as the result of the operation of forces outside of the self. Such processes of growth or "quantum change" seem to be allowed and received rather than achieved. Such conversions and transformations have

---

1. Diana Fosha, "Emotion and Recognition at Work: Energy, Vitality, Truth, Desire and the Emergent Phenomenology of Transformational Experience," *The Neuropsychotherapist* 2 (July–September 2013): 44.

a clear demarcation of self before and self after—the landscape has been reconfigured, and almost universally for the better.

As a Catholic psychologist I will attempt to place *Confessions* book 8 in dialogue with findings in the field of phenomenological psychology to compare and contrast the phenomena of spiritual conversion with the phenomena of a transformational therapy known as Accelerated Experiential Dynamic Psychotherapy as developed by Fosha. Reference will also be made to William James's groundbreaking field work in *The Varieties of Religious Experience* and its exploration of the phenomenology of conversion and Miller and C'de Baca's more recent revisiting of this same project in their work *Quantum Change*. Fosha's theory, building on the findings of James, Miller, and C'de Baca, draws upon and synthesizes a growing body of work in neurobiology and social neuropsychology regarding the role of attachment and the emotions in human development, a body of work which has also garnered the interest of contemporary theologians.[2] It enlists the power of these in a therapeutic process designed for the healing of defensive dissociative states that result from ruptures in attachment and impede growth. The desired outcome of Fosha's work is the restoration of the connection to the core True Self and its vital drive for transformation and authentic engagement in the world. Such transformational processes are aided, "midwifed," by the accompaniment of a True Other.[3]

In exploring the phenomenology of both psychological transformation and spiritual, particularly Christian, conversion, attachment theory provides a useful heuristic. Both give an accounting of the primacy of relationality and attachment that allows the person to come into being as his true, intended self in the world. Both attempt to account for the painful disruption of attachment which leads to a fragmented false self, a self-out-of-joint, dissociated, in both self and self-other relating. Finally, each observes the operation of the "restless heart," the affective, appetitive drive for restoration of the core, true self and its rightly ordered relating to the field of being.

Hopefully this side-by-side comparison of Augustine in book 8 with Fosha's client can add to our understanding and appreciation of the dynamics and markers of the journey of the self to greater wholeness and how to help occasion or support such growth. To avoid the risk of reducing either field into the

2. Martin Bieler's "Attachment Theory and Aquinas's Metaphysics of Creation" (*Analecta Hermeneutica: International Institute for Hermeneutics*, vol. 3: 2011) provides an integrative sample of this exploration of attachment theory and theology.

3. Diana Fosha, "Emotion, True Self, True Other, Core State: Toward a Clinical Theory of Affect Change processes," *Psychoanalytic Review* 92, no. 4 (2005): 513–552 at 517, 540. Fosha explains that her term "True-Self/True-Other relating" are her version of Buber's I/Thou.

terms of the other, we will propose that the project of transformational psychological healing might be seen as a fractal instantiation, guided perhaps by prevenient grace, of the larger soteriological drama.

1. Emergence of True Self in Attachment

In *Unless You Become Like This Child*, Hans Urs von Balthasar draws deeply from attachment theory developed in the work of James Bowlby and those who have elaborated Bowlby's theory.[4] He frames the mother-child bond as central to the emergence of the child's true self into the field of hopeful attuned relationship, which opens the child's psyche to the possibility of a loving God.[5] The child leaves mere symbiotic relating—mother and I are one—to enter an awareness of the mother's caring "otherness."

Bowlby's research and subsequent neurobiological studies have demonstrated that mother-child bonding activated by gazing, voice, and touch activate hormonal processes which result in the healthy wiring of the brain and nervous system. Fosha, drawing upon the work of investigators in the field of emotion and social neuroscience, summarizes this understanding: "Positive, attuned, dyadic interactions are the constituents of healthy secure attachments and the corelates of neurochemical environments conducive to optimal brain growth."[6]

From the beginning of our development, the gaze is what helps the child to "feel felt" and to see herself; and to see the world as safe and full of possibility. This is the beginning of a felt sense of true self and true other and opens the field of relationship. The child sees that in her vulnerable need and desire she can trustingly reach across the breach of aloneness and be met. The relational field is the ground of the unfolding of the self.

> As a spiritual being, the human creature is defined through interpersonal relationships. The more authentically he or she lives these relations, the more his or her own personal identity matures. It is not by isolation that man establishes his worth, but by placing himself in relation with others and with God.[7]

---

4. Bieler, "Attachment Theory and Aquinas."

5. Hans Urs von Balthasar, *Unless You Become Like This Child*, trans. Eramo Leiva-Merikakis (San Francisco: Ignatius Press, 1991), 16–17.

6. Diana Fosha, Daniel Siegel, Marion Solomon, eds., *The Healing Power of Emotion* (New York: W.W. Norton, 2009), 177.

7. Pope Benedict XVI, *Caritas in veritate* (June 29, 2009), §53, at www.vatican.va/holy_father/benedict_xvi/encyclicals/documents/hf_ben-xvi_enc_20090629_caritas-in-veritate_en.html.

The disruption of this process has dramatic consequences in fracturing the self's relationship to self, and recursively, to the relational field in general.

2. Dissociation and Original Sin

Looking back at his fragmented and distorted past, Augustine knew that "I was at odds with myself, and fragmenting myself. This disintegration was occurring without my consent, but what it indicated was not the presence in me of a mind belonging to some alien nature but the punishment undergone by my own . . . the punishment for that other sin committed with the greater freedom; for I was a son of Adam" (8.10.22). In Christianity, we understand our fractured state first to be the result of original sin, the primordial self-willed hiding from the gaze of God out of distrust of his gratuitous love.

In contemporary psychology, this could be understood as a state of dissociation.[8] It is a shutting-down, hiding or splintering of aspects of the self and its drive for connection in attempt to protect the self from being overwhelmed by helplessness, abandonment, shame or danger. Dissociation can be seen, both spiritually and psychologically, as fundamentally an injury to relational attachment which necessarily results in a splintering of man's identity which is received and matured through man's relational nature.

Balthasar warns that if the original unity described above is disturbed the results are often dire:

> Any disturbance the child begins to sense—whether between the parents or one parent and the child—confuses and clouds over the horizon of absolute being, and, therefore, also its bestowal of all creaturely being as a gift of God. . . . Any violence in this realm of wholeness inflicts wounds in the child's heart which for the most part will never heal.[9]

This invites consideration of Augustine's own upbringing in the midst of his parents' conflicted marriage as one precipitator of his own divided state, though we will not develop that here. In such circumstances even at the neurobiological level the child's development and integration are compromised. The

8. I am using the term here in the sense used by Fosha to describe a significant impairment or interruption in the self's integrative capacities due to experiences that overwhelm and threaten the self. For an excellent discussion of this see Diana Fosha, "A Heaven in a Wild Flower: Self, Dissociation, and Treatment in the Context of the Neurobiological Core Self," *Psychoanalytic Inquiry*, 33, no. 5 (2013): 504–512.

9. Von Balthasar, *Unless You Become Like This Child*, 19.

brain and nervous system default to a protective system rather than its more open and vulnerable seeking and receptive system.

This results in an obscuring of the true self and a confusion about the true value and positive possibility of creation and Creator. The impact generalizes, leaving the individual with a compromised relationship with the rest of reality. As Fosha observes of this negative pole of change: "Trauma [including, and perhaps especially, early attachment injury] is the definitum of quantum transformation: in one fell swoop, everything changes. Nothing is ever the same again."[10]

As with trauma, so with original sin: in one fell swoop, everything changed. Experience was truncated, blunted, or distorted because the self shut down and turned away from both its true desires and its fundamental dependency on the God who lovingly and gratuitously provided for them. In a misguided attempt at self-protection and agency, the vulnerable need for God is shut down in favor of the delusion of becoming like him through self-sufficiency. As a result, the moral realm loses its relational grounding and becomes one of calculation. To quote the *Catechism*,[11]

> The harmony in which they had found themselves, thanks to original justice, is now destroyed: the control of the soul's spiritual faculties over the body is shattered; the union of man and woman becomes subject to tensions, their relations henceforth marked by lust and domination (Cf. *Gen* 3:7–16). Harmony with creation is broken: visible creation has become alien and hostile to man (Cf. *Gen* 3:17, 19).

Augustine's struggle with chastity certainly is reflected in this. Without acting from his "true self," he cannot be in true relationship with true subjects. And compounding the dilemma, without true relationship, man loses connection with his true self. The particular causes of original sin and psychological dissociation may be different, but the results are analogous: the lack of an experience of reality in its wholeness and goodness, with the self and the relational field fragmented and "seen through a glass darkly." Raniero Cantalamessa makes this self-observation regarding our dissociative postlapsarian state: "If Jesus were to ask me, as He did that poor demoniac in the Gospel, 'What is your name?' I too would have to reply, 'My name is legion, for there are many of us.'"[12]

---

10. Diana Fosha, "Quantum Transformation in Trauma and Treatment: Traversing the Crisis of Healing Change," *Journal of Clinical Psychology: In Session* 62, no. 5 (2006): 569.

11. *The Catechism of The Catholic Church, Second Edition* (Washington: United States Catholic Conference, 2011), §400.

12. Raniero Cantalamessa, OFM Cap., trans. Charles Serignat, *Virginity: Positive Approach to Celibacy for the Sake of the Kingdom* (New York: Alba House, 1995), 29.

For our purposes, we offer that the state of psychological dissociation is an instantiation of the effects of that primordial spiritual split through original sin. Conversion or transformation, then, is the vulnerable turning back of the true self into the relational field of true others. The passage to repair is fraught with re-entering the fear of vulnerability which led to the initial dissociation and the grieving of the costs of that rupture. In the face of this ambivalent state, the desire for such restoration is propelled, Augustine tells us, by the teleologically ordered restless longing of the heart. Diana Fosha would describe it as neurobiological drive for transformance.[13]

3. The Role of the Will in Transformation and Conversion

In this framework, transformation and conversion can be viewed as the healing of dissociative states:

> The result [of a transformative change or (to use the authors' term) Quantum Change] is a new, dramatically reorganized identity. One might draw an analogy here to the development of multiple personality disorder, where early trauma is so great that one's identity is segmented, dissociated into separate parts. In quantum change, it is almost the opposite process. Strained and separate aspects of identity are reordered in one brilliant moment.[14]

It is commonly observed that in book 8 Augustine's "second conversion" is essentially a moral one, building on the intellectual conversion of book 7. In our framework, this moral reordering of the second conversion could be seen as essentially a deep healing of relational capacities. Augustine's restless heart propels his desperate searching and his being searched. His transformation in book 8 is not discontinuous with book 7 in its desired object—a chaste life ordered to God—but in its process. Rather than a willful journey up an intellectual summit, it is the surrendered falling, or perhaps jumping, off a cliff. If book 7 is an intellectual assent with the ascent of the will towards the unchanging God, book 8 is the whole-hearted vulnerable surrender into relationship with Christ. James makes two important points in his comparison of more gradual, volitional, workmanlike conversions and the more dramatic, surrendered type we have here:

> Even in the most voluntarily built-up sort of regeneration there are passages of self-surrender interposed; and in the great majority of cases when the will

---

13. Fosha, "Emotion and Recognition," 30.

14. William Miller and Janet C'de Baca, *Quantum Change* (New York: Guilford Press, 2001), 157.

had done its uttermost towards bringing one close to complete unification aspired after, it seems that the very last step must be left to other forces and performed without the help of its activity. In other words, self-surrender then becomes indispensable.[15]

This presents problems for a psychology which attempts to locate change in the control of self-initiative. It fits well with Aquinas's understanding of the self's secondary cooperation with the operation of actual grace.[16]

In book 7, Augustine comes to conclude "So totally is it a matter of grace that the searcher is not only invited to see you, who are ever the same, but healed as well, so that he can possess you" (7.21.27). Augustine has found that even in the light of this deeper intellectual conversion at the end of book 7, he is unable to reorder himself, to will himself, body and soul, in line with his ideal of self-gift in chastity. Though his intellect can give him the view of its desired object, it alone cannot embrace it.

In book 7, the discrepancy between Augustine's growing enlightenment and his old attachments builds to a crescendo. His new apprehension of the ways of God has left him indeed apprehensive. His declaration at the end of book 7 sets the stage for the transformation to follow "In the awe-inspiring ways these truths were striking deep roots within me as I read the least of your apostles: I had contemplated your works and was filled with dread" (7.21.27).

Fosha in her clinical observations notes that there is a "sometimes thin line between trauma and healing . . . between, on one side, *fear* and, on the other, *excitement and curiosity.* . . . Being taken by surprise means there has been a violation of our expectations. Such disruptions generate intense emotions."[17]

Augustine states: "All I knew was that I was going mad, but for the sake of my sanity and dying that I might live" (8.8.19). Given the combination of attraction and fear, what keeps the experiencer moving forward? The answer lies in the potent mix of desperation and desire, and again the line of distinction between these is quite thin.

---

15. Miller and C'de Baca, *Quantum Change*, 157.

16. Thomas Aquinas, *Summa theologiae* I-II, q. III, aa. 2–3, in *Summa Theologica*, trans. Fathers of the English Dominican Province, at www.newadvent.org/summa/2111.htm.

17. Fosha, "Quantum Transformation," 570.

4. The Crisis of Desire as a Precursor to Transformation

"Ring the bell that still can ring / Forget your perfect offering / Everything
has cracks in it / That's how the light gets in."

LEONARD COHEN, "ANTHEM"

"I say it is not enough to be drawn by the will; you are drawn even by delight
... not by necessity, but pleasure; not obligation but delight."

AUGUSTINE[18]

Miller notes, "The most common antecedent [to Quantum Change] as we have
seen was the intense pain of emotional distress, *a point of desperation or hit-
ting bottom, and that seems to be one important source of receptivity*"[19] (emphasis added). The balance of the calculus for survival suddenly shifts—the self-
protective strategy of dissociation is now felt to be too costly, opening the
possibility of taking relational risk.

This receptive opening-up and reaching-out is a crucial element in risk-
ing relational reintegration. Miller and C'de Baca note, "Besides personal pain,
another common theme involves some conscious decision to be open to the
spiritual, although few anticipate what would follow that decision."[20] Fosha's
work echoes this, stating, "Crisis and intense emotional suffering, *when experienced in conditions of safety*, [provided by a True Other] can be a great boon to
transformation strivings: The alchemy of transformation strivings together with
the drive to relieve distress is an unbeatable mix for change."[21]

What is the source of our desire? Fosha, always favoring the neurobiological explanation, references the wired-in, dopamine-rewarded pleasure system
as the driver of our desire to seek wholeness, resources and meaning in the
world. "Drive and fuel for the self's interactions with the mind–body–world
comes from seeking system, the motivational aspect of the neurobiological
core self."[22] For Augustine, this drive is an indication of our telos, of our nature
as beings created not only in God's image but also towards it.

When this drive is frustrated and its energies are dammed up, it seems it
becomes latent potency. Moments of heightened desperation, desire, and possibility can crack the dissociative barrier releasing the torrential transformative

---

18. Augustine of Hippo, *Tractates on the Gospel of John* §26 (on John 6:41–59), at www
.newadvent.org/fathers/170126.

19. Miller and C'de Baca, *Quantum Change*, 174.

20. Miller and C'de Baca, *Quantum Change*, 174.

21. Fosha, Siegel, and Solomon, *The Healing Power of Emotions*, 176.

22. Fosha, "Heaven in a Wildflower," 500.

flow of energy, power, desire, and grace rapidly reordering the interior landscape. At a felt risk to the current self, once the calculus of safety has shifted, surrender may be allowed.

Fosha's identification of the neurobiological processes which register the teleological tug has an appealing beauty in honoring of the body's created nature in the role in spiritual yearning. However, the neurobiological explanation by itself seems inadequate to bring us to the realm of meaning or spiritual desire—it pinpoints its somatic registration in the self, but not its source. The following concept of recognition of the true self contains similar intimations and limitations.

5. Recognition of True Self

"And so two wills fought it out, the old and the new. . . . I was aligned with both, but more with the desires I approved of, for in these [other] I was not really the agent . . . I was enduring them rather than acting freely . . . the prospect of being free from all these encumbrances frightened me."

AUGUSTINE (8.5.10-11)

"I (just realized) that what's on the edge of my vision is . . . .the person who I was always meant to be, who I just can't seem to get to . . . .That's what's on the edge of my vision. It's a . . . . [*long pause*] . . . if I let go of all the shit I carry around with me . . . it's not fear exactly . . . I get this feeling . . . I used the word 'searing' . . . There is this brilliant possibility and just the thought of it . . . I don't know . . ."

DIANA FOSHA quoting from transcript session
with middle-aged male client[23]

In the face of this dilemma, letting go of the self-as-I-know-me for the self-I-am-meant-to-be, Fosha makes a keen observation regarding the crisis of transformation: if transformation contains in it the terrifying sense of undoing of the self, it also contains, in the midst of this undoing, a recognition of the true self that is coming into view. She calls this sense the "click of recognition," noting "I refer to this as the felt core self. At the moment of the felt core self-experiencing the individual has the sense that 'this is me'. Such experiences are accompanied by a strong subjective sense of truth."[24]

Unfortunately, but consistently, Fosha later adds, "The truth sense that accompanies the experience of the *felt core self* experience is a crucial aspect

23. Fosha, "Emotion and Recognition," 47.
24. Fosha, "Heaven in a Wildflower," 497.

of such experiences. Although, indeed, there is no such thing as The Truth, there is such a thing as the *experience of truth* in the moment."[25] Her client's own language seems to be somewhat disregarded here. His awareness of a self he was "supposed to be" suggests a "Supposer" and a given sense of purpose to his existence. Perhaps we could more readily honor Fosha's unwillingness to consider an ontically true self as an act of modesty, staying in her domain as a psychologist, not a theologian, if she had not in the same paragraph so dogmatically denied its possibility.

Like Fosha's client, Augustine wrestles with this surrender of the disordered, dissociative self in the garden: "The nearer it came, the moment I would be changed, the more it pierced me with terror" (8.11.25). He then hears the singing child's voice instructing him to "pick up and read." (8.12.29) As he picks up the Bible and does so, he is struck by Romans 13:13–14 exhorting him "Not is dissipation and drunkenness, nor in debauchery and lewdness, nor in arguing and jealousy; but *put on the Lord Jesus Christ . . .* " (8.12.29). Much more than an admonishment, Augustine receives this as an ontologically transformative invitation. This far supersedes the psychological enterprise of recovering and healing of the core true self. Rather than Fosha's click of recognition of the true self, Augustine's "click" is the recognition of his heart's deepest desire. Joseph Ratzinger speaks of this phenomenon of recognition:

> When the heart comes into contact with God's Logos, with word who became man, this inmost point of his existence is being touched. Then, he does not merely feel, he knows within himself this is it, that this is HE, that is what I was waiting for. *It is a kind of recognition.* For we have been created in relation to God.[26]

And how fitting it is that a child's voice calls Augustine to "pick it up and read" (8.12.29). As Balthasar observes in *Unless You Become Like This Child*:

> This demands of Jesus' listener a reawakening to his true origin, to which he has turned his back, a spiritual turnabout ("unless you convert and become like children") that will enable him to become aware of himself. And since this turning about takes place in obedience to Jesus, it must count on the illuminating light of his grace is to succeed.[27]

25. Fosha, "Heaven in a Wildflower," 503, emphasis original

26. Joseph Cardinal Ratzinger, *Pilgrim Fellowship of Faith: The Church as Communion* (San Francisco: Ignatius Press, 2005), 23–24, emphasis added.

27. Von Balthasar, *Unless You Become Like This Child*, 27–28.

As the recognition of the true self helps guide the crisis of transformation, Fosha's client celebrates a new ease: "I have let go of little chunks of misery . . . but now I think there is the possibility of letting go of all of it . . . my eyes are filled with tears . . . but what a thought!!! . . . that my misery is like a carapace that I can take off like a big scab."[28] The client is no longer identified in himself with past trauma and past mistakes. A sense of the true self is emerging. Augustine similarly celebrates the freedom and ease of this self newly transformed in Christ "How sweet did it suddenly seem to me to shrug off those sweet frivolities and how glad I was to get rid of them—I who had been loath to let them go!" (9.1.1).

For Augustine, the transformation goes beyond transformative restoration of the true self, beyond the healing of any core wounds, and proceeds to a higher transformation, that of the self not only through but in Christ. As Ratzinger states, "whenever we encounter Christ, there takes place what theology would call a 'dialogic communication,' a mutual inner exchange in the great new I into which I am introduced and assimilated."[29] We will explore this further as we turn now to the necessary presence that accompanies and helps midwife the emergence of a healed, true self both in the natural and spiritual domain, the True Other.

6. The True Other: The Relational/Dialogical Character of Transformation

"Attachment decisively tilts whether we respond to life's challenges as opportunities for learning and expansion of the self or as threats to our integrity, leading to constriction of activities and withdrawal from the world."

DIANA FOSHA[30]

"You were more intimately present to me than my inmost being." (3.6.11)

"You inspired in me the idea that I ought to go to Simplicianus, and even I could see the good sense of this." (8.1.1)

---

28. Fosha, *Emotion and Recognition*, 47.

29. Joseph Cardinal Ratzinger, *Co-Workers of the Truth* (San Francisco, Ignatius Press, 1992), 235. See also Monika Szetela and Grzegorz Osiński, "The Concept of 'Dialogical Soul' by Joseph Ratzinger Against the Latest Concepts of Neuroscience," *Scientia et Fides* 5, vol. 2 (2017): 199–215, for a discussion of Ratzinger's attempts to address reductionistic impulses in the findings of neuroscience.

30. Fosha, "Quantum Transformation," 570.

If dissociation is at its base a rupture in our relational self, it is fitting that the relational accompaniment of a true other is essential to finding our way back. For Fosha, the term designated for this counterpart in the emergence of the True Self is the True Other. The true other is one the self comes to trust as one (or several) who can see and speak into the self's distress, align with its true desire, support the self through the navigation of the tumultuous emotions of healing, and welcome the true self as it emerges in greater wholeness.

For Augustine, throughout the *Confessions*, but at a crescendo pitch in book 8, his true others not only accompany him, but also invite him more deeply into his internal discrepancy, the fault line between his current reality and his heart's deep desire, along which the transformative conversion can erupt. They do so in part, and perhaps not with such intention, by telling stories that appeal to the desire of his heart, that show its lived possibility. Simplicianus relates to Augustine the story of Victorinus's conversion; Victorinus, a man whose gifts and station in life were similar to that of Augustine.

After hearing this story, Augustine states, "A new will had begun to emerge in me, the will to worship you disinterestedly" (8.5.10). This continues in his encounter with Ponticianus telling him of the court officials who converted: "Ponticianus went on with his story; but, Lord, even while he spoke you were wrenching me back toward myself, and pulling me around from that standpoint behind my back" (8.7.16). These stories of others' conversions help deepen the felt longing, hope, and needed tension between current state and where his heart desires to be in a manner that intellectual discourse did not.

It is important to note that none of these "true others" seek to confront or persuade Augustine, nor do they seek to comfort or affirm him. There is nothing forceful in these powerful and transformative encounters. There is a caring invitation into the possibility of true freedom. These true others do not engage in a battle of the wills. This allows Augustine room and support as he contends with his own divided will. Nor is any easy reassurance being offered. Our current culture, which can have a tyranny of affirmation, may not be well equipped to help another deepen this life-saving discrepancy. This certainly has implications for pastoral counseling and formational work.

Later, on the cusp of his surrender in the Garden, Augustine is quite aware of being accompanied: "So I went out into the Garden and Alypius followed at my heels; my privacy was not infringed by his presence, and in any case, how could he abandon me in that state?" (8.8.19). For his part, Alypius stays close when proximity is needed and allows the distance that Augustine desires as he falls into his weeping and greets him with great receptivity when he seeks him out to process and share the joy of this transformation. Alypius's way of being with Augustine is attuned to Augustine's shifting needs from moment to moment as his conversion unfolds.

So also in the work of therapy with Fosha. In narrating a vignette from a session, she observes, "It is hard to capture the fullness of somatic experiencing going back and forth between patient and therapist. Held by the therapeutic dyad, having moved through resistance and avoidance, the patient now surrenders to his experience."[31]

There is a lovely dance of accompaniment by one acting as a true other that allows the self enough support and safety to surrender to its transformation. As the true other generously and with great attunement accompanies the emerging true self, defenses and resistance are honored and allowed, even as new safety begins to help them loosen and the self to allow their surrender. Shifts in emotional and somatic states are acknowledged and honored with interest and curiosity. Painful and positive emotions are welcomed, validated, and allowed to deepen so that they can have their transformational value for the emerging self. Fosha notes, "The key to the way things go is the presence—or the absence—of a trusted other. There is a world of difference between being alone with overwhelming emotions and being with a trusted other in the affect storm."[32]

If a true other is instrumental to those going through an integrative transformation, what of those who report navigating this journey when alone? Fosha's work, by its nature, does not give an accounting of this. In the findings of James and Miller, however, there are many accounts of conversion or quantum changes occurring when the person was alone, and often alone in a desperate state. Yet in this seeming aloneness, Miller and C'de Baca note that most of those they interviewed had the sense of a holy Other that accompanied their epiphanies. They add, "It was rare for quantum changers to feel afraid in the presence of the Other. Rather they felt utterly safe. . . . The almost universal experience of the Other presence . . . was of utter love and total acceptance, even if the person felt a heightened awareness of past shortcomings."[33]

This spiritual sense of the True Other is doubly evidenced in Augustine's account of envisioning Lady Chastity and her encouragement to Augustine to trust Christ as the True Other: "Why try to stand by yourself, only to lose your footing? Cast yourself on him and do not be afraid: he will not step back and let you fall. Cast yourself upon him trustfully; he will support and heal you"

31. Fosha, *The Healing Power of Emotion*, 195.
32. Fosha, "Quantum Transformation," 570.
33. Miller and C'de Baca, *Quantum Change*, 188.

(8.11.27). In this sense, for Augustine both the true self and true other are constituted in Christ.

There is another missing component in Fosha's accounting: the integrative role of participation in an ongoing community of true others, of believers in which this transformation can take root and bear fruit. This lack of accompaniment and grounding may explain Miller and C'de Baca's finding that many of the experiencers were quite secretive about their experience, in part out of concern that others might consider them to be "crazy."[34]

In Augustine's case the community of the Church allows the conversion experience to be integrated into the living body and wisdom of the Church community in a way that moves it beyond a merely private and potentially idiosyncratic expression. The energy with which Augustine lives out his life in the Church also reflects the spiritual nature of his transformation which leads to self-gift, rather than stopping with self-actualization or a private faith. As Ratzinger notes: "Conversion does not lead into a private relationship with Jesus, which in reality would be another form of mere monologue. It is the delivery into the pattern of doctrine .... or ... entrance into the "we" of the Church. ... Only the concrete God can be something other than a new projection of one's own self."[35]

7. Affective Movements and Markers of the Transformation Process

"Then God, the gentle first Truth, spoke: O dearest daughter whom I so love, you have asked for the will to know the reasons for tears and their fruits. . . . I want you to know that all tears come from the heart. Nor is there any other bodily member that can satisfy the heart as the eyes can."

CATHERINE OF SIENA[36]

"Emotional occasions . . . are extremely potent in precipitating mental rearrangements. The sudden and explosive ways in which love, jealousy, guilt, fear, remorse, or anger can seize upon one are known to everybody. Hope, happiness, security, resolve . . . can be equally explosive. And emotions that come in this explosive way seldom leave things as they found them."

WILLIAM JAMES[37]

34. Miller and C'de Baca, *Quantum Change*, 173

35. Joseph Cardinal Ratzinger, Adrian Walker, trans., *The Nature and Mission of Theology*, (San Francisco: Ignatius Press, 1995), 59

36. Catherine of Siena, trans. Suzanne Noffke, *The Dialogue* (New York: Paulist Press, 1980), 161.

37. William James, *The Varieties of Religious Experience* (London: Longmans, Green, and Co., 1902; s.l.: Renaissance Classics, 2012), 147–148. Citations refer to the Renaissance Classics edition.

In the painting of Augustine by Flemish artist Phillipe de Champaigne circa 1650, Augustine's heart, held in his hand, and God's truth, "Veritas," are depicted as full of light and flames being pulled towards each other. The head is in the middle of them and is illumined by this dialogue between the light of Veritas and Augustine's restless heart burning for God. Dietrich von Hildebrand in his work on affectivity, *The Heart*, credits Augustine as the one Western Father of the Church who gave the heart, the affective life, its rightful place noting, "St. Augustine's work from the *Confessions* onward is pervaded by deep and admirable insights concern the heart and the affective attitudes of man."[38]

Augustine's portrayal of his affective movements in book 8 are compelling, and phenomenologically closely parallel Fosha's careful observation regarding the affective markers of the transformational process. Throughout her work, she observes these movements of the heart, the affective life, to be a key dynamism in transformation as well as a signaler of the transformational process. This does not diminish the role of the intellect in the process; rather it provides a powerful, visceral experience of the integration of the sensitive and intellective appetites for intellectual reflection and meaning-making.

Ongoing developments in the neuropsychological science of emotion help us map and track the role of emotions in growth and transformation, giving these affective experiences some pride of place as agents of change. It is important to note that emotions are not only rich intrapersonal events, alerting us to respond to danger and opportunity; they are also important interpersonal signals sent by the individual to those around him. They help signal our need for proximity and distance, they cue our closedness and our receptivity. When signaling for assistance, they also help the one signaling enter a zone of vulnerable, even if ambivalent, receptivity. In Augustine's case, it may be his pained heart's desperate call out to God—"'Oh Lord, how long?' . . . I uttered cries of misery: 'Why must I go on saying 'Tomorrow . . . tomorrow?' Why not now? [8.12.28]"—that both signals and assists his heart's surrender to the transformative power of Veritas.

We will explore some of the key emotional movements and markers in book 8 and compare these with Fosha's mapping of emotional processes in transformation. To use Fosha's model, by the time we encounter Augustine in book 8, he has already left his earlier defensive secondary emotions (which we will not treat here), and he is entering the experience of such vulnerable primary core affective states as desire, pain, regret, and longing.

---

38. Dietrich von Hildebrand, *The Heart: An Analysis of Human and Divine Affectivity* (South Bend, Indiana: St. Augustine's Press, 1991), 5.

The main affective movements we find in book 8 are initially waves of those that Fosha would term transformational affects, which include the tremulous affects; the mourning-of-self affects; and the healing affects, which include recognition, gratitude, and tenderness.[39] These are followed or accompanied by alternating waves of core state affective states such as energy, openness, empathy, clarity, and the "truth sense" that are experienced with the emergence of the true self. This new sense of the true self is further integrated through the joyful sharing and celebrating of this transformation with true others who can help make meaning and root this new reality so that it can continue to broaden, build, and bear fruit.[40]

Tremulous affects. In their physical experience, the tremulous affects have a quality similar to that of fear, and yet also attraction. They signal both danger to the current state of things and rich possibilities for growth. They are exemplified in a passage we already examined in which Augustine states, "In awe-inspiring ways these truths were striking deep roots within me as I read the least of your apostles: I had contemplated your works and was filled with dread" (7.21.27). The functioning false self is fearfully sensing that it is facing its "undoing" and the true self is even more compellingly desiring it. Further on, this continues to draw him in, "The nearer it came, that moment when I would be changed, the more it pierced me with terror" (8.11.25). And again, he writes, "a revelation was coming to me from that country toward which I was facing, but into which I trembled to cross. There I beheld the chaste, dignified figure of Continence" (8.11.27). And he sees that Continence beckons him to make the passage. Tremulous affects are crucial harbingers of change, they tell us something big is afoot. They benefit from attuned accompaniment so that they can be tolerated and allowed to do their work and continue to draw us forward.

The mourning-the-self affects are also represented in Augustine's *Confessions*. The mourning-the-self affects occur in tandem with the transformational process and are often the experience of deep, even gut-wrenching grief, and yet accompanied with a rather peaceful and convicting sadness. "But as this deep meditation dredged all my wretchedness up from the secret profundity of my being and heaped it all together before the eyes of my heart, a huge storm blew up within me and brought on a heavy rain of tears" (8.12.28). Entering this experience of the legitimate sense of past pain caused to the self and others, and the grief over lost time and the past wasting of life, allows these hard realities

39. Fosha, "Quantum Transformation," 571.
40. Fosha, "Emotion and Recognition," 50.

to be safely experienced and their truth integrated rather than numbed in the dawning light of transformational process.

Healing affects. If the tremulous affects are the harbingers and the motivational dynamism at the threshold of transformation, the healing affects are a common experience after a wave of transformation has been passed through. They signal a place of new arrival and they seek to be shared and integrated. As Fosha describes it, "The healing affects possess simplicity, clarity, innocence, freshness, sweetness, and poignancy. The individual is in a state of openness and vulnerability, but a shimmering vulnerability without anxiety and without the need to defend against it."[41]

Upon his transformative reading and surrendering to the admonition "put on the Lord Jesus Christ, and make no provision for the flesh of the gratification of your desire" (Rom 13:13–14), Augustine states, "No sooner had I reached the end of the verse than the light of certainty flooded my heart and all darkness of doubt fled away. . . . My face was peaceful now" (8.12.29). Later, recounting his conversion, he notes, "How sweet did it seem to shrug off those sweet frivolities. . . . Childlike, I chattered away to you, my glory, my wealth, my salvation, and my Lord and God" (9.1.1).

Core state affects and the metaprocessing of transformation: shared joy and meaning making. After Augustine joyfully recounts to Alypius the story of what happened in the garden, the two friends go and bring their shared joy to Augustine's mother in book 9, and by extension, to mother Church. Fosha employs the term metaprocessing to describe this process of sharing the sense of mastery, arrival, joy, gratitude, energy and meaning arising from the transformational experience. This mutual reflection between the true self and true others allows for the deepening, broadening, and integration of profound positive affects and dawning understanding that helps fuel the desire for and openness to continued growth. Such growth does not satiate the self, but platforms further growth in a manner that Fosha terms "appetitive."[42]

This processing of what just happened also gives the head the opportunity to catch up to the heart. The rational processes apprehend and assist in making fuller meaning from the experience, integrating it into the person's life narrative, looking both to the past and towards the future as the "new self." A community of meaning-making is also vital in this. For Augustine this community is the Church, and the broadening and building occurs throughout a life time of

41. Fosha, "Emotion, True Self, True Other," 539.
42. Fosha, "Emotion and Recognition" 49–51

living out his conversion in that community of shared sacrament, meaning and mission which continues to broaden and build along with him.

8. Post-Transformation Sequelae

An important but less-developed subject is the aftermath of transformative conversions. Fosha's work is of less use here as its primary purview is the moment-to-moment transformational process as it unfolds in the therapy office between therapist and client. We will instead turn to some of the findings of James and Miller and C'de Baca who pull the camera back to look at the larger frame of the integration and durability of transformational and conversion processes over time in the lives of those who experienced them.

Miller and C'de Baca observe, "A common theme in the aftermath of quantum change is a decentering of the self, an abrupt move away from an 'I-me-my-mine' self-centered view of the world."[43] The experience leads away from any defensive posturing, ego-enlargement, or self-asserting and towards self-surrender and self-gift. They report:

> A common thread running through the stories is that after such an experience, people often view the material world as merely a small part of a much greater reality, and a relatively unimportant part. This insight does not send them into monastic withdrawal from society. To the contrary, it often inspires their devotion of significant time to compassionate service for others.[44]

And further:

> The biggest single gain was in the priority given to spirituality . . . both men and women also reflected large increases in the value they place on forgiveness, generosity, God's will, growth, honesty, humility, loving and personal peace, all of which were reported in the bottom half of priorities before quantum change.[45]

Even for the many whose experiences were not expressly Christian or religious, Miller and C'de Baca note these spiritual themes espoused in the stories of their respondents. [46] Even if these are outside of the baptized Christian experience, such transformations seem to show evidence of prevenient grace and the gifts of the Holy Spirit.

43. Miller and C'de Baca, *Quantum Change*, 186.
44. Miller and C'de Baca, *Quantum Change*, 172.
45. Miller and C'de Baca, *Quantum Change*, 130–31.
46. Miller and C'de Baca, *Quantum Change*, 190.

Though I do not know of outcome research on the durability of change resulting from Fosha's therapy, my own clinical experience with her process has been that core state transformative experiences tend to be irrevocable—they cannot be "un-known." As James observed,

> So with the conversion experience: that it should for even a short time show a human being what the high-water mark of his spiritual capacity is, this is what constitutes its importance—an importance which backsliding cannot diminish, although persistence might increase it. As a matter of fact, all the more striking instances of conversion, all those, for instance, which I have quoted, HAVE been permanent.[47]

James also notes of his colleague, Prof. Starbuck, that of one hundred subjects followed, "only six percent relapsed from the religious faith which the conversion confirmed."[48] These are watershed moments around which the "before and after" narrative of the person's life become organized.

All of this both confirms a moral and spiritual value in these experiences and readily differentiates it from any histrionic, delusional or grandiose defensive operations of a self. If a transformational experience resulted in ego gratification rather than a de-centering from the ego, it would give lie to itself. Again, from James:

> As Professor Coe well says . . ., "The ultimate test of religious values is nothing psychological, nothing definable in terms of HOW IT HAPPENS, but something ethical, definable only in terms of WHAT IS ATTAINED" . . . . we shall see that what is attained is often an altogether new level of spiritual vitality, a relatively heroic level in which impossible things have become possible, and new energies and endurances are shown. The personality is changed; the man is born anew, whether or not his psychological idiosyncrasies are what give particular shape to his metamorphosis.[49]

9. Concluding Summary and Reflections

In our exploration, we have seen how phenomena described by psychology's investigations of conversion and transformational processes and those in Augustine's Christian conversion experience recounted in book 8 bear a number of striking parallels. The concepts of man's fundamental relationality as evidenced in the neurobiological processes of attachment, dissociation, and its

---

47. James, *Varieties of Religious Experience*, 190.
48. James, *Varieties of Religious Experience*, 191.
49. James, *Varieties of Religious Experience*, 178.

healing; and the dynamism of the affective life, the heart, in driving and surrendering to the restoration of man's true relationality are compelling.

But what of this? Once science can give some accounting of the observable or measurable "how" of an experience there is the danger of reductionism, reducing the spiritual to its psychic phenomenon or the neurobiological operations of that experience. The post-modern mind, as seen in Diana Fosha's work, could too easily conflate the mechanism and somatic registration of a spiritual reality with the wholeness of that reality itself, reducing, for example, the sense of "true self" to midline cortical structures in the brain.[50]

The error of this reductionism is that it risks overlooking the very thing that phenomena it uncovers seem to point to—the frequently reported sense of an objectively intended true self—"the self I was meant to be," to quote Fosha's own client—and the frequently reported awareness of the operation of a loving transcendent force in the transformational experience. In this denial, these experiences would lose their profound power as sign. This could leave the experiencer trapped in his subjective self and without a higher, transcendent opening to being. With such limiting beliefs, those acting as "midwife" to such an experience may stop short of allowing or affirming the full birth, leaving it unaccompanied and thus not fully realized. Augustine provides this cautionary note about transformation outside of the Lord, "The trouble is that they want to be light not in the Lord, but in themselves, with their notion that the soul is by nature divine, and so they have become denser darkness still, because by their appalling arrogance they have moved further away from you, the true Light" (8.10.22). As Ratzinger observes of the fully converted: "[Christ] is the new 'I' which bursts open the limits of subjectivity and the boundaries dividing the subject from object, thus enabling me to say: 'It is no longer I who live.'"[51] This is the healing of all dissociation.

On the other hand, religious conversions which assent dutifully and intellectively to their true object, Christ, without transformation and integration in Christ at the level of the heart through the operations of the intellectual and sensitive appetites also stop short of full conversion, leaving the self still potentially split and dissociated. Those pastorally guiding such believers would need to be aware that such dutifully willed faith may be closed to fuller transformation and conversion in actual grace and the invitation to participate in Trinitarian love.

50. Fosha, "Heaven in a Wildflower," 499.

51. Joseph Ratzinger, trans. Adrian Walker, *The Nature and Mission of Theology* (San Francisco: Ignatius Press, 1995), 58–59.

If properly understood, these findings in neurobiology and the psychological insights into the phenomenon of transformational processes honor the role and meaning of the body and emotions as voices and dynamic forces in our teleological journey. These insights and understandings could help inform and deepen the capacities of those in formational or pastoral work who seek to accompany others in this journey. This could sensitize us to see glimmers of the operation of prevenient grace in our secularized society and welcome it into its fuller birth in the Church.

These findings could help those accompanying others to be more helpfully attuned to the movements in the affective states and the stages of transformation. They could better assist others in deepening the felt discrepancy between the person's current state and their heart's desire, ripening the movement towards conversion. In short, it could help those attempting to be true others be aware of the psychic and somatic registration and signals of the workings of the Spirit.

Fosha borrows a line from William Blake's poem "Auguries of Innocence" for the title of her article "Heaven in a Wildflower." This image suggests that even the smallest glimmer of transformation contains in it the elements and possibilities, fractals, of the pattern of the whole. Perhaps even in the "natural" experience of transformation into greater psychic wholeness through a therapy such as Fosha's, God's indwelling in his creation can be seen represented in this fractal form if we are open to the true sign of that phenomenon. In that manner, all true, positive transformations—those that evidence the gifts of the Spirit—could be viewed as a spiritual movement towards God, even if not fully realized and integrated. In any case, transformational and conversion process are never an end in themselves. They are a point of arrival that is also a point of departure. They are a new beginning for the ongoing unfolding of the journey out of dissociation, out of sin, which always divides and separates, to assist the true self coming back into communion with true others in creation and Creator in the heart's restless journey towards his gaze in the Beatific Vision.

Christian Transcendentalism

John Peter Kenney

The ninth book of the *Confessions* brings Augustine's retrospective autobiography to a close. Although it will be followed in book 10 by an examination of the current spiritual condition of its author, the long sweep of the historical narrative concludes with the death and burial of Monica. That denouement is carefully plotted and finely wrought, reaching back to the death of Augustine's unnamed childhood friend in book 4, and even further to book 3, to Monica's premonitory dream and the sage advice of an unknown bishop to wait out the son of her tears. For Book 9 is, in truth, as much Monica's book as it is Augustine's.

Book 8 had ended with the surprise announcement of Augustine's conversion both to Catholicism and asceticism. Monica reacts with joyful equanimity—happy at her son's decision to return to the spiritual home of his childhood and accepting of the loss of legitimate grandchildren for whom she had naturally yearned (8.12.30). Book 9 follows by offering the reader Monica's own biography, sketched by her son in terms at once tender and honest. Among its details is the telling but neglected fact that she had been a martyr for Catholicism during Holy Week of 386, willing to die with her bishop Ambrose in defense of his cathedral against the imperial troops of the young emperor Valentinian II and his Arian mother Justina. That act of civil disobedience was a telling vignette revealing her steely character and manifest sanctity, but, more importantly, it underscored the source of her spiritual authority in the Catholic community.

Into the midst of that biography, Augustine interweaves what is perhaps the most striking event in the *Confessions*, the so-called "vision at Ostia," the joint ascent of his soul and Monica's to divine Wisdom. That event bisects Monica's biography, separating the events of her life from the account of her death. But it is the extraordinary account of this mutual vision, or audition, that I want to consider here. In doing so I will look at the text itself and also some important antecedent passages as well a few references that Augustine offers in the later books. My larger purpose is to reflect on the continuing significance of Augustine's ascension narrative, especially his claim to unmediated knowledge of Wisdom in a *momentum intelligentiae*—a moment of nondiscursive knowledge (9.10.25). I want to consider how Augustine's account of divine and human transcendence might help us understand Christianity in our contemporary age, marked as it is by rapid and sweeping secularism in the Western world. And so this paper might be regarded as an informal exercise in the *ressourcement* tradition, retrieving elements from a founding authority of Catholicism.

1. Secularism and the "View from Nowhere"

We begin where we are, amidst a culture in which the default position has become increasingly some sort of secularism. Charles Taylor has, of course, done extraordinary work in defining that phenomenon, tracing its genealogy and disaggregating some of its strains.[1] One of the salient points of his work is his characterization of what he calls the "exclusive humanism" of our age, the now culturally imbedded notion that we live in a closed, materialist universe. The key to this new dispensation is "immanentization," the gradual cultural process by which the world as we understand it has come to be characterized as restricted to the material universe.

Belief in a transcendent God, once the common assumption of Western culture, has now receded, becoming a contested option in some places in the West, and in others, especially among the progressive elites, a largely dead option. In its place have come claims to finding meaning in a purely immanent account of human reality, one that centers on nature and human solidarity independent of any non-material source. As Taylor shows, this momentous and continuing shift to exclusive humanism was no accident but the product of a sustained effort: "The development of this purely immanent sense of universal

---

1. Charles Taylor, *A Secular Age* (Cambridge, MA: Harvard University Press, 2007).

solidarity is an important achievement, a milestone in human history."[2] The project of finding meaning in this material world has become "the charter of modern unbelief."[3]

There are two important aspects of this exclusively immanent outlook on reality that bear consideration in reference to Augustine and Catholic Christianity. The first is the closed perspective of anti-transcendental humanism. Central to contemporary secularism is the assertion that we live in a closed universe, one that is envisioned as sealed off from extrinsic, non-material influences. The modern self is seen as "buffered," personally autonomous and radically enclosed in its interiority, in contrast to the pre-modern "porous" self, which was vulnerable to external forces, whether divine or demonic.

As Taylor notes, this sealing-off of the individuated self had immense significance for cultural and social structures as well as far-reaching changes in Christian theology. The idea that a transcendent God could have access to the privacy of the inner self and exercise direct providential causality has become increasingly implausible and even deeply repugnant, causing the abandonment of theism by some and its modification by theologians within Christianity itself. That theological retreat from a personal God—who might be said to lead us into temptation—is still ongoing.

Beyond the buffered self is the even more critical issue of the nature of knowledge, a matter that is bound up in complex ways with this cultural shift towards secularism. Taylor argues that modern secularism rests upon an epistemology grounded in an impersonal outlook on reality, one that rigorously removes the human self from the nature of knowledge in the interest of an "objective" perspective. The natural sciences have come to seen as paradigmatic in this regard and their effectiveness attributed to this epistemic outlook. Knowledge must be objective and universal, free from the idiosyncratic and the personal. Indeed, it must be conducted as if by an impartial spectator, what Taylor calls the "view from nowhere." As he points out, "the protocols of modern 'scientific' and analytic thinking privilege the impersonal 'view from nowhere.'"[4] As a result, natural science has come to be the most prestigious form of knowledge, and with this development, materialism has become more deeply embedded in Western culture. And so the idea of transcendence, of openness to a higher level of reality, becomes just magical thinking.

Into the spiritual vacuum of this modern materialism have come many

2. Taylor, *A Secular Age*, 255.
3. Taylor, *A Secular Age*, 257.
4. Taylor, *A Secular Age*, 555.

efforts to supply non-transcendental substitutes for God. These include rhapsodic depictions of the physical universe, ecological pantheism, refined aestheticism, dialectical materialism, socialistic humanism, and so on. But the question remains whether these accounts do anything but provide an unsupportable patina of meaning over the ultimate nihilism of materialism. This point has been made in the starkest possible way by Alex Rosenberg, a philosopher and advocate for scientific naturalism:

> Naturalism is the label for the thesis that the tools we should use in answering philosophical problems are the methods and findings of the mature sciences—from physics across to biology and increasingly neuroscience. It enables us to rule out answers to philosophical questions that are incompatible with scientific findings. It enables us to rule out epistemological pluralism—that the house of knowledge has many mansions, as well as skepticism about the reach of science. It bids us doubt that there are facts about reality that science cannot grasp. It gives us confidence to assert that by now in the development of science, absence of evidence is *prima facie* good grounds for evidence of absence: this goes for God, and a great deal else.
>
> I think naturalism is right, but I also think science forces upon us a very disillusioned "take" on reality. It forces us to say 'No' in response to many questions to which most everyone hopes the answers are 'Yes.' These are the questions about purpose in nature, the meaning of life, the grounds of morality, the significance of consciousness, the character of thought, the freedom of the will, the limits of human self-understanding, and the trajectory of human history. The negative answers to these questions that science provides are ones that most naturalists have sought to avoid, or at least qualify, reinterpret, or recast to avoid science's harsh conclusions. I dissent from the consensus of these philosophers who have sought to reconcile science with common sense or the manifest image or the wisdom of our culture. My excuse is that I stand on the shoulders of giants: the many heroic naturalists who have tried vainly, I think, to find a more upbeat version of naturalism than this one.[5]

Rosenberg is brutally honest here in exposing what lies beneath the outward face of contemporary scientific naturalism, the linchpin of exclusive humanism. Materialism, relativism, skepticism—these are at the core of contemporary secularism, even if they are seldom brought clearly to the surface and their larger significance exposed. If we are to be honest about the

---

5. Alex Rosenberg, "The Disenchanted Naturalist's Guide to Reality," at nationalhumani tiescenter.org/on-the-human/2009/11/the-disenchanted-naturalists-guide-to-reality/. Cf. Lloyd Gerson, "Platonism versus Naturalism" in *Defining Platonism*, ed. John F. Finamore and Sarah Klitenic Wear (Steubenville, OH: Franciscan University Press, 2017), 291–311.

foundations of modern progressive secularism, we need to be cognizant of the full dimensions of what is at stake. We should also be aware of the extent to which this robust scientific naturalism rests upon what Taylor called the "view from nowhere," the putatively objective vantage point that leads, in the end, to nihilism.

I raise this matter not to offer a detailed critique of this outlook on reality but only to throw into relief an alternative: the Christian transcendentalism of Augustine. As readers of the *Confessions* are aware, Augustine was no stranger to materialism, relativism, and skepticism. At the end of book 5, he tells us that his materialism had left him unable to conceive of any other sort of reality. As such, he could find no adequate solution to the problem of evil and no ability to address the turmoil of his own inner life. At that point he admits he had fallen into skepticism, doubting almost everything and living in a fluctuating state of suspended judgment. We might now turn to consider what brought him out of this skeptical state, and what we might learn from Augustine's discovery.

2. Prolegomena to Ostia

In the narrative of the *Confessions,* the vision at Ostia concludes the story of Monica's life and offers an anticipation of her postmortem existence among the saints. In that respect it frames the final account of her death and her son's Christian attitude towards it. But that visionary episode is also the conclusion of the theological journey of Augustine, describing the union of his soul with the divine Wisdom. It offers the reader an eschatological account of transcendence, of the immediate presence of God to the soul. In that respect it is Augustine's strongest claim to absolute certainty about the existence of God who transcends materiality and finitude, a God to whom the soul can return out of the distension of time. Thus the texts that make up the Ostian narrative draw many strands of philosophical and theological thought together at once.

To understand Augustine's account of Christian transcendence at Ostia, it might be helpful to review some antecedent passages that prepare the reader for that culminating event. It is especially important to realize the full dimension of Augustine's account and its specifically Christian character.

In book 5, Augustine explains that his thinking throughout his life had been hampered by a total inability to conceive of nonmaterial reality, what he calls *spiritalis substantia*, spiritual substance (5.14.25). The antidote to that materialist thinking and the discovery of transcendence will be provided—paradoxically—by pagan Platonism. Augustine is candid in making this attribution and very careful in setting out the sequence by which it came about.

Indeed he regards his discovery of spiritual reality through his readings of the books of the Platonists as providential.

Augustine tells us that he had thought Catholics regarded God as existing in the form of the human body. That was the basis of his rejection of his childhood religion during his Manichaean period (6.3.4). So, from the time of his African adolescence as a catechumen through his early thirties, he had no conception of divine transcendence.

When he heard the preaching of Ambrose, Augustine discovered an allegorical method of reading scripture, distinct from his earlier literal approach. Yet, although this new method removed the "mystic veil" of scripture, Augustine still had no conception of transcendence, nor was he moved to drop his skepticism. It was his failure to grasp the notion of *spiritalis substantia* that was the problem (6.3.4). Nonetheless, he later insists that this painstaking development was providential. He explains this in a fascinating passage that may seem to many contemporary Christian readers to be counterintuitive:

> If I had first become well informed about your holy writings and you had grown sweet to me through my familiarity with them, and then I had afterward chanced upon those other volumes, they might perhaps have torn me loose from the strong root of piety, or else, if I had held firm in the salutary devotion I had absorbed, I might have supposed that it could be acquired equally well from those books, if everyone studied them and nothing else. (7.20.26)

If Augustine had read the Scriptures without the insight of transcendence, and had subsequently read the Platonist books, then those pagan works might have seemed more powerful and persuasive than sacred Scripture. Or he might have supposed Platonists held much the same theology as Christianity. But instead, a providential sequence brought him first to the recognition of transcendence through his reading of Platonism and then to the study of sacred Scripture, whose deeper meaning could be discerned in light of his recognition of *spiritalis substantia*. Reading the Bible alone would not, therefore, have opened the full meaning of the Scriptures to him. That was only possible when he had grasped the nature of transcendence through the reading of Platonic philosophy. Then he could turn to the reading of sacred Scripture, in particular Paul: "It was therefore with intense eagerness that I seized on the hallowed calligraphy of your Spirit, and most especially the writings of the apostle Paul" (7.21.27). Now these texts made sense based on the exegesis of Ambrose and the Platonic conception of transcendence. That had been the divine intent behind the providential sequencing of their discovery all along.

There are several important observations that follow from this account.

The first is that Augustine tightly conjoins his discovery of transcendence with the exegesis of scripture. The two are deeply interconnected in his thought and are not really separable. Augustine was not a member of a Platonic school, did not pursue philosophical dialectic with his associates, and did not write commentaries on Platonic texts.[6] Especially after his ordination, Augustine began to center his reflection and writing on scripture in the style of Ambrose, leaving behind the earlier Ciceronian style found in the Cassiciacum works. This is a point he himself makes in *Reconsiderations*, where he takes exception to his earlier philosophical style in contrast to his subsequent writings which were rooted in the language of the church.[7] Like Ambrose, reading the books of the church in light of the discovery of spiritual reality was now his path to wisdom, and it was the guidance of scripture that he regarded as dispositive for his soul. Throughout his life as a bishop and preacher, scriptural dialectic and exegesis were now the core of his intellectual and spiritual practice, an ecclesial path to wisdom.

Platonism was, therefore, a necessary part of Augustine's story, but he did not consider its philosophy sufficient to achieve the goal of transcendence that the school expounded. But with that being said, it should also be emphasized that the philosophical conception of transcendence was something that Augustine acquired from the Platonists. That is the point of his lengthy account of its providential discovery. Prior to that point, during his Catholic adolescence in North Africa, as a Manichee, and then as a catechumen in Milan, Augustine read the Bible literally and without that philosophical understanding of transcendence. So although Augustine's understanding of transcendence nested in his project of biblical exegesis, it cannot be literally discovered there.

The power of his reading Platonism can be quite evident in his contemporaneous writings that are still extent. Book 9 mentions his pre-baptismal retreat in the autumn of 386 and winter of 387 at Cassiciacum, where he wrote his earliest extant works. He relates his excitement at discovering Plotinus:

> After reading a few books of Plotinus, for whom I gather you are very keen, I compared them as best I could with the authority of those who handed down the divine mysteries, and I was so inflamed that I'd have broken away from all anchors, if the judgment of several men hadn't forced me back.[8]

Both his excitement at reading Plotinus and his concern to correlate his thought with scripture are evident here. He goes on to describe his excitement

6. J.J. O'Donnell, *Augustine: Confessions*, vol. 2 (Oxford: Oxford University Press, 1992), 416.

7. *retr.* 1. 3. 2.

8. *De beata vita* 1.4. Author's translation.

in another Cassiciacum treatise, *Against the Academics*, dedicated to his hometown patron and old friend Romanianus. At II.2.5 he addresses Romanianus, who had become a Manichee, about the books of the Platonists:

> And notice, when certain rich books exhaled over us, as Celsinus says, costly substances from Arabia, and poured a few tiny drops of the most precious perfume onto that little flame, incredibly, Romanianus, incredibly, and even more powerfully than you might believe about me—what more can I say?—unbelievable even to me, those books excited within me a conflagration. What now was honor to me? Or human pomp? Or lust for empty fame? And, finally, what consolation or bond in this mortal life then moved me? Truly I was returning completely to myself. As if on a journey, I confess, I looked back upon that religion which had been grafted into us as boys and entwined in our marrow. Indeed it was taking hold of me but I didn't realize it. And so, hesitatingly, I grabbed the works of the apostle Paul. For I must admit that surely those apostles could not have lived—as they really did live—if their writings and their reasons were opposed to such a good. I read all of it intently and carefully.[9]

The main point here is the interstitial relationship between Augustine's discovery of the Platonic notion of transcendence and his desire to reconsider the scripture of Catholic Christianity in light of his new recognition. So Plotinus is to Augustine what Aristotle was to Aquinas; important but not by any means the whole story.

All this evident excitement brings us to the grammar of transcendence as Augustine understood it in the wake of reading the *libri Platonicorum*. Two crucial advances made by Platonists, especially Plotinus, are especially salient: intelligible reality and ontological infinity. We need to consider each of these briefly in anticipation of Ostia. The first of these, intelligible reality, is what Augustine was referencing with his term *spiritalis substantia*. Platonists were committed to an ontology of degrees of reality such that the real world of being was understood as invisible, immaterial, nonspatial, and eternal. It was accessible only through the intellect, not the physical senses. It is in this sophisticated, philosophical sense that Augustine came to understand the notion of spiritual reality. This is the core of his account of divine transcendence and the basis of his spiritual exegesis of scripture. It bears mention that Platonists regarded the intelligible reality not as a higher and inert level of reality, but as the source for lower levels of reality. This fecund productivity brought with it a recognition that the transcendence of the intelligibles was, in a sense, balanced by their

---

9. *contra acad.* 2.2.5. Author's translation.

immanence within lower sorts of reality whose existence was conferred and sustained by the intelligibles.

Transcendence and immanence were thus interwoven into the tapestry of reality. Moreover, by late antiquity this Platonist account of transcendent reality had developed its own sort of monotheism centering on an ultimate transcendent source of all reality, the One or the Good. That divine One was, according to Plotinus, infinite. This positive account of infinity reversed the ancient association of infinity with irrationality, chaos, and numerical regression. Instead Plotinus and his school came to regard the infinity of the One as the chief token of its absolute transcendence, separating it entirely from all forms of finite existence. Yet the infinity of the One so removed it from spatiality that it could thereby be conceived as being present to finite reality in a radically new way. Its presence was ontological, conferring existence to finite beings. The mere fact of existence betokened the presence of the One, which was spatially nowhere but ontologically everywhere. There was, therefore, no escaping the presence of the One.

This philosophical conception of transcendence was radically new and conversionary for Augustine. It was not to be found literally in the Bible though it could be discerned through spiritual reading along the lines of Ambrose. The resulting understanding of God can be seen in the prologue to the *Confessions* where Augustine sketches some answers to the question, what is God? Here the Platonic conceptions of intelligible being and ontological omnipresence, are skillfully interwoven with biblical attributes, subtly transposed into a new metaphysical key. Here is Augustine's inventory:

> Most high, excellent, most powerful, omnipotent, supremely merciful and supremely just, most hidden yet intimately present, infinitely beautiful and infinitely strong, steadfast and elusive, unchanging yourself though you control the change in all things, never new, never old, renewing all things yet wearing down the proud though they know it not; ever active, ever at rest, gathering while knowing no need, supporting and filling and guarding, creating and nurturing and perfecting, seeking although you lack nothing. You love without frenzy, you are jealous yet secure, you regret without sadness, you grow angry yet remain tranquil, you alter your works but never your plan; you take back what you find although you never lost it; you are never in need yet you rejoice in your gains, never avaricious yet you demand profits. You allow us to pay you more than you demand, and so you become our debtor, yet which of us possess anything that does not already belong to you? You owe us nothing, yet you pay your debts; you write off our debts to you, yet you lose nothing thereby.
>
> After saying all that, what have we said, my God, life, my holy sweetness?

What does anyone who speaks of you really say? Yet woe betide those who fail to speak, while the chatterboxes go on saying nothing. (1.4.4)

This passage, full of paradoxes and conceptual enjambment, captures Augustine's Christian transcendentalism: an account of God rooted in the foreground of scripture but also built on the architecture of Platonic metaphysics. Many of the anthropomorphic and materialistic aspects of the biblical account of God that had once put him off when read literally are now understood as part of the fragile semantics of finite discourse about the infinite. Moreover there is, behind those paradoxical attributes, a recognition that discourse about God can never be adequately descriptive, that the project of appraising the infinite is inherently flawed.

This point will be essential for reading of the vision at Ostia. We should perhaps pause for a moment and reflect back to the initial section of this paper on exclusive humanism. There were two central conceptions that were foundational to that theoretical outlook: the buffered self and the objective-spectator account of knowledge.

As we begin to look more closely at Augustine's transcendentalism, we should be alert to how sharply different his approach is from naturalism. This is not, after all, surprising since he was drawn to Platonism precisely because it was the most powerful anti-materialist and anti-skeptical tradition in antiquity. It is evident throughout the *Confessions* that the Augustinian self is certainly not conceived as buffered, privatized, or atomistic. Indeed to describe it as porous would also hardly do it justice. The soul for Augustine is a saturated self, suffused with the presence of the divine. In fact, Augustine is quite aware that such thinking is itself too spatial to capture the omnipresence of the infinite God. As he notes, again at the very beginning of the *Confessions*:

No, my God, I would not exist, I would not be at all, were you not in me. Or should I say, rather, that I should not exist if I were not in you, from whom are all things, through whom are all things, in whom are all things? Yes, Lord, that is the truth, that is indeed the truth. To what place can I invite you, then, since I am in you? Or where could you come from, in order to come into me? To what place outside heaven and earth could I travel to, so that my God could come to me there, the God who said, *I fill heaven and earth?* (1.2.2)

Divine transcendence radically eclipses spatiality, shifted the conceptual ground of our representation of the self in reference to the infinite One. Thus the Augustinian self is always in the ontological presence of God, even if in its fallen state its attention is too morally limited to recognize this.

Moreover the soul is not a spectator of the infinite. The Augustinian soul nests in the infinite reality that is God and exists by participation in God. Its knowledge of God is advanced as it centers itself on God, sharing more deeply in the source of its finite and contingent existence. In this sense its knowledge of God is participatory and not observational, not directed at the theoretical appraisal from afar, not a form of *scientia*, not a view from nowhere. It is instead deeply personal and centered on the ontological enhancement of the soul and the recovery of its prelapsarian condition in the divine presence. Hence the paradoxicality of Augustine's representation of God just reviewed is designed to press the soul forward in its recovery of the presence of God, not to offer an accurate description of God.

It is for this reason that Augustine's recognition of divine transcendence in book 7 is depicted as an act of self-transcendence, as his soul does not just discover the idea of spatiotemporal transcendence but experiences it. The moments of recognition that secure the certainty of divine transcendence are also occasions of the soul's ontological deepening as it advances towards higher levels of reality discovered within the soul. These ascension narratives serve as pilot schemes for the vision of Ostia.

At 7.10.16, Augustine describes how he was given by God the power to enter his innermost self. There he discovers the intelligible light of divine being transcending his mind before his soul is pulled back into ordinary conscious-ness. At 7.17.23, the inner ascension is plotted out in greater detail. Once again his soul is drawn up to the divine, passing through the sense impressions of the body, then through discursive reasoning that is carried out in time and change. Finally the soul reached momentarily to the unchanging, to the uncreated, to "that which is," to being itself, only to be dragged down into time and change by the weight of its moral condition. This depiction suggests not only that there are levels accessible within the self but that the soul might exercise a "cursive" function, choosing which level on which to focus.

Crucially, it is divine aid that catalyzes this inner ascension. It should be clear, however, that the Augustinian account of knowledge and the self that we have uncovered thus far is an entirely different mode of reflection from modern secularism. To clarify that point in greater depth, we must turn now to the pre-eminent account of Christian transcendentalism, the vision at Ostia.

3. Vision at Ostia

Book 9 begins with Augustine's gradual cessation from teaching and his retire-ment, along with an entourage of family, friends, and student, to a country estate at Cassiciacum in the north of Italy that he borrowed from a wealthy friend (9.3.5-6). Having converted to Catholic Christianity, he remained there from the late summer of 386 until he returned to Milan to be baptized by Ambrose on April 24, 387. He tells us it was during this period of contemplation that he read the fourth Psalm. His comments upon it are especially revealing of his new spiritual reading of Scripture:[10]

> The next verse wrung a cry from the very depths of my heart: *In peace!* Oh, *In Being itself!* What did it say? *I will rest and fall asleep.* Yes, for who shall make war against us when that promise of scripture is fulfilled, *Death is swallowed up into victory?* In truth you are Being itself, unchangeable, and in you is found the rest that is mindful no more of its labors, for there is no one else beside you, nor need our rest concern itself with striving for a host of other things that are not what you are; rather it is you, *you, Lord, who through hope establish me in unity.* (9.4.11)

Out of the text of this psalm emerges the absolute being of God, immutable, self-same, and in a state of quiescence. Augustine employs the term *idipsum* here, translating the notions of being and the self-sameness (*auto kath' hauto*) of the Platonic forms, the same term he will use later in the Ostian narrative. This passage vividly exposes how the notion of divine transcendence has become a metaphysical template for Augustine's understanding of God and the cornerstone of his scriptural hermeneutic.

We turn now to the Ostian narrative. The account is constructed to foreshadow Monica's impending but unexpected death. The setting is a conversation between Monica, a woman schooled in the discipline of the church, and her son, a learned rhetorician and teacher in the liberal arts. The interlocutors are looking out into a garden in Ostia, the port city of Rome, where they are resting after a long journey amidst civil strife from Milan. They await passage to North Africa, where Augustine plans to set up his monastery on a farm in his hometown. Here is how Augustine describes the topic of their conversation (9.10.23): "We were alone, conferring very intimately. Forgetting what lay in the past, and stretching out to what was ahead, we inquired between ourselves in the light of truth, the Truth which is yourself, what the eternal life of the saints would be like."

Two depictions of this moment of union with divine Wisdom follow. The first articulates the levels of reality and the inner self that the two contemplatives traverse—apparently simultaneously. Although the ascension has a more abbreviated account of those levels than found at 7.17.23, the general pattern

---

10. Cf. *conf.* 9.10.24.

is the same. The primary difference between the accounts is the tranquility of these two souls, whose spiritual motion is gentle and measured, especially in their return to ordinary earthly consciousness. The abrupt falling back of the soul in that earlier pre-baptismal ascent, driven by the weight of its moral state, is now absent. This is an essential point. It underscores that the extraordinary knowledge Augustine describes here is a direct outcome of the spiritual state of these Christian souls. Yet the ascension is not ascribed to some inherent power latent within those souls but rather is due to the gravity of grace. The longing of these contemplatives for transcendence is answered by its being granted to them. This is clear from the opening of the first account of the vision:

> Our colloquy led us to the point where the pleasures of the body's senses, however intense and in however brilliant a material light enjoyed, seemed unworthy not merely of comparison but even of remembrance beside the joy of that life, and we lifted ourselves in longing yet more ardent toward *That Which Is*, and step by step traversed all bodily creatures and heaven itself, whence sun and moon and stars shed their light upon the earth. Higher still we mounted by inward thought and wondering discourse on your works, and we arrived at the summit of our own minds; and this too we transcended, to touch that land of never-failing plenty where you pasture Israel for ever with the food of truth. Life there is the Wisdom through whom all these things are made, and all others that have been or ever will be forever. Rather should we say that in her there is no "has been" or "will be," but only being, for she is eternal, but past and future do not belong to eternity. And as we talked and panted for it, we just touched the edge of it by the utmost leap of our hearts; then, sighing and unsatisfied, we left the firstfruits of our spirit captive there, and returned to the noise of articulate speech, where a word has a beginning and end. How different from your Word, our Lord, who abides in himself, and grows not old, but renews all things. (9.10.24)

The long autobiographical arc of the *Confessions* has led to this moment of transcendent union with divine Wisdom. But Monica and Augustine have come to it under different auspices. In one sense, Augustine might seem the more obvious candidate, having read Platonic philosophy and learned the theoretical discourse which he uses to describe this ascent. He has now been baptized, and all the "dread" of his previous life had dropped away (9.6.14). His baptism has washed away his sins, though not his moral limitations, which he will admit and catalogue in book 10.

In contrast, Monica exhibits an evident sanctity, having been formed in that schoolhouse of souls, the Church, even if she was not conventionally learned. Her courage as a martyr for her faith, mentioned earlier, commends her as well. Yet these qualifications, which exemplify different paths to Wisdom, are nonetheless insufficient to accomplish transcendence. Divine grace remains, in the Augustinian account, necessary.

With a view towards contemporary appraisal, we might reflect further on what might be called the "interiority" of this ascension. The central theme of the *Confessions,* introduced in the first paragraph is, of course, that the human heart is restless until it rests in God. That appears to be accomplished in the text before us, albeit only for a moment. The souls of Monica and her son have been led to being itself, to *idipsum,* to what is absolutely real and unchanging. Transcendence is the only rest worth having for the Augustinian soul. And it is achieved with cognitive surety as their souls are described as touching the divine Wisdom, an image that is not so much spatial as epistemic. The type of knowledge that each soul enjoys is immediate and unmediated, a participation in Wisdom that is certain and complete. It is not in any way like a sense experience that occurs in time. Nor is it an experience on the basis of which inferences can be drawn. Everything associated with empirical knowledge has been withdrawn. So this contemplative knowledge is a priori, free from sensory input and removed from empirical consciousness. And its inner logic is that of closure between knower and known. Anything to do with *scientia,* with knowledge understood as intentional and about something distinct from the knower, is no longer apposite. Participation in infinite Wisdom is thus true knowledge for Augustine.

That interior vector is made clear in Augustine's succinct description of the levels of the reality through which the contemplative souls ascend: first the pleasures of the bodily senses; then material level of space-time, including all creatures both terrestrial and heavenly; then the summit of the mind, the rational intellect. The final stage is the transcendental one, into eternity and the divine Wisdom. All these are understood, therefore, to be levels both of reality and of the interior self, so that the subjective ascent does not pass through the geography of the inner psyche alone, but through the nature of reality. This is a crucial point, for the Augustinian self, having been created in the image of divine Wisdom, can discover within itself the degrees of reality that emerged from God. Thus the inner ascension of the soul in contemplation is an act of recovery, of knowledge that exposes the depth of the divine Wisdom within the soul. This conjunction of theological epistemology and metaphysics is, therefore, essential to Augustine's insistence on the importance of interiority in the *Confessions.*

The passage ends as the souls return to the temporal sequence of language, but not before leaving the "firstfruits of the spirit" there in the eternity of Wisdom. This beautiful image shifts the passage to eschatology, to Romans 8:23 and the expectation of the Christ's coming. It reminds the Christian reader of the limits of transcendence, for the soul as a fallen creature has no inherent hold on eternity during its temporal existence. The unmediated knowledge of Wisdom enjoyed at Ostia was conferred and not within our human cognitive capacity alone. Monica's presence is thus a powerful token of divine grace, both the grace that brought her to this moment of transcendental knowledge of Wisdom and the grace that foreshadows her post-mortem return to her place in the divine Wisdom. But for her son, the vision at Ostia is premonitory, helping him to discern the nature of his continued exile from eternal Wisdom. Christian transcendence is, therefore, ambivalent: bringing the soul into momentary communion with God, but also sharply underscoring the fallen soul's distance from God.

The second account of the vision offers a distinctive perspective on the same mutual interior ascension. Here is the text:

> Then we said,
> "If the tumult of the flesh fell silent for someone,
> and silent too were the phantasms of earth, sea, air,
> silent the heavens,
> and the very soul silent to itself,
> that it might pass beyond itself by not thinking of its own being;
> if dreams and revelations known through its imagination were silent,
> if every tongue, and every sign, and whatever is subject to transience were
>   wholly still for him
> —for if anyone listens, all these things will tell him,
> 'We did not make ourselves;
> he made us who abides for ever'—
> and having said this they held their piece
> for they had pricked the listening ear to him who made them;
>   and then he alone were to speak,
> not through things that are made, but of himself,
> that we might hear his Word,
> not through fleshly tongue nor angel's voice,
> nor thundercloud,
> nor any riddling parable,
> hear him unmediated, whom we love in all these things,
> hear him without them,
> as now we stretch out and in a flash of thought

touch that eternal Wisdom who abides above all things;
if this could last,
and all other visions, so far inferior, be taken away,
and this sight alone ravish him who saw it,
and engulf him and hide him away, kept for inward joys,
so that this moment of knowledge—
this passing moment that left us aching for more—
should there be life eternal,
would not *Enter into the joy of your Lord*
be this, and this alone?
And when, when will this be?
When we all rise again, but not all are changed?" (9.10.25)

Here the dominant imagery is auditory rather than visionary. The passage emphasizes the initial ontological separation of the contemplative souls from Wisdom and the necessity for silence among created things in order to hear the divine voice. The din of the world that must grow silent includes the soul itself, whose outer voice and inner noise drown out the distant Word. The silence of the soul must include all discursive thought in time. But beyond this initial quietude, there is the deeper silence of the soul as it surpasses itself and no longer thinks of itself. This withdrawal of the incessant assertion of the self marks a reversal of the *superbia*, the pride and self-focus that lie at the core of original sin and pride. To hear the divine Wisdom, that self-assertive focus too must cease. In doing so, the instruments the soul uses in time both to assert itself and to know about the world must cease. The voice of divine Wisdom can only be heard by the soul in a state of self-transcendence. But then, in that absolute silence, the soul can achieve humility and admit that it did not make itself but is instead a temporal product of eternal Wisdom.

It is then that Wisdom can speak without mediation. That voice supersedes all temporal forms of communication, even the symbolic discourse of scripture. Then the soul can extend itself and make contact with the eternal Wisdom that transcends all finite creation. That moment out of time is an intensification of divine omnipresence, a deepening of the soul into the infinite being in which already exists. Put differently, it is a radical conjunction of transcendence and immanence, as the soul discerns more fully its own abiding presence in Wisdom, in being itself. But the temporal condition of its created nature immediately asserts itself and this moment of unmediated, participatory knowledge, this "*momentum intelligentiae*," ceases, leaving only an eschatological hope (9.10.25). That theme is again emphasized, as the passage concludes with a reference to 1 Corinthians 15:51, a Pauline resurrection text, alerting the Christian reader to the larger frame into which this moment of contemplation must be set.[11]

A more complete analysis of the contemplation at Ostia would require a detailed discussion of those fascinating later books of the *Confessions* where Augustine reflects repeatedly on contemplation, with references back to the Ostian narrative. I have discussed these several times elsewhere, particularly the discussion of time and the soul in book 11, and the heaven of heaven in book 12.[12]

But there is one final aspect to contemplation in the *Confessions,* discussed in book 13, that must be mentioned in seeking to bring Augustine's concerns to our contemporary world. That is Augustine's understanding of the Christian practice of contemplation in the wake of Ostia. It might well be thought that the vision at Ostia was as a singular, one-off event, from which little can be drawn besides its significance for the participants. But that would be a mistake. *Confessions* 13 builds on the centrality of scriptural contemplation. For Augustine, the practice of transcendence is grounded in the church and its scriptures, not in philosophical dialectic. What happened at Ostia, although extraordinary in many ways, is not different from the routinized practice of the divine presence available in the life of the church. If Platonic philosophy was a way of life for some pagans who sought transcendence through its practice, so was Christianity for Augustine the true path to transcendence, to be pursued through the practices of the church. *Confessions* 13.18.22 states this quite clearly:

> Let us break our bread for the hungry and bring the homeless poor under our roof, let us clothe the naked and not spurn our own kin. When these fruits are burgeoning on the earth, take heed and see that it is good. Then may the dawn break for us, so that rising from this lowly crop of active works to the delight of contemplation, we may lay hold on the Word of Life above, and appear like luminaries for the world, firmly set in the vault that is your scripture. There you school us to mark the distinction between realities of the mind and sensible things, as between day and night, or between souls devoted to the life of the mind and others preoccupied with sensible matters.

This ecclesial dimension helps to clarify the extent to which that contemplative moment at Ostia was, in fact, a confirmation of the practice of transcendence

---

11. The Ostian narrative features a series of such references, e.g. 1 Corinthians 2:7, Philippians 3:13, and Romans 8:23.

12. J.P. Kenney, *The Mysticism of Saint Augustine: Rereading the Confessions* (New York and London: Routledge, 2005), chap. 8; and *Contemplation and Classical Christianity: A Study in Augustine* (Oxford: Oxford University Press, 2013), chap. 5.

available to all Christians within the life of the church. That path to transcendence is not an individual quest, but a communal one, a disciplined set of practices instituted to restore the soul to full communion with its transcendent source.

4. Concluding Observations

It is time now to pull the strands of this essay together by returning to where we started, with exclusive secularism and naturalism. A major theme of Taylor's work is that secularism has seeped deeply into the cultural aquifer of the West and is now commonly accepted even though it lacks philosophical warrant. It has come to be regarded as the most plausible account of reality largely because of the technological success of science. To be deemed an intelligent and sophisticated person in elite circles often requires giving surface credence to its main tenets.

And yet, at the same time, there is substantial data indicating that although religious identification has fallen across the West, belief in some sort of spiritual reality has persisted. There seems to be an inchoate theism beneath the cultural surface, along with many alternative forms of spirituality. This spiritual recidivism might be regarded as emerging from the misease that springs from setting aside positive answers to all those issues that Rosenberg iterated: the meaning of life, purpose in nature, the grounds of morality, the foundations of values, etc. There seems to be a muted cultural recognition of the limitations of naturalism. Surprising events, such as the public response to the 2019 Holy Week fire at Notre Dame in Paris—much of it overtly religious—indicate that the sovereignty of secularism is not complete.

It is in this cultural environment that the Christian transcendentalism of Augustine seems especially salient. It is a compelling expression of ancient contemplative Christianity, of Nicene Catholicism. And it stands in sharp contrast to naturalism. It denies the disembodied epistemology at the core of naturalism, the view from nowhere, and places the moral condition of the human observer at the center of the pursuit of knowledge. Indeed, from the Augustinian standpoint, naturalism is a contrived theory with unacknowledged aesthetic and ethical dimensions. As Augustine recognized in reference to ancient materialism, such theories are cognitive choices and bear the mark of their adherents. The view from nowhere is not itself a scientific fact but a contrivance, an evacuation of the self that disguises the judgment behind the theory. For Augustine all views are from somewhere and the moral state of the observer conditions what is known.

In the *Confessions,* Augustine worried about the complex connection between his materialism and his dissolute moral state, having become, he says, "a problem to myself" (4.4.9; 10.33.50). The transcendentalism of Augustine invites us to remove the buffering surrounding the atomized modern self and search out the interior depths of the soul, directing the soul through meditation on scripture and disciplining it through the ethical precepts found there. In that sense, the interior turn of the soul is a communal one, nesting in the book and the ethical practices of the Church. By breaking out of the buffered model of the self, the soul can come to recognize the ontological omnipresence of God and deepen its participation in the divine reality. This Christian contemplative path, the *via antiqua* of Augustine, is there still, a still live option, a vision of a deeper reality, behind our contemporary view from nowhere.

Memory, Individualism, and the Collected Self

Hilary Finley

Book 10 of St. Augustine's *Confessions* continues the author's examination of the process by which humans come to know God. In this book, titled "Memory," Augustine focuses on memory as a vehicle for coming to know God. He segues from realizing his own existence in God (books 1 through 9) to understanding that all things exist in God (books 11 through 13). Books 1 through 9 deal with Augustine's past, which his own memory brings to his consciousness in order that he may "confess," so that in book 10 he considers his present. Finally, book 11 and following consider all of time and eternity.

For Augustine, memory is a distant pointer toward, or image of, eternity and God's omnipresence, since it brings together the past and the present simultaneously. Augustine carefully lays out the processes of the inner self's reflection upon images within the mind, which becomes an indication of a universal truth: humans universally recognize accuracy in images of recollection (for example, correctly recalling a person's name). Augustine uses this reality to establish a universal search for truth, and thereby a common human nature. This begins his search for God, the Source of all Truth, which Augustine considers possibly to exist in the human mind, as well.

Augustine's search ascends from the physical world to the spiritual, and then into a mystical union with a personal God. He determines that God could not possibly be contained merely in the mind alone, but that access to friendship with God is possible for every human being through interior reflection.

This discussion of book 10 will begin by presenting the basic tenets of Augustine's account of human recollection and how it may lead an individual soul to God, with a view to the second part of this chapter. The second part will reflect on the common images within contemporary culture and how these affect the communal memory. The virtual community created by the internet seems to be a mimetic spirituality, as several aspects of virtual reality mimic Augustine's description about how the mind comes to know God.

First, a brief account of book 10. Augustine begins by setting out his purpose: "You love the truth because anyone who 'does truth' comes to the light. Truth it is that I want to do, in my heart by confession in your presence, and with my pen, before many witnesses" (10.1.1). The author locates man's ability to recognize truth in the mind, so he begins his search for God there.

Augustine commences his philosophic inquiry into the mind with an account of memory. He starts with the function of the physical brain essentially as a repository for images. He describes the five senses—touch, taste, smell, hearing, and sight—to describe how each physical sense provides substantial information to his brain, stored there as images. His experiences in temporal existence become new realities, or impressions, stored as memories: "It was not these things themselves that entered me, but only the images of them" (10.8.15).

Augustine also includes abstract "ideas" and "emotions" as other contributors to his memories. He describes a "liberal education," or the collection of ideas from the classical authors, as well as the arts, such as rhetoric, for example, as other sources of impressions in his memory. The abstract "rules" of various arts are inherently different from the sensations that impress upon his senses; nonetheless, these are all retained somewhat similarly as memories within the storehouse of his mind.

Finally, he includes "emotions" as a contributing component to his memories. He lists specifically desire, joy, fear, and sadness as the four fundamental emotions (10.14.22). Augustine observes that humans may recollect emotions without experiencing them all over again (10.14.22): "Who indeed would discuss these passions if every time we mentioned sadness or fear we were forced to mourn or feel frightened?" This contrasts with book 4, in which Augustine talks about how he would go to the theater precisely in order to be carried away by the emotions presented vicariously through the actions of the actors. This later description in book 10 points to something more divine in humans, since we can know the emotions without necessarily being affected by them.

Augustine wonders how "ideas" and "emotions" are etched on the physical matter of his brain despite entering his body differently from the way information is gathered by his senses. Abstract principles about realities, and specifically numbers, for example, do not leave the same physical markings in his memory, and he wonders where is the space for these memories of abstract ideas. He muses, "The sounds are one thing and the truths themselves something else" (10.12.19), and again: "When we hear [a] word, what we want is the reality behind the name, for the sound in itself holds no attraction for us" (10.20.29).

Augustine notes that all of the recollected images are located somehow in a different arena of mental space than what is provided for the original impressions, since recollection and reflection are entirely different functions than merely receiving impressions. Here, Augustine describes the "mind" as the location of dual functions: one is what he calls the "huge repository" and "enormous recess" of images, the other is the capacity for reflection on these images.[1] Irrational animals also have a brain and an ability to remember, as he says: "Animals and birds also have memories; they would not otherwise return to their accustomed lairs and nests, rather than randomly to others, and indeed they would never be able to grow accustomed to anything without memory" (10.17.26). But Augustine pushes further to describe how humans alone become aware of God.

Since the brain is a treasure-house for ideas and emotions, Augustine wonders where these abstract notions are retained, as ideas and emotions are recalled just as are the images from sense-impressions.

Augustine also wonders what power or capacity enables him to recognize ideas within his mind. He meticulously describes the process of reflecting upon received images. He wonders how he may recognize and think about memories without either currently re-engaging in the substance of the memories, or without their bumping into each other, so to speak, in his mind.

He gives examples from each sense to prove definitively that each does not interfere with the others: his eyes receive colors, though he sees them in his memory while sitting "in the dark." Similarly, he sings familiar tunes though his tongue is silent; he distinguishes the scents of lilies from violets while not smelling; honey from grape juice, without tasting; smooth from rough, without feeling; and none of the memories interferes with the others: colors do not interrupt his song, for example, even though they exist simultaneously in his memory with the music (10.8.14).[2]

---

1. Keeping with Augustine's long-standing tendency, I too shall use mind (*mens*) and memory (*memoria*) interchangeably..

2. Aristotle and his tradition, including Aquinas, speak of the four "interior senses": the *unifying sense*, which is that by which we're aware of sensing through, for example, eyes or

Augustine describes the unique ability in humans to decipher and recognize accurate recollections from inaccurate ones. He observes,

> When the memory itself loses some item, as for instance when we forget something and try to remember, where are we to search in the end but in the memory itself? And if some other thing is offered us there, we brush it aside, until the thing we are looking for turns up. When it does, we say, "That's it!" (10.19.28)

Remembering a person's name is one example; this is not Michael, this is Thomas, yes, Thomas. Alighting on an accurate memory is an abstract ability; it sorts and recognizes incorrect answers from correct ones, or false ones from the true. For Augustine, this indicates the reality of truth. The small but accurate recollection reveals, for Augustine, a larger picture, namely that he is meant to seek Truth.

Moreover, discovering truth creates a sense of happiness internally. In the example of recalling someone's correct name, the agitating search is over, and the one remembering rests peacefully knowing he has found the correct match. This interior happiness, or peace, which results with respect to a small truth (a correct answer) indicates that a larger happiness may exist when the Source of Truth is found; deep happiness and peace result.

Augustine's writings here articulate a universal human nature. Since humans universally seek the accuracy of a recollection in the way he describes, and readers relate to and understand his descriptions, then a sense of accuracy, or truth, seems to exist in every human mind. Moreover, everyone universally has access to the interior distinction between truth and falsehood. Since truth universally brings a type of happiness, such as in the recognition of a correct name, Augustine suggests a similarly universal human desire for happiness exists: "Absolutely all of us want to be happy" (10.21.30).

In the case of recalling someone's name, one must know the name first in order to recall it accurately later. For example, I must know Thomas in order to recall correctly his name in my memory when I am not in his presence. With

---

ears—it also thus distinguishes brown from sweet from loud; *imagination*, which stores sense images and is able to associate them in true and false ways; *memory*, which recognizes some sensed reality as having been encountered previously; and *instinct*, which tells us whether some sensed reality is painful or pleasant (Aristotle. *De Anima*. books 2 and 3; Thomas Aquinas, *Summa theologiae* I-II, q. 78, a. 4). None of these is yet intellect/mind, and thus higher animals possess all of these. Aristotle would speak of "imagination" and "memory" as distinct functions of sense (retention and remembrance), while only "intellect" could reflect upon images and memories, properly speaking. Augustine tends to speak of memory, mind, and will as three rational faculties, though memory seems to bridge sense and reason/mind.

more profound happiness, due to the vaster knowledge of God, Augustine wonders, "Unless we had some sure knowledge of it, our wills would not be so firmly set on gaining it. But how can this be?" (10.21.30). In other words, Augustine muses that humans had to know, or somehow to have experienced, happiness in God before they could search for it in time on earth, or even to know to search for it while on earth.

Convinced of the existence of God, Augustine offers a notion of beatitude, as he prays: "This is the happy life, and this alone: to rejoice in you, about you and because of you" (10.22.32). If happiness ultimately exists in rejoicing in God, then, he wonders, how do humans have prior knowledge of God in order to know to look for Him, and to recognize Him when they find Him? This is a great question. Augustine surmises that the knowledge of happiness may have existed somehow primordially in every human through Adam and Eve, occurring possibly when the first parents were in friendship with God, in a way similar to humanity's inheritance of original sin. He hypothesizes that humanity had an experience of friendship with God but lost it, and that human life is entirely the process of recollection to find again the friendship with God and be able to say, essentially, "That's it!"

Augustine does not explain how this hypothesis could be possible, or what it really means. It seems that his account of the universal human ability to recollect and make judgments of accuracy is the basis for inferring the reality of God, a Source of truth recognizable in a similar way in every human. Reflection and judgment are possible in humans only if humans subsist in some way in a metaphysical space, beyond the bounds merely of animal recollection. Augustine explains:

> As I remembered you [God], I left behind those parts of [my memory] which animals also possess, because I did not find you there amid the images of material things. I came to those regions of memory to which I had committed my emotional states, but I did not find you there either. Then I arrived at that place in my memory where my mind itself is enthroned, for indeed the mind must reside there, since it can remember itself; yet not even there were you to be found. (10.25.36)

Eventually, Augustine concludes, "You are not the mind itself: you are the Lord and God of the mind, and though all these things are subject to change you abide unchangeably above them all. And yet you have deigned to dwell in my memory from the first day that I learned to know you" (10.25.36).

Augustine uses a beautiful prayer to transition from his philosophic inquiry of the matter and purpose of memory as a way to come to know God, to a discussion of how humans unite with a living God, whom Augustine is convinced is the Source of happiness. The initiation into truth, his awareness that truth is so evidently a part of the human experience, begins Augustine's deeper conversion. Truth in recollection advances to truth of right living, so that actions are understood as good or evil, having truth in ethical appropriateness. The poem becomes a crux in the *Confessions*, taking the reader from Augustine's vain search for happiness in the sensible world (a recapitulation of books 1 through 9) to the fountain within. He expresses himself in this beautiful insight,

> Late have I loved you, Beauty so ancient and so new,
> late have I loved you!
> Lo, you were within,
> but I outside, seeking there for you,
> and upon the shapely things you have made I rushed headlong,
> I, misshapen.
> You were with me, but I was not with you.
> They held me back far from you,
> those things which would have no being
> were they not in you.
> You called, shouted, broke through my deafness;
> you flared, blazed, banished my blindness;
> you lavished your fragrance, I gasped, and now I pant for you;
> I tasted you, and I hunger and thirst;
> you touched me, and I burned for your peace. (10.27.38)

God becomes a concrete reality, reaching Augustine by deliberate design. Appealing to all of Augustine's senses, God uses the physical aspects of reality to point Augustine toward the ultimate Good.

The verbs that express God's motions here are significant. The first verb describing God is in line three, a conjugation of the state-of-being verb "to be," namely "you were" (see also line seven). This echoes the eternal presence of God described in Genesis that he existed before creation and is its prerequisite, "In the beginning, God created . . . and the Spirit of God was moving over the face of the waters" (Gen 1:1),[3] as well as God's revelation to Moses in the burning bush that He is existence, "I Am" (Exod 3:14), echoed again in John's Gospel that creation finds its origin in rational existence: "In the beginning was the Word, and the Word was with God, and the Word was God" (John 1:1).

---

3. *The Holy Bible*, Revised Standard Version, 2nd Catholic ed. (San Francisco: Ignatius Press, 2001).

In his poem, Augustine first establishes God as the Cause of all of existence, and simultaneously permeating existence, and then Augustine wonders how he could have been so blind to God who was similarly intimately and thoroughly within Augustine himself. Augustine describes God's numerous advances, in order that Augustine would recognize him; God "called, shouted, broke . . . flared, blazed, banished . . . lavished . . . [and] touched."

The order of verbs within the poem is significant, describing God's intentional movements toward Augustine. At first, God displays his power and strength, as He "called, shouted, broke through" (line eleven). Once he has Augustine's attention, God displays who He is with impressive agility and power: He "flared, blazed" (line twelve). Then He takes a more loving paternal or teaching role, as He "banished his blindness" (line twelve). Finally, once Augustine recognizes God, God becomes attractive, lavishing fragrance, and generous, as well as subtle (line thirteen). In keeping with the catalogue of sense-impressions, the verbs indicate God's appeal to all five of Augustine's senses: he "broke through deafness," "banished blindness," "lavished . . . fragrance," let Augustine taste him, and finally "touched" Augustine, who burned for His peace.

As Augustine is transformed, the tense of the verbs that describe his own actions moves from the past to the present: "loved . . . rushed . . . was not . . . gasped . . . tasted" become "pant . . . hunger . . . thirst," the latter verbs of hunger and thirst having obvious references to the Eucharist, the perfect mystical union between the physical and the spiritual within humans. The present tense verbs mirror Augustine's new desire to exist actively present in the presence of God.

The final verb returns to the past tense: "burned" (line fifteen), but the object here is active inner peace. Since flames are intensely active, this signifies the intensity of Augustine's desire to unite himself to God. Ironically, the activity he seeks is interior peace, which we think of as calm. Yet, this active peace recalls the tongues of fire at Pentecost, an image of the Holy Spirit of serene peace and burning, active love. This also provides a contrasting image to the fire that Augustine spoke of in book 2 as representative of Hell, when he was in love with sin and desired the flames of Hell. In book 5, Augustine called God a "devouring fire," asking Him to consume his vain ambitions and prepare his heart for eternal life (5.3.4). Momentarily, in book 10, Augustine will repeat this very image of the refining fire, the way by which the human heart is transformed in God: "O Love, ever burning, never extinguished, O Charity, my God, set me on fire" that "you will bring your merciful dealings in me to perfection, until I attain that utter peace which all that is within me and all my outward being will enjoy with you" (10.29.40; 10.30.42).

In this purgative process and with zealous desire, Augustine moves from false pursuits to the pursuit of God, from fragmentation to the collected self. Fragmentation indicates a dangerous existence whereby the internal self seeks various idols apart from God. The fragmented person is scattered and anxious, neither collected with a unified integrity, apart from the biological space in which he or she inheres—along with his or her memories—nor recollected interiorly. Such a person is generally uncomfortable or disdains the humble acceptance of existing as a dependent creature and the subservience implied therein.

For Augustine, God is the unitive focus or cohesion of the collected interior self. All of Augustine's memories are also present in the mind of God, but only Augustine himself in recollection can place himself intentionally in that awareness and offer gratitude, eventually inviting God to become more and more present in order that Augustine may magnify God. This becomes a conversation, a personal dialectic, between Augustine and God. Augustine reveals this friendship for the sake of the reader when he includes his prayers to God, and this is partly why he weaves poetry and prayer into his philosophical observations; he is in conversation with God while talking with the rest of us. As a bishop, he is simultaneously offering an example of what personal prayer can look like, as well as offering words that his readers may pray with him.

As Augustine pivots toward a discussion of virtue as the locus of interior peace, he recalls how each sense contributes to his development in either vice or virtue. When speaking of sight, Augustine compares physical light, necessary to illumine material objects, with spiritual light, necessary to determine accurate moral judgments. Augustine explains that "true insight" is the ability to judge rightly by "the vision that guided . . . within" (10.34.52). He unites several biblical examples and explains, "All these enjoyed the same Light, the Light that is one in itself and unites all who see and love it" (10.34.52). He concludes that God is "that abiding Light" and "nowhere amid all these things which I survey under your guidance do I find a safe haven for my soul except in you; only there are the scattered elements of my being collected, so that no part of me may escape from you" (10.40.65).

Although some knowledge of God existed somehow in Adam and Eve, their knowledge of God is not the necessary cause of every person's search for happiness. In other words, an awareness of God exists in every human heart not necessarily because the first humans had an intimate friendship with God and somehow passed on that prior knowledge to all of their offspring via a spiritual inheritance. All of reality exists in God, so happiness is coming to know God through our very selves. Conscience is the mysterious union by which a person judges the accuracy of his or her actions in terms of what will lead him or her to God via inner happiness and peace. Like Augustine, all humans may search the world and their interior selves to become aware of God's presence. Once God's reality is inferred from nature and experience, every human has the ability to say with Augustine, "From that time when I learned about you I have never forgotten you, because wherever I have found truth I have found my God, who is absolute Truth, and once I had learned that I did not forget it" (10.24.35).

One brief example illustrates humanity's subsistence in God. Augustine asks,

> If I am anxious that my neighbor shall profit by praising me, why am I less concerned when some other person is unjustly criticized than when I am myself? Why does an affront offered to myself bite more deeply than one flung at another person in my hearing, given that the injustice of it is the same in either case? (10.27.62)

Augustine replies that he is more offended by an affront to himself because he is deceived about his own value, since pride makes him consider his own injustice more acutely than the injustice to his neighbor. The gloss suggests this is a reference to Galatians 6:3, in which St. Paul says, "For if any man think himself to be something, whereas he is nothing, he deceives himself." It seems Augustine desires in humility to esteem all injustice equally. This follows Paul's exhortation to bear one another's burdens.

In human contemporaneity, we cannot live in full awareness of the presence of others' insults, with full understanding of what goes into every insult, and bear it in perfect justice and equanimity. It is too much for one temporal mind, even with all of its awesome abilities of comprehension and awareness, to understand the complexity of even one insult in its fullness. The context of Augustine's reflection invites the difficulty of what it would actually mean to take on one another's every burden, apparently impossible for one finite mind; only an infinite mind is even capable of this, necessarily, as Augustine explains of the mediator Christ as Redeemer.

God's immutable omnipresence comes to the fore in Augustine's discussion. Regarding his memories, Augustine says he may "summon them equally well, if I wish, and find them present at once" (10.8.14). In God's omniscience, every moment is eternally present; even the attempts at recollection within each individual are contemporaneously present in God's awareness. The vast processes of thought within each human mind exist in the subsistence of all of reality in (the mind of) God, who retains all of created time in His perpetually present memory, so that God knows every moment of every thing without being confused and may without confusion or interruption reflect on the myriad potential aspects relevant to every moment or action.

Another way to look at this is to consider the realm of human consciousness in one person and the requirements of that inner self with regard to what Augustine calls "the abyss of human conscience" (10.2.2). As our consciousness collides with others, we have a further responsibility to others for what we put in their treasure-house of memories. We find a parallel in Fyodor Dostoevsky's *The Brothers Karamazov*, as Father Zosima explains:

> Every day and every hour, every minute, walk round yourself and watch yourself, and see that your image is a seemly one. You pass by a little child, you pass by, spiteful, with ugly words, with wrathful heart; you may not have noticed the child, but he has seen you, and your image, unseemly and ignoble, may remain in his defenseless heart. You don't know it, but you may have sown an evil seed in him and it may grow, and all because you were not careful before the child, because you did not foster in yourself a careful, actively benevolent love.[4]

The responsibilities that confront one's consciousness are so vast, how are humans capable of understanding all of this?

Augustine wonders at the ability of his mental powers: "This faculty of memory is a great one, O my God, exceedingly great, a vast, infinite recess. Who can plumb its depth?" (10.8.15). Offering a type of Virgilian image, he compares the vast spaces of the mind with "lofty mountains, huge breakers at sea, crashing waterfalls, vast stretches of ocean, and the dance of the stars" (10.8.15). For Augustine, the vastness of the natural world finds its parallel in the interior, mental and spiritual life of the human mind, which elicits his wonder: "This is a faculty of my mind, belonging to my nature, yet I cannot myself comprehend all that I am" (10.15.8).

What does one person do with the images, sense-impressions, ideas, and emotions which confront and depart from his or her inner self? The task is enormous. For Augustine, all of the material and immaterial avenues to the mind of each human existence serve primarily and ultimately to unite the individual soul inhering in dust, with the omnipotent Source of that conglomeration of love.

The self is an amazing miracle, capable of immense activity and thought, and every self is this potentiality. Yet each eternal being does not exist alone;

4. Fyodor Dostoevsky, *The Brothers Karamazov*, trans. Constance Garnett (New York: W.W. Norton & Co., 1976), 298.

all humans live in community. Augustine honors God's inhering presence not only in his own mind, but also within the minds of others, especially among all who strive for virtue. Those who live intentionally with God in friendship is the collection of persons called the Body of Christ, a body united in holy friendship, the fraternal love of those whom Augustine describes as having a "brotherly mind" (10.4.5).

Christians are not the only ones who live in community, although the Body of Christ is the holiest community. All people exist in community. The family is a community, for example, and with respect to society, one boundary of a community is geography. The people, places, and work of various communities are, as Christopher Dawson suggested in 1950 in *Religion and the Rise of Western Culture*, joined by natural boundaries but also separated from others, or fragmented. Dawson suggests that the idea of Christianity is a bonding agent which understands the universal human nature of the individuals who compose mankind, engaging everything in an understandable and ultimately unified cosmos. For example, Christianity offers an organic explanation for the dignity of every individual, regardless of country of origin, economic status, color, intelligence, or whatever category society determines for grouping communities.

Out of natural geographic communities come civilizations, a community of people sharing certain ideas. A good civilization provides good, true, and beautiful, accessible images for its members. In this way, as many individuals as possible have access to real things and ideas that create within each person a number of similar internal memories. These may provide interior access to the knowledge of God and eventually lead to friendship with Him; at the very least, they offer God something to work with in the interior memory of a human. These substantial social realities include speeches, statues, plays, public art, and so on.

Contemporary society needs substantive objects and images in public places to form the treasure-house of our common memories. Public images create sense-impressions on everyone within the community, so the images which a society honors publicly in art, sculpture, movies, songs, and speech become the common memories within people. Which images allow for human reflection and awareness of God's presence? Which, when meditated upon, can turn the recollected interior mind to God? Society's responsibility should be to provide images through which more and more individuals may live in God and magnify his presence.

Yet, contemporary society seems easily distracted from its location in God. One difficulty is the ubiquitous presence of personal devices which create a lack of common images, as individuals search remote images disconnected from what others are seeing.

As mentioned, the global community is in one way necessarily fractured due simply to geography. But this is merely a physical boundary. In the Christian cosmos, all of humanity is unified in Christ, both as the organizing principle of the natural world and, spiritually, in a mystical union through the heart of every human.

Within contemporary society is an apparently growing rejection of Christianity. The result is a fractured global community without a conscious understanding of a unifying agent, or at least without the acknowledgment of a unifying Agent who, as a Person, is the Wellspring of love, mercy, and generosity. Moreover, contemporary society is largely forgetting the antidote to personal fragmentation. People remain in sin, unable to overcome the gluttony, lust, and other desires which Augustine suggests divide human beings interiorly and separate them from God. In this social climate, how might an individual and a society reclaim friendship with God?

The reality of human corruptibility is not a new or profound observation, but two unique aspects of contemporary society reflect this problem in a new way. First, the internet and other technological advances mimic rational human thought and unify the world but without God; and second, contemporary science allows biological changes and fragmentation at the most intimate levels of the human person, thus challenging the very notion of the self.

The first aspect of contemporary society that challenges human friendship with God includes certain aspects of the internet. The internet unifies disparate geographical regions, with the result that the world seems smaller, or unified, or collected somehow. Certainly, vast geographical distances which would previously have taken months or weeks to circumnavigate are accessible now at the click of a button. This is not necessarily a bad thing, but like many things, it can be good or bad, depending on how it is used; it has dangerous implications, for example, regarding power.

FaceTime is an interesting and unifying phenomenon, since people living in previously inaccessible regions are able to livestream visual communication immediately. Another example is the Google Translate app, which allows users to hold a personal device, such as a phone, over a word in another language and the word is automatically translated. This amazing unity in communication apparently eliminates the language barrier of a global society. The connectedness of humans via the internet mirrors a collected self at the communal level; it mimics, for example, the Body of Christ, as a potential universal communal body. Previously, omnipresence was attributed only to God, but with cameras and the internet, another different sort of reality ascribes to itself a similar omnipresence, depicted in such films as *The Circle*, starring Tom Hanks and Emma Watson.

In addition, the internet creates a space which mimics the spiritual center in humans, as the internet exists in a virtual plane. Like the human brain, a computer motherboard has circuits and a system of memory. The 1s and 0s lack the original rational capacity to create or independently interpret, but they may be programmed to do so. Combining humans and robots is no longer relegated to science fiction; billionaire Elon Musk has launched a venture to merge human brains with artificial intelligence.[5]

At the personal level, Facebook now creates memories. Without permission or invitation, phones tell users that they have "a memory" and present an image or picture to the user. Users may share these "memories" or keep them private; ignoring the forced memory entirely is difficult but still possible, although one does have to swipe it away quickly to ignore it, which means not entirely ignoring it. The interface imitation of the human mind is uncanny. What if one does not like or want the image? How does the forced memory affect a user's spiritual development, since it is presenting a personal image to one's consciousness without proper placement within one's own self's continuity and reflection therein? Of course, anything may trigger an unwanted memory, or be an unwanted original image, but the language of the social media interface is purposefully forced and personal.[6] The "memory" does not appear in an insulting or threatening manner—and thus all the more likely is a user to consider it and let it become constitutive of one's memory, and one's self.

One predominantly imperceptible yet staggering problem with this elusive virtual personality, namely the social-media interface, is that the workers who orchestrate these memories in, say, Silicon Valley, or the less-personal algorithm, are not the omniscient, benevolent, all-good Creator-God. Augustine praises God as the Source of memory, biology, moral judgment, virtue, joy, and freedom:

> O my God, for me you are loveliness itself; yet for all these things too I sing a hymn and offer a sacrifice of praise to you who sanctify me, because the beautiful designs that are born in our minds and find expression through

---

5. Reuters, "Elon Musk on Mission to Link Human Brains with Computers in Four Years: Report," at CNBC (April 21, 2017), at www.cnbc.com/2017/04/21/elon-musk-on-mission-to-link-human-brains-with-computers-in-four-years-report.html.

6. Jeff Bulas, "7 Ways Facebook Keeps You Addicted," at www.jeffbullas.com/facebook-creates-addiction/.

clever hands derive from that Beauty which transcends all minds, the Beauty to which my own mind aspires day and night. Those who create beauty in material things, and those who seek it, draw from that source their power to appreciate beauty, but not the norm for its use. The norm is there, and could they but see it they would need to search no further. (10.34.53)

To invoke such a prayer to the gods of social media is hard to imagine. In China, the police force uses technologically connected glasses to identify suspects, record visual images, and publish criminals' pictures on billboards by uploading their photos and crimes onto public screens.[7] This seems counterproductive to the change of heart that the privacy of the confessional protects.

Social media outlets create memories and potentially addictive dependence on psychological approval from other members of the online virtual community. What is the corporate motivation of social media? It does join people in community, which is a great thing. Ultimately, it is not likely the eternal salvation of the human soul, as it is with God, the norm for beauty's use. The Apple emblem is an apple with a bite taken out, an obvious reference to the Tree of Knowledge from the Genesis account of man's creation. Perhaps this indicates a desire for immediate knowledge instantaneously; perhaps, however, it is dubiously more relevant to Satan's temptation to humanity: "You shall be like gods" (Gen 3:5).

The danger on the individual level, and necessarily by extension to the community, is living in the ability to "create beauty" and "appreciate beauty" to the exclusion of beauty's Creator. With accuracy and loveliness, Augustine ascribes the acknowledgments of beauty to God. His ability to determine this, however, comes in recollection; the plugged-in culture of the early twenty-first century is losing the sense of recollection, as silence evades even the most intentional of those who seek it.

A space for silence is fundamental for God's entry into our souls. Either individuals must create a space for silence, or God forces silent moments upon individuals. A danger of our society is the endless noise and cacophony, made omnipresent by portable electronic devices. Nowadays, children stare at screens from infancy. Not only are their minds receiving an unnatural amount of fleeting, incongruent images, but the content of the images is often banal or even detrimental. These are the images which will form the substance of the memories available to them later in recollection. Imagine trying to find God

---

7. Jon Russell, "Chinese Police Are Using Smart Glasses to Identify Potential Suspects," at TechCrunch (February 8, 2018), at techcrunch.com/2018/02/08/chinese-police-are-getting-smart-glasses/.

amid an array of cartoon images of Captain Underpants. How will insipid cartoons lead anyone to wonder, and a natural admiration of beauty?

Offering anyone, and especially children, beautiful images to form the storehouse of their memories is immensely important. Young minds are sponges, eagerly soaking up their environment in an attempt to understand the world. As Dr. Maria Montessori, an Italian pioneer of education, explains in her fascinating book *The Absorbent Mind*, a child's environment begins a process of forming his or her personality. Introducing a child to the natural environment allows the child to develop fully his or her personality, carrying early images of God's handiwork into adulthood.

Exposure to the natural world is particularly important, as the natural world is a sign of God. Augustine's metaphors of the mind include oceans, mountains, the sea, waterfalls, and the stars. He draws on expanses and power within nature. As Christians, we know the natural world is a reflection of the Divine Creator. But for those who are immature in the process of life, either children or fragmented adults, the natural world offers visual vistas to indicate the power and vastness of the Almighty. Spending time close to the earth or in the presence of boundless space reminds us of the multiplexity of God, a perfect environment for creating sense-impressions which may lead to Him.

In contemporary culture, scientists discover and manipulate even the DNA of substantial things here on earth, including human beings. Although many important discoveries and cures have been uncovered, some processes result in unwarranted effects. Transgender surgeries, for example, attempt to eliminate medically the inherent biologically given gender within human anatomy, attempting to alter the most intimate aspects of the human self. Whereas the integrity of the human person is under scientific scrutiny, God maintains the lovely stars at a generous distance, where they are free from the probing scientific reach of human manipulation.

Pythagoras, the ancient Greek philosopher and mathematician whom Augustine references early in the *Confessions*, speculated that the stars and planets moved according to mathematical equations that corresponded with musical notes, potentially thereby producing a symphony. To think what this might have sounded like is overwhelming. In 1918, Danish composer Rued Laangard attempted such a composition and created a beautiful symphony titled "Music of the Spheres."

Shakespeare, who is similarly attuned to the incredible fathomless depths of the night sky, in "The Merchant of Venice" also beautifully articulates the powers lying hidden in nature, with a surprising correspondence to Augustine's book 10. In Act Five, Lorenzo tells Jessica that the music of the spheres, similar to the beautiful music she hears in Venice, has the effect of colleting her interior self:

> Here will we sit and let the sounds of music
> Creep in our ears: soft stillness and the night
> Become the touches of sweet harmony.
> Sit, Jessica. Look how the floor of heaven
> Is thick inlaid with patines of bright gold:
> There's not the smallest orb which thou behold'st
> But in his motion like an angel sings,
> Still quiring to the young-eyed cherubins;
> Such harmony is in immortal souls;
> But whilst this muddy vesture of decay
> Doth grossly close it in, we cannot hear it.[8]

Like Augustine, Lorenzo blames his inability to hear the divine on man's fallen nature, the "muddy vesture of decay." Also like Augustine, Lorenzo suggests mastery over the self is an important element of reaching divinity. Jessica replies that she is never merry when she hears sweet music, and Lorenzo says:

> The reason is, your spirits are attentive:
> For do but note a wild and wanton herd,
> Or race of youthful and unhandled colts,
> Fetching mad bounds, bellowing and neighing loud,
> Which is the hot condition of their blood;
> If they but hear perchance a trumpet sound,
> Or any air of music touch their ears,
> You shall perceive them make a mutual stand,
> Their savage eyes turn'd to a modest gaze
> By the sweet power of music: therefore the poet
> Did feign that Orpheus drew trees, stones and floods;
> Since nought so stockish, hard and full of rage,
> But music for the time doth change his nature.
> The man that hath no music in himself,
> Nor is not moved with concord of sweet sounds,
> Is fit for treasons, stratagems and spoils;
> The motions of his spirit are dull as night
> And his affections dark as Erebus [the son of Chaos]:
> Let no such man be trusted. Mark the music.[9]

8. William Shakespeare, *The Merchant of Venice*, Act V, Scene 1, lines 52–63.
9. Shakespeare, *The Merchant of Venice*, 5.1.68–86.

This passage encapsulates Augustine's focus on the collected self, both in books 1 through 9, and again in book 10, coinciding with Augustine's observation that moderation is a necessary first step on the road to the collected self.

Lorenzo uses music poignantly to explain the power of continence, highlighting this virtue as part of the tradition of Western civilization in his reference to classical mythology, and personalizing the message to his beloved. The focus on the "wild and wanton herd" is not a perfect metaphor, as the horses do not come to know the trumpeter, but Augustine sympathizes; when he loves God, Augustine says he will "leave behind that faculty whereby I am united to a body and animate its frame. Not by that faculty do I find my God, for horse and mule would find him equally, since the same faculty gives life to their bodies, too, yet they are beasts who lack intelligence" (10.7.11). However, Lorenzo's metaphor perfectly depicts the collection of the soul. Jessica is not "merry" when she hears sweet music, but she is not necessarily sad, either. It is likely that she is focused, and her self is composed. Augustine, writing on moderation with respect to sound, says, "Without pretending to give a definitive opinion I am more inclined to approve the custom of singing in church, to the end that through the pleasures of the ear a weaker mind may rise up to loving devotion" (10.33.50).

The people who create such lovely verses and music, such as Shakespeare and Laangard, epitomize Augustine's notion that the human mind is more vast than the stars of the sky. More than mirroring the natural world, the creative, rational impulse within combines more powerfully, as the human soul shares the divine nature. To repeat from a quotation above, Augustine writes, "Those who create beauty in material things, and those who seek it, draw from that source their power to appreciate beauty, but not the norm for its use. The norm is there, and could they but see it they would need to search no further" (10.34.53).

The pulse of contemporary society suggests the public space for God is narrowing. As a result, the public memory of God and the path to joy may be careening toward extinction. For example, Justin Bieber and others drone crudely from malls across the country promoting erotic lust. Political battles wage to protect the lives of completely dependent baby humans. The month of June, dedicated traditionally to the Sacred Heart, has become Pride Month, symbolizing a cultural shift regarding human sexuality. Google's home page, rather than the Catholic Church, has become the harbinger of national holidays. In *The Abolition of Man*, C. S. Lewis predicts some of the gender ideologies of contemporary society, which seem to fulfill an idea in Graham Greene's 1940 novel *The Power and the Glory*, in which the whiskey priest explains to the atheist Mexican lieutenant that if he hates God and wants to destroy Him, he will end up destroying himself, because man is the *imago Dei*.

Bawdy elements of life have always existed, immortalized by playwrights and poets such as Aristophanes, Chaucer, and Shakespeare—Falstaff is a notorious drunk and comic foil, for example. Yet something deeper seems to be at stake today, which is more permanent and widespread. Nietzsche may rightly have forecasted the death of God, whose image is fading from society's social fabric.

In his reflection on memory, Augustine observes, "If we remember that we have forgotten something, we have not forgotten it entirely. But if we have forgotten altogether, we shall not be in a position to search for it" (10.19.28). Our contemporary culture seems to be at a crossroads with respect to civic praise of Christian principles. We know, with Augustine, that all men—and all creation—live and move in the Spirit of God. The question becomes how to keep humanity aware of the moving Spirit. Of course God is working in the lives of every individual, but if society closes churches, removes holy statues, and promotes evil ideas and images, the avenues to God become fewer. How may the individuals of a society recollect God in quiet moments if their minds have no images to search? Of course God can break through any barrier, but He does work within the system He created. The danger is that souls will be lost in the meantime, famished for images, seeking illicit pleasure like Augustine had done. If society has forgotten God altogether, where will the soul find God? It will not be in a position to search for Him.

How might a society recollect God? In Brad Bird's 2004 Pixar film "The Incredibles," the heroes—the Incredibles—are forced to live under cover, stifling their superhuman abilities because society does not want them anymore. Mr. Incredible saves a man's life, but in a wry twist, the man sues Mr. Incredible for interrupting his suicide: "I didn't want to be saved!" The scene metaphorically summarizes the element of self-destruction abounding in contemporary culture. Later, Mr. and Mrs. Incredible visit Edna, the designer and tailor of their super-suits, a woman full of creativity and ideas, and she laments, "I used to design for gods, but now . . . " The film briefly alights on an enormous bronze statue of a faceless god, framed by the sky and clouds. She laments the loss of the hero!

This nod to the Greek tradition of gods and heroes seems to be a brief homage to the tradition of human excellence, which formed the foundation of Western society and thought for centuries. Soccer's World Cup and other sports events highlight human physical excellence, but where are the spiritual heroes? Fifty years ago, Flannery O'Connor used bizarre images to shout to society's deafness in her attempt to recall for her contemporaries the spiritual realities. T. S. Eliot exclaims, "HURRY UP PLEASE ITS TIME" to remind readers of his poem "The Waste Land" to return to the dignity of the human person and reject the wasteland of contemporary culture. As in "The Incredibles," the public heroes may be hiding, but, like Edna, one may encourage—or even be—one of the needed heroes at work.

Sanctity is very difficult. Augustine observes, "Many have there been who tried to make their way back to you and finding themselves insufficient by their own powers . . . lapse into a fancy for visions that tickled their curiosity" (10.42.67). Humans by themselves are incapable of sanctity, but with God's help, through the intercession of Christ, sanctity is possible. Augustine describes Christ as the "true Mediator between God and humankind . . . like us he was mortal, but like God he was just" (10.43.68). Human sanctity is possible by imitating Christ. Augustine reminds us, "I am mindful of my ransom. I eat it, I drink it, I dispense it to others, and as a poor man I long to be filled with it among those who are fed and feasted" (10.43.70). The sacraments, and in particular the Eucharist, are the primary avenues to grace and virtue.

In some ways, the times are bleak in a new way, as men are taking hormones to become women and vice versa; children are asked by doctors whether they are boys or girls; and within ten years, artificial wombs are predicted to begin raising "responsibly" created new humans.

With the Internet, possibilities for sin and sinful images are exponentially available in ways never before imaginable. Despite all of this, grace holds the world in existence and is continually incarnated, both at Mass and in the good actions of people. Like Mary and Joseph fleeing Herod's commitment to evil as they hide in Egypt, Christianity thrives as intentional minds and hearts collect themselves in the Lord.

Augustine reminds us: "This is the happy life, and this alone: to rejoice in you, about you and because of you" (10.22.32). Augustine wants to find others to share his joy, with whom he can be in pilgrimage: "Let a fraternal mind love in me what you teach us to be worthy of love, and deplore in me what you teach us to be deplorable. But let it be a brotherly mind that does this, not the mind of a stranger . . . believing men and women" (10.4.5-6). To recognize an "other," striving to live in this case in the justice and mercy of God, can be the beginning of holy community. When a third, or several others, are also recognized, the community becomes a society.

Christians may find holy communities in a variety of ways. Today, people speak of the Benedict Option, of being secluded from the world to follow God in small intentional communities, or of the Marian option, to be in the world but not of it. In our dignity as sons and daughters of God, we Christians must set the vast array of our own stars, internal oceans and waterfalls, the beautiful mountain top vistas of our thought, to the service of good in the world and of God's will, in order that God's kingdom may be "on earth, as it is in Heaven."

Throughout book 10, as elsewhere, Augustine weaves prayers to God in and out of his philosophic observations. This seems to be his intentional echo of the movements of God in his own life, weaving in and out of his consciousness. The poems, or hymns, in elevated language, beautifully reflect a heightened and articulate awareness of his dependence on and love for God, improved with the divinization of his personhood.

God is always present in people, calling their minds and hearts to Him. Always, at least a small band of people will respond with love, like Mary and St. John at the foot of the cross, even if all the rest call out (Matt 27:17), "We want Barabbas!" God tells Abraham, "If there are only ten [faithful] people in the city, for the sake of the ten, I will not destroy it" (Gen 18:32). Civilization begins with a community of persons, seeking beauty, goodness, and truth. To enhance spaces, public and private, with beauty honors the dignity of each person, filling each one's mind with memories of images and truths through which each person may find God and use the incredible inheritance of human experience to join with Augustine and, ultimately, to confess the Lord.

Sacramental Time or the Never-Ending News Feed?

Veronica Roberts Ogle

As everyone knows, book 11 of the *Confessions* is the book about time. Much ink has been spilled over the viability or coherence of Augustine's theory of time, its origins and its purpose. In this chapter, I want to focus on its purpose. In brief, I will argue, Augustine thinks that we tend to think of eternity in temporal terms, which is a problem because we tend to think of time in spatial terms, and thinking about eternity in spatial terms just doesn't work. That is to say, when we think of time, we tend to imagine it as something with a length, and so when we turn to eternity, we just extend that length, positing that it is infinite.

But why is Augustine dissatisfied with this approach? Perhaps surprisingly, I will argue that he associates a spatial notion of time with the very fragmentation of mind and heart that pulls us away from God. Spatial time, Augustine argues, flattens our horizon, so that passing things more easily occupy us and take our attention away from our eschatological goal. Book 11's project of dissolving *the time that is* down to a vanishing point, I argue, is designed to draw the reader's attention to the simultaneous reality and ephemerality of the temporal present, and so makes it possible for that reader to conceive of eternity as the true reality of the present—that which the temporal "now" fails to fully be. In glimpsing the true nature of eternity, Augustine hopes, we give ourselves knowledge that we can constantly recollect, using it to enliven our desire for eternity, and so to persevere on the journey home.

This chapter proceeds in three sections. First, I give a brief survey of the literature, demonstrating that there has been a significant reintegration of Augustine's philosophy with his spirituality, and arguing that this is a good development. Second, I embark on an exploration of book 11 itself, with a view to understanding why Augustine is so interested in re-framing time for us. Third, and finally, I reflect on the contemporary relevance of Augustine's reframing of time, focusing first on the ways our culture exacerbates the human experience of *distentio* and the resulting flight into screen time that this encourages, and then focusing on what advice Augustine can offer us today.

As will become clear, I am convinced that the fundamental conceptual juxtaposition in book 11 is between *distentio* and *extentio*. Here is how I am thinking about the two terms. By *distentio*, I mean something like fragmentation—the state of being pulled apart by fractured desire. The neutral translation of the term as a kind of tension, I believe, is merely secondary. Fundamentally, it evokes the myriad of concerns that life in the world presupposes. By *extentio*, on the other hand, I mean the state of reaching out towards God. It is what the Psalmist inhabits as he exclaims (Ps 130:1; *conf.* 11.2.3), "O Lord, I cry to you from the depths," and what Augustine echoes as he adds, "for unless your ears be present in our deepest places where shall we go and whither cry?"

1. Literature Review

Famously, Bertrand Russell once referred to book 11's meditations on time as "the philosophical part" of the *Confessions*.[1] For a philosopher who insisted on the separation of reason from revelation—and then the jettisoning of revelation, this was in a way, a mark of approval for the passage, though one quickly undermined by his subsequent claim that Augustine relegated time to the realm of the subjective—that, problematically, Augustine's account suggested that time did not exist outside of the mind.

In the 1990s, Roland Teske, taking Russell's challenge seriously, sought to rescue Augustine from the charge of subjectivism by appealing to his Neoplatonism.[2] Again reading the passage on time as a philosophic meditation *tout court*, Teske used Augustine's Neoplatonist philosophy as a way to get out of the bind that Russell had found Augustine to be in. Augustine's meditation on time, the argument went, raises three paradoxes, each of which Augustine resolves

---

1. Bertrand Russell, *Human Knowledge: Its Scope and Limits* (New York: Simon and Schuster, 1948), 212.

2. Roland J. Teske, *Paradoxes of Time in Saint Augustine*, The Aquinas Lecture (Milwaukee: Marquette University Press, 1996).

with Neoplatonist resources. The third and most difficult, Teske argued, does not lead the reader into subjectivism because the soul that measures distended time is the world soul—the soul in which all rational souls participate. Thus, because we all share in the world soul which measures time, time does have a kind of objective reality. This trend of reading the philosophic Augustine as Augustine the Neoplatonist, has, however, had its day, and its passing has been heralded by Jim Wetzel's observation that if and when Augustine philosophizes, he "philosophizes by praying."[3] That is, without denying the Neoplatonic skeleton upon which much of Augustine's metaphysical and moral theory hangs, the trend in recent scholarship has been to admit that Augustine saw Neoplatonism as a partial and distorted framework, surpassed by Christian revelation. Not only has the ideal of philosophic ascent been replaced in Augustine with the notion of spiritual pilgrimage, but contemplation itself looks different.

Thus, clever though Teske's theory was, and Neoplatonic as Augustine's theory of time is, after Teske there has been a general shift in approach to book 11. As we will soon see, the so-called philosophical bit of the *Confessions* is sandwiched between a prayer for illumination and a mediation on the distended human condition. This being the case, recent scholars have tended to argue that that the meditation, philosophical though it may be, cannot be extricated from its spiritual context—hence Wetzel's abovementioned objection that Augustine only ever philosophizes by praying. This understanding is nothing other than the rediscovery that, for Augustine, the truth is only ever revealed to us to the extent that we hear it from the Inner Teacher. Indeed, much of Augustine's meditation on time, the beginning of his meditation on creation which stretches throughout the last three books, is punctuated with appeals for divine help, that God's light might shine through the chinks in his mind (11.9.11). Augustinian contemplation, ultimately, is a kind of communion. Knowledge and love goad each other on.

With this shift in the scholarly discourse, there has arisen a greater emphasis on the existential import of Augustine's exploration into the nature of time. For example, Mateusz Strozynski has argued that Augustine's meditation on time is best read as a spiritual exercise within the tradition identified by Pierre Hadot. By and large, I find this reading convincing. The section is clearly performative, beckoning the reader into a shared enterprise which involves confusion (aporia), prayer and discovery.[4] Why, though? Strozynski argues that

3. James Wetzel, "Time after Augustine," *Religious Studies* 31, no. 3 (1995): 341–357, 345.

4. Mateusz Strozynski, "Time, Self, and Aporia: Spiritual Exercise in Saint Augustine," *Augustinian Studies* 40, no. 1 (2009): 103–120. Incidentally, Strozynski resolves the subjectivist

time, being as it is, makes it impossible to see eternity; as such the spiritual exercise of book 11 is an attempt to lift the veil, if only for a moment.[5] In this way, Augustine hopes to give his readers a glimpse of the eternity for which they ought to long. The study of time orients them home.

Taking a different approach, Rowan Williams has read the discussion on time as a continuation of book 10's emphasis on the pilgrim's essential unfinishedness. Arguing that books 10 and 2 are designed as an antidote to the hagiography, Williams reads Augustine as emphasizing the degree to which he remains a work in progress, requiring the charity of God and his fellow travelers to persevere to the end. In particular, he argues, Augustine's emphasis on the strangeness of time—his rendering it unfamiliar—is designed to teach us that we are constantly surrounded by mystery, and that the mystery we associate with God is not an exception, but the rule.

Perhaps most pertinent to my theme is that scholarship which seeks to reintegrate Augustine's theoretical conclusion—that time is a tension of the mind (*distentio*)—with the spiritual condition of disintegration (also *distentio*) that he laments in the concluding chapters of book 11—an echo of book 10's conclusion. There are three insights I would like to draw and build upon from this literature. The first is Gerard O'Daly's careful and compelling demonstration that Augustine's juxtaposition of *distentio* and *extentio* is rooted in Scripture, and, more specifically in Ecclesiastes 3:10-11 and Philippians 3:12-17.[6] The second is Thomas Humphries' recognition that the discussion of time in book 11 cannot be extricated from his discussion of memory in book 10, and the third is Jim Wetzel's insight that sin's sense of time, somehow, is not time at all, but, as he puts it, "time's absence."[7]

Turning to the first of these, O'Daly persuasively shows that *distentio* is a significant Scriptural theme that Augustine intentionally appropriates in books 10 and 11 of the *Confessions*. As we will see below, Augustine ends both books by lamenting how life in this world constantly threatens to distract us from prayer, sweeping us away into the hustle and bustle of daily life. O'Daly reads this as a development of Ecclesiastes 3:10, translated in Latin as "*deus distensionem magnam dedit hominibus, ut distendantur in ea*," and, in one English version

problem by arguing that for Augustine reality is real; time is just the human way of seeing reality. See Strozynski, "Time, Self, and Aporia," 116.

5. Strozynski, "Time, Self, and Aporia," 117.

6. Gerard J.P. O'Daly, "Time as Distentio and St. Augustine's Exegesis of Philippians 3, 12–14," *Revue d'Etudes Augustiniennes et Patristiques* 23, no. 3–4 (1977): 265–271.

7. Thomas L. Humphries, "Distentio Animi: Praesens temporis, imago aeternitatis," *Augustinian Studies* 40, no. 1 (2009): 75–101; Wetzel, "Time after Augustine," 355.

as, "I have seen the business that God has given to the children of man to be busy with."[8] The anxiety that comes with falling headlong into busyness, what I will ultimately call alienated time, is a significant theme that ties together not only books 10 and 11 (though principally so) but also the story of Augustine's conversion as a whole. It is the abyss over which a converted life always looms.

Yet, notably, Ecclesiastes goes on, "He [God] has made everything beautiful in its time. Also, he has put eternity into man's heart, yet so that he cannot find out what God has done from the beginning to the end" (Eccl 3:11). The fact that God has put eternity into man's heart, of course, means that the *distentio* that Augustine so laments is only the inverse of the possibility of *extentio*. For O'Daly, Augustine really roots his notion of *extentio* in the Pauline declaration from Ephesians, "I continue my pursuit toward the goal, the prize of God's upward calling, in Christ Jesus" (Eph 3:14). O'Daly calls the verse "a leitmotif when[ever] [Augustine] broaches the theme of man's calling to the eternal and liberation from the temporal, the reaction of faith to the disturbing fragmentation of temporality."[9]

It is therefore quite rational, I think, that Humphries reads time in Augustine as at once an icon of eternity and a fall into multiplicity. Connecting Augustine's concept of *distentio* with his meditation on memory only a book before, he highlights the ambiguity of our power to make past or future present—and so brings us back to Wetzel's original contention that time and sin's time are not the same. Our sense of time is utterly bound up with our spiritual condition and is, at best, in a perpetual yet precarious state of *extentio* until we reach our true home.

Thus to conclude this foray into the secondary literature on Augustine's discussion of time, what we see is a progressive movement from a concern with the philosophizing Augustine, an Augustine stripped down to his Neoplatonic bones, to a praying Augustine: first, an Augustine who philosophizes by praying, thus signaling that true Augustinian contemplation is a graced endeavor requiring humility and charity from the start, and second, an Augustine who philosophizes to facilitate praying, thus signaling that the true goal of contemplation is to know and love God, and so to praise Him. Clearly, for Augustine, knowledge and love are inextricably bound together; Augustine seeks to love so that he and his readers can know, and he seeks to know so that he (and his readers) can love.

---

8. *English Standard Version*; cf. O'Daly, "Time as *Distentio*," 267.
9. O'Daly, "Time as *Distentio*," 269.

2. The Trajectory of Book 11

Having reviewed the trajectory of recent meditations on book 11, it is now for us to dive into the text itself, with a view to ultimately connecting it to the effects of our modern lifestyle on an already distended human condition. I would like to proceed by first, examining book 11 on its own terms, and then commenting on the questions it raises for our contemporary experience. In the textual examination, I will argue that Augustine's main theoretical goal, to reframe time in relation to eternity, is ultimately of spiritual import. That is, his attempt to effect this paradigm shift cannot be extricated from his attempt to draw himself and his readers out of distended time into a state of *extentio* by enlivening their desire for their eternal home. As we see, Augustine presents the conflict between *distentio* and *extentio* as the paradigmatic drama of pilgrimage. Longing for heaven, the pilgrim remains in constant danger of being pulled back into the stream of alienated time, just as Augustine confessed himself to be at the end of book 10. The pilgrim's ability to remain on the path home is a matter of grace certainly, but, significantly, it is also a matter of recollection.

In fact, I will argue, it is in the activity of recollection that we find the true significance of time's reframing. Notably, Augustine begins book 11 by stepping back from the project of confession in order to ask why he has been telling God things that He undoubtedly already knows. In brief, Augustine's answer is that this activity arouses our devotion to God. Thus, we find, Augustine has engaged in the project of recollection in order to recall, and so love, the God who has loved him first. As we will discover towards the end of book 11, the practice of recollecting God mysteriously allows God to recollect us—not in the sense of remembering us, but in the sense of gathering us back together out of our fragmented or distended state. This re-integration is a significant object of hope for Augustine, tied to his very idea of eternal life—for, as he writes at the close of the book, "In the most intimate depths of my soul my thoughts are torn to fragments by tempestuous changes until that time when I flow into you, purged and rendered molten by the fire of your love" (11.29.39). Then, he writes, he will finally stand still.

It is, therefore, in order to sit still that Augustine embarks on a seemingly theoretical discussion of time—for it is only in sitting still that we can see how time points to eternity. I have already mentioned that Augustine begins book 11 by asking himself why he is telling God things that He already knows. In this question, the relationship between time and eternity, man and God, already takes central stage. At the very least, any catechized reader would know that God stands outside of time, and therefore knows what Augustine will say before he says it, just as he knew everything that Augustine would do before he did it. To be sure, as Augustine argues elsewhere, this does not undermine human freedom but simply means that God sees time all at once, as if a thousand years were a single day.

Yet, this basic teaching about divine foreknowledge, presented in terms of spatial time, can be a stumbling block to Christian readers. Consider what connotations arise as I say the following: God knew *before* I acted. In the beginning, God created heaven and earth. God *awaits* us in his eternal home; we will see him *after* our journey is done. This tendency to think and speak of God in terms of before and after time is symptomatic of our tendency to think of eternity in terms of time, rather than time in terms of eternity. Why does Augustine worry about this? Tentatively, I would suggest, Augustine believes that this habit contributes to our tendency to fall into alienated time—the state where linear time occupies our whole attention. When eternity is understood in temporal terms, we think of it as an infinite epoch stretching back beyond the dawn of time and stretching forward far beyond its end. Yet, where is God in the present? At best, we think of Him as being perched in some upper reaches of space, looking down on our temporal world with a bird's eye view. So far away, how can God be intimately involved in the drama of our lives?

All this is encapsulated in the difficulty we have in understanding how it could be that we can and should speak to God. Normally, it seems, communication is predicated on the desire to inform someone about something. Yet, God does know what we will say before we speak, and somehow, mysteriously, it still matters that we do. I have already alluded to Augustine's way of resolving this problem: human beings must speak in order that their love for God may grow. Communication with God, then, mirrors the fundamental asymmetry of our whole relationship with God: whatever we do out of love for God draws *us* closer to God and so works for our good; it does not assuage some neediness on His part. God, it turns out, hears and desires that we speak to Him, but does so in order that we might return to Him.

Indeed, the project of recollection in which Augustine has engaged over the last ten books is really a reaching out to God—an *extentio*. It is the work of love working to rouse love by recalling and praising the activity of God in his life. Now, Augustine turns to another work of love—contemplation. In his life of episcopal responsibility, Augustine explains, he has but few moments to spare and his heart yearns to spend them contemplating the wonders of God's law. Accordingly, having written enough of his life story to glorify God, he is now in a position to turn to these mysteries. If this were a different paper, I would elaborate on how Augustine begins his meditation with a hymn, intersperses his musings with prayer, and generally models what he considers to be the proper disposition for Christian contemplation. However, since my concern is to tie Augustine's meditations on time with his diagnosis of our distended condition, and so to elaborate on the way this distention is aggravated by life in the modern world, I will invoke these points only tangentially.

Beginning at the beginning, Augustine wonders about creation. The fact that heaven and earth were created, he argues, is evident from the fact that they "undergo change and variation" (11.4.6). Things subject to change and variation, he knows with certainty, could not have made themselves because they are contingent. Yet, above all, it is their beauty, goodness and existence that bear witness to their Creator:

> It was you who made them Lord: you are beautiful, so it must have been you, because they are beautiful; you who are good must have made them, because they are good; you who are because they are. Yet not in the same way as you, their creator, are they beautiful and good, nor do they exist as you exist; compared with you they have neither beauty nor goodness nor being. We know this, and we thank you for the knowledge, yet compared with your knowledge ours is but ignorance. (11.4.6)

Augustine, in looking at created things, sees traces of God's own qualities in their qualities. This will become important later. For now, it is enough to note that this construal marks the beginning of his attempt to shift our perspective from one defined by those things that are first for us to one defined by that which is first *per se*. Consonant with this effort, Augustine goes on to dispel anthropomorphic visions of how God created heaven and earth by invoking Scripture's revelations about the Word through whom all things were made. Thanks to God's self-disclosure, Augustine is able to understand that "all things are uttered simultaneously in one eternal speaking. Were this not so, time and change would come into it, and there would be neither true eternity nor true immortality" (11.7.9). The Word through which God made the world, then, was not an audible word with beginning and end, but something silently and mysteriously uttered in eternity, out of which a whole world came forth. Again, we see, Augustine does not seek to understand the divine in terms of the human, but models what it means to let God reframe human thoughts.

It is not surprising, then, that soon after making this point, Augustine chastises those who would ask, "But what was God doing before He decided to create the world? Surely if God willed to do something He had not done before, then there would be some change in Him, and He would not be truly eternal" (11.10.12). In the way he has his interlocutor pose the question, Augustine clearly means to present him as a foil, displaying a disposition far from that which Augustine has been very consciously modeling. Indeed, it is as if this interjector seeks to catch Augustine out, naysaying orthodox Christian teaching by invoking clever logic. Yet, Augustine remarks disparagingly, those who do this "strive to be wise about eternal realities" without understanding the Wisdom Who is the Light of the mind (11.11.13). Striving for wisdom in the wrong way, he writes, "their heart flutters about between changes of past and future found in created things," and, therefore, remains empty (11.11.13).

In writing about these objectors' hearts, Augustine again drives home the idea that contemplation is an essentially spiritual practice; true wisdom, he is convinced, comes only when the light of God shines through the chinks in our mind. Ultimately, Augustine argues, this kind of contemplation requires sitting still and listening—not being clever. When our heart remains fettered to the created things of time, we do not sit still, cannot receive the light of God, and so begin to imagine God and God's eternity in our own image. Thus, if it has not already become evident, the question of the relationship between time and eternity is as much a spiritual as an intellectual problem: to see is to be filled from above, and to be filled, one must sit still.

Yet, he asks, who will take hold of the human heart and

> peg it down, so that it may stand still for a little while and capture, if only briefly, the splendour of that eternity which stands for ever, and compare it with the fugitive moments that never stand still, and find it incomparable, and come to see that a long time is not long except in virtue of a great number of passing moments which cannot run their course all at once? (11.11.13)

With trepidation, Augustine takes up the challenge—or at least something akin to it, asking if his hand has strength to "take hold of the human heart to make it stand still and see how eternity, which stands firm, has neither future nor past, but ordains future and past times" (11.11.13). In my opinion, it is this passage that best explains Augustine's apparently philosophic foray into time. If, embedded in the objector's question, is what I have called a linear or, if you will, spatial view of time—something stretching before and after—it is only too natural to think of eternity as something which stretches even further before and after. Yet, this would be to take the ways of created things and project them onto the Godhead. Recall, for Augustine, it is not the ways of created things that map onto nature of the Godhead, but that created things speak of the Godhead; their existence, goodness, and beauty point to the God Who *is* Being, Goodness, and Beauty. Precisely because creatures only participate in these qualities, possessing them in partial shares, they evoke the One who instantiates them completely—and, importantly, our desire for that One.

Looking at the world sacramentally, as something that points upwards, Augustine sees eternity, not as extended time, but as that which time *points* to in its incompletion. If, as he puts it, a long time is long because of the myriad of passing moments that make it up, then a long time is far from the best way of thinking about eternity. In fact, it is quite wrongheaded, for, he explains, in eternity nothing passes because the whole is present all at once. The difficulty of grasping what this means is obvious: it involves an entire paradigm shift. His readers must come to see that eternity is the true focal point of all that is—that it is, in Eliot's words, "the still point of the turning world" (*Four Quartets,* Burnt Norton, II.62).

Yet, because it is only too natural to think of eternity in terms of what we know, Augustine cannot deny the questioner who genuinely asks, "But what *was* God doing before he created?" His short answer is nothing. There was no time, and therefore no "before," until God created the world. Yet, lest we read this as a mere semantic point, suggesting that what we *call* time only began when God got up out of His metaphorical chair and began to create, Augustine clarifies what he means. Ultimately, Augustine argues, the very concepts of before and after are only conceivable in a world of becoming, and Eternity simply *is*. In other words, it is not as though, at a certain point on eternity's never-ending timeline, God decided to create a world with a beginning and an end, whose epoch of discrete length would alone bear the name of time. For Augustine, there is no "time before time" because there is never any change in God; God created from all eternity, and it is only the coming-into-being of a created world, which resulted from this perpetual willing-into-being that can properly be called temporal. Change is the characteristic of the created world alone, and so, therefore, is time. To speak of "before" and "after," or of particular moments at all in eternity is to drag the nature of changing things into the Godhead. Ultimately, Augustine believes, the difference between time and eternity is not the difference between finite and infinite length, but between becoming and being.

But how to convey this to his readers? This is where Augustine's exploration into the nature of time comes into the picture. Arguing that time is at once a most familiar concept, yet also a most obscure one, Augustine embarks on the project of getting his readers to see time anew. He begins by getting his readers to sit still. In pausing the flow of time, substituting it with stillness, Augustine dissolves our everyday sense of time as something always in motion—something that we are "in"—our very horizon, and allows us to look at it in its constituent elements: past, present, and future. Again, we see that past and future are rooted in the changing nature of created things, for there could be no "past time" if nothing passed away, and there could be no 'future time' if nothing came into being. It is only the present that transcends these constraints, for to exist in the present, one must simply exist.

Though Augustine can easily identify these parts of time in freeze-frame, as soon as he turns his attention to their individual natures, he finds that the flow of time has resumed, and he cannot hold them in his grasp. Looking for the past, he discovers that it is not anywhere because it is no more, and looking for the future, he finds the same, for it has not yet come. In the stillness of the present moment, Augustine and his readers come to realize that only the present ever actually *is*, and that each present moment goes by so fast that it is constantly being replaced by a new one. Although, it seems, all we have access to is the present moment, we can never pause to examine its nature because each present moment is perpetually slipping through our fingertips.

Thus, through this curious guided exercise into the being of time, Augustine has managed to give his readers an experience of time that is deeply ephemeral. Remarking that "the present's only claim to be called time is that it is slipping away into the past," he concludes that time can only be said to exist "because it tends to non-being" (11.14.17). This is a strange thing to say. What Augustine means is that the temporal present, which perpetually slips into the past, has one characteristic that separates it from the eternal present: namely, that it slips into the past. In other words, through our experience of the fleeting present, Augustine gives us a foretaste of what the eternal present might be—for, Augustine tells us, if the temporal present "never slipped away into the past, it would not be time at all; it would be eternity" (11.14.17). Accordingly, just as the creature who participates in goodness, beauty and being can evoke a desire for the Goodness, Beauty, and Being of God, time in its partial mode of existence can evoke a desire for eternity, even as it is distinguished itself from eternity by its very same. Notice that in making this claim about time, Augustine has resituated it in its proper relationship to eternity. Now, we see, time points beyond itself. Eternity becomes, more clearly, an object of hope.

Nevertheless, in order to truly help his readers see their life in time as a pointing to eternity, Augustine must explain how our experience of time relates to what he has just demonstrated. Human beings, after all, rarely think about time in terms of the stillness of the present moment. Instead, we think about periods of time; we talk about the dinner party we will go to this evening, the wedding that happened a year ago, and how long it will take before an eagerly anticipated guest arrives. On the face of it, the time that we measure seems far more real than the time Augustine has just presented, but is it? What exactly are we measuring, when we measure periods of time? It cannot be the past or the future, Augustine argues, for something must exist in order to be measured, yet neither can it be the present, for this has been whittled down to a fleeting, immeasurable moment (11.14.17).[10] Having ruled out these three, Augustine invites his readers into the experience of being puzzled.

Pausing frequently to ask God for help, Augustine considers whether he was mistaken to argue that the past and future do not exist, especially since they seem awfully real to us (11.17.22). For Augustine, the answer lies in the nature of mind and memory. The person who tells a true tale about the past has before her mind's eye not the past itself, but images impressed upon it during the event. Similarly, the person who anticipates the future has before her mind's eye, not the future itself, but current realities that signal what the future will likely bring. It is worth noting that both of these are decidedly contingent: our recollection of the past can be spotty, depending on how well we were paying attention, and our prediction of future off the mark, depending on the degree to which we foresaw and understood the causes of future events.

Yet, Augustine does not introduce these complexities here. It is enough for him to grapple with the strangeness of past and future, which seem to be and not to be at the same time. Ontologically, he has established, past and future do not exist. Yet, they do seem to have some kind of existence in the mind's eye, for Augustine is able to see in the present what the future holds and what the past held. The same goes for all kinds of things that we anticipate and recall—the birth of a child, the start of a school year, the marriage of a friend. This would seem to suggest that the past and future do have a kind of reality after all, and so Augustine's conclusion is as follows: properly speaking, "there are three tenses or times: the present of past things, the present of present things, and the present of future things. These are three realities in the mind, but nowhere else as far as I can see, for the present of past things is memory, the present of present things is attention, and the present of future things is expectation" (11.20.26).

At this point we can pause and ask ourselves, is this true? Indeed, where else *is* the past and the future made present but in our mind's eye? In the mind of God? Perhaps, but Augustine will later establish, God does not see time in a distended way (11.31.41). In claiming that the past only becomes present through recollection and the future only through expectation, Augustine has gained the title of a subjectivist. Yet, if we really think about it, unless we have stumbled out of a Tardis, every time we go out into the world, we go out into a world

---

10. Famously, Augustine argues that, just as a century cannot be present all at once, neither can a day, and nor can a minute (11.15.19–20).

that exists as it exists *now*. We may encounter the world of the past through photographs, ruins, or keepsakes, but it is only because these things remain in existence now that we experience them as realities outside of the mind. Some things are simply gone from the world forever; though we may recall the old roof of Notre-Dame, see photographs of it, and perhaps even build a replica of it, we will never again see it as it was. Time, simply put, marches on, and it is we who remember, we who anticipate.

All this having been worked out, Augustine remains confused about the implications of his conclusion, wondering, in particular, how it is possible to measure time if time's length is not spatial. He writes:

> My mind is on fire to solve this most intricate enigma. O Lord, my God, my good Father, through Christ I beg you not to shut against me the door to these truths, so familiar yet so mysterious. Do not slam the door in the face of my desire, nor forbid me entrance to that place where I may watch these things grow luminous as your mercy sheds its light upon them, Lord. (11.22.28)

Again drawing his readers into his confusion, Augustine attempts to enliven their curiosity, so they that really pay attention to the difficulty. Perhaps, he backtracks, time is spatial after all; after all, a wise man once told him that time is constituted by the movement of the celestial spheres. Yet, thinking through the possibility, he concludes that it cannot be true—if the sun moved through its whole trajectory in the space of an hour, everyone knows that it would still take less time than its route's usual duration of a day. Time, he famously concludes, must instead be "a kind of strain or tension"—*distentio* (11.23.30). At this point in the text, this conclusion is opaque, seemingly arising out of nowhere. Though he has successfully separated time from distance, so that the reader can see how a faster motion is *shorter* than a slower one of the same distance, Augustine has more work to do before the tension hypothesis makes sense. Indeed, he admits as much, saying,

> I confess to you, Lord, that even today I am still ignorant of what time is; but I praise you, Lord, for the fact that I know I am making this avowal within time, and for my realization that within time I am talking about time at such length, and that I know that this "length" itself is only long because time has been passing all the while. But how I can know that, when I do not know what time is? Or perhaps I simply do not know how to articulate what I know? Woe is me, for I do not even know what I do not know! (11.25.32)

To gain some clarity, Augustine embarks on a phenomenology of time-keeping through an examination of poetry. Though we may contrive units for measuring the length of poems—syllables, lines, stanzas, and movements, to name a few—he quickly notices that these forms of measurement do not determine how long the poem takes to be read. Everyone knows, for example, that the recitation of a poem takes longer if the performer has a drawl, yet this has nothing to do with the word-count of a poem. As such, Augustine concludes that the length of the poem is not the same as the length of the poem read and again returns to the idea that time is a tension, this time clarifying that he believes it to be a tension of consciousness itself. Yet, how does the example illuminate the meaning of this claim, and how does this use of the term *distentio* fit with the anxiety-ridden meaning invoked by Ecclesiastes?

Essentially, what Augustine has just done is demonstrate that the way in which we know whether a poem's duration is longer or shorter is not spatial, but through our *experience* of time passing. In other words, when I measure the length of a poetry reading, there is one thing I cannot do: zone out.[11] Otherwise, without the help of a time-keeping gadget, I do not know whether it was long or short at all. Indeed, even if I do use a watch to measure its length, I have to remember what time it was when the poetry reading began. A half-hour it may have been, but even this number would have no meaning for me if I had not the experience of paying attention for half an hour. Memory and attention, incontrovertibly, ground the possibility of measuring time.

In an effort to further dissolve our attachment to the spatial units that we use to measure time, Augustine highlights the fact that the poem whose length we are measuring never actually exists all at once.

> Where is the short syllable I was going to use as a standard? What has become of the long one I want to measure? Both have made their sound and flown away . . . yet I do my calculation and confidently assert . . . [that] the short is half the long, the long twice the short; and obviously I am speaking about a space of time. (11.27.35)

Augustine's answer is that they are both in the mind, which, as he has already established, is the only place that passing phenomena leave their impressions for human beings to measure and compare.[12] In the end, our ability to measure time is part and parcel of our human consciousness, which remembers, pays attention, and anticipates.

---

11. To be more precise, Augustine returns to the question of what kind of time he is measuring, and concludes that the future, the present, and the past are all unmeasurable; only periods of time are measurable. To measure a period of time, we must be attentive from its beginning to its end.

12. Addressing his own mind, he concludes, "What I measure is the impression which passing phenomena leave in you, which abides after they have passed by" (11.27.37).

Now, it is incontrovertibly true that in drawing this conclusion, Augustine describes the human ability to measure time as a gift, which means that the meaning of the term *distentio* might be a bit more ambiguous than I've let on. After all, if it were simply a bad thing, surely it would be a product of the Fall and not a gift from God. *Distentio*, it would seem, is simply the way human beings experience a changing world—because life in time unfolds in succession, we recall what has happened, pay attention to what is happening, and look forward to what might happen next, all the while measuring various periods of time that have meaning for us. Yet, *is* Augustine's account as neutral as it first appears? Perhaps Augustine's answer comes in his thoughts on what it is like to recite a poem.

Now, if I were to describe what it is like to recite a poem, I would say the following: Before you begin, it is as if the idea of reciting the poem is anticipated in your mind, but the parts of the poem are somehow hidden from view. As soon as you start, though, your focus narrows to the recitation, and you find each word popping into your consciousness in more or less correct order all the way until the poem is done. Then, what remains is the memory of having recited it, whole and parts included. While Augustine's account is similar, it is a little more complex: "Before I begin," he writes,

> my expectation is directed to the whole poem, but once I have begun, whatever I have plucked away from the domain of expectation and tossed behind me to the past becomes the business of my memory, and the vital energy of what I am doing is in tension between the two of them: it strains towards my memory because of the past I have already recited, and to my expectation on account of the part I still have to speak. (11.27.36)

What Augustine notes that I did not is the strain his attention undergoes as he recites the poem, tending to both past and future at once. Whereas I argued that during my recitation, I was focusing on the recitation alone, Augustine reminds us that, even as we are concentrating on the next word or phrase, we are simultaneously aware of what we have already done and what we still have to do. We are, in other words, more mentally divided than my account let on.

Perhaps this perennial pull of past and future seems is of little consequence when it comes to reciting a poem, but imagine what it means when applied to human life and history. Insofar as our attention is pulled in these various directions, we experience life in this world as something fragmented. What is more, insofar as what occurs is liable to change, we can experience the goods of this world as tentative. Finally, insofar as what occurs in this world is less than perfectly good, we can experience its goodness as inadequate. By ending his meditation with the observation that "what is true of the poem" is equally true of a person's entire life, Augustine reveals that his phenomenology of poetry recitation is of greater existential import than it first appears (11.28.28).[13]

Indeed, this becomes even more evident as we approach the closing passages of book 11. Here Augustine reflects that his life is "no more than anxious distraction," hearkening back to the world-weary confessions that closed book 10 (11.29.39). His attention, he now confesses, continues to be "pulled many ways by multifarious distractions," and, were it not for Christ, he fears he would be pulled apart by them. Here, presumably, he is referring to his continuing struggles against gluttony, pride, and concupiscence of the eyes. Yearning to be "gathered in from dispersion," Augustine begs to be given the grace "to pursue the One, forgetting the past and stretching undistracted not to future things doomed to pass away, but to [his] eternal goal" (11.29.39).

To stretch undistracted, it seems, is Augustine's deepest desire, and the dissatisfaction he feels with his current state is palpable. The beauty of created things, while pointing to God, don't always point quickly enough for Augustine, and it is clear that he feels the weight of the time lag (see, for example, 10.35.47). Here, then, we see the dichotomy between *distentio* and *extentio* in its full clarity. Life in time is, on Augustine's account inevitably distracting, but, recollecting our true home, we can reach out towards it love. It is therefore, he declares, "with no distracted mind but with focused attention [that] I press on to the prize of our heavenly calling, to that place where I yearn to hear songs of praise and contemplate your delight, which neither comes, nor slips away" (11.29.39).

Throughout my exposition of Augustine's philosophical meditation on time, I have suggested that Augustine goes to great lengths to divest his readers of a spatial notion of time in order that they might glimpse eternity as that to which time points. I have also suggested that this paradigm shift is of spiritual import, and, having seen Augustine conclude that time is measured through our awareness of its passing, we can begin to see how this awareness ought to evoke a longing for that which does not pass away. Put in a more familiar way, this is a longing for rest. Because it is only in sitting still that we notice the degree to which time is always passing away, Augustine gives his readers an experience of time stood still, only to show that nothing of time does stand still. Theoretical as Augustine's meditations on time may first appear, they are, most

---

13. One implication is immediately obvious: if, throughout my life, I am aware that the future is perpetually being used up, I am aware that eventually, all of my time will be used up. I am aware of my own contingency and death.

definitely, meant to recall us to ourselves, to remind us of our current state, and to give us a foretaste of our true home.

3. Contemporary Significance

Having gone through Augustine's meditations on time in book 11, we are now in a position to see the degree to which they speak to contemporary culture. Certainly, if we follow Augustine's meditation, we can see how the passage of time does create a negative tension in our psyche; its flow pulls us in different directions at once, so that a single event can at once evoke nostalgia about the past, fear about the future, and anxiety about the present. Indeed, the more that we stop and reflect on our experience of time, the more anxiety-laden it appears. How can we sit still, given so many constant and competing demands on our attention? Is there something about our culture that makes this so especially difficult? These are the questions I would like to explore in the last section of this paper.

First, I would like to explore how our current condition exacerbates already existing tendencies in the human psyche. To be sure, as Augustine tells us, the human condition is one of distention in every day and age—it is simply part and parcel of our fallen state. Unable to see God, we are perennially wont to be engrossed in the things of this world, and they, being many, carry parts of our heart with them in different directions. Some of them bury a part of our heart in the past, so that we have a hard time embracing the present for what it offers. Others bubble forth from memory to stir our desire, compelling us to seek anew what we once enjoyed. Still others greet us as something novel, tugging at our hearts and occupying our attention for the first time. Yet it is not only the things we love that pull us in different directions; it is also our responsibilities. Indeed, Augustine often laments the tediousness of his administrative duties, transfigured into works of love to be sure, but nonetheless tiresome for pulling him away from the contemplation in which he yearns to engage.

In this way, Augustine's lament that his life is "an anxious distraction" is a timeless one. In every day and age, we are faced with responsibilities that take us away from those activities which most fulfill us. Yet, it is also true that the sentiment pertains in a particular way to life in contemporary America. Children, we often complain, are overscheduled, and adults rush around with their to-do lists, anxious to complete the tasks set before them. Many, it seems, are either overwhelmed at work or bored by their everyday routine—sometimes both. When we catch up with our friends, we frequently talk about how busy things have been, and how long it will be before they settle down again. This busy-ness, at once, becomes our purpose, and drains us of purpose. A life spent moving on from task to task is exhausting. We might ask, what is it all for?

Although there are a variety of movements in America encouraging us to ask this question, many if not most of us seek refuge from it by absorbing ourselves in our screens instead. The reason is, perhaps, obvious. As anyone who has tried to begin or to recover the habit of sitting still knows, the mind, unsaddled, runs in all kinds of directions— to grocery lists, to bills unpaid, to emails unanswered, and beyond. This is not the case when we turn to our phones or computer screens. Instead, we experience a kind of haze—a pleasant escape from the very responsibilities that nag us in our everyday lives. We are, simply, in the screen.

And yet there are a myriad of studies documenting the detriments of this escape into screen time. These days, it is a well-known fact that there is a link between social media use and depression, and who can genuinely claim to emerge from a Netflix binge feeling rejuvenated?[14] Again, studies show that those who binge-watch have higher rates of stress, anxiety, and depression—the very states that we watch Netflix to escape.[15] Whether or not this is correlation or causation, cure it is not. It is not surprising, therefore, that there are so many articles on the internet documenting people's struggles with video streaming and social media addiction. Yet few name the deeper reasons that we turn to these platforms. We seek to procrastinate, to be sure, to be affirmed, without a doubt, to kill time, obviously. But Augustine would have us ask, what is *underneath* it all? This question is especially necessary today, when we so easily substitute a parodic rest of screen time for the sacramental rest of prayer, which can truly sustain our lives in time.[16] By recalling us to ourselves, Augustine forces us to confront the degree to which we are restless because a desire for *eternal* rest is at the very center of our being; this is something that our culture, for all its therapeutic resources, often fails to understand.

Thus, Augustine helps us see that we have, as a society, plunged headlong

---

14. One *New York Times* blogger has called the "post-binge-watching blues" one of the most common maladies of our times. Matthew Schneier, "The Post-Binge-Watching Blues: A Malady of Our Times," *New York Times* (December 5, 2015), at www.nytimes.com/2015/12/06/fashion/post-binge-watching-blues.html.

15. J. Mitchell Vaterlaus, Lori Andersen Spruance, Kala Frantz, and Jessica Sloan Kruger, "College Student Television Binge Watching: Conceptualization, Gratifications, and Perceived Consequences," *The Social Science Journal* 56, no. 4 (2019), 470–479, at 472.

16. I think this substitute in the modern consciousness is particularly evident when we start watching contemporary science fiction. One need only think of the *Black Mirror* episode "San Junipero" and its reception to see this.

into time alienated from eternity. In today's world, we do not consider life in time to be contextualized by anything beyond itself; instead, we strive to give our lives meaning by the stories we tell about them—we talk of our hopes for the future and defining events in the past. We post them on Instagram. Yet, however polished our narratives are, and however many likes our posts yield, we can still be deeply unhappy if our daily lives do not correspond to the narrative that we give them—and life rarely does. Thus, we see, Augustine's objection to the spatial notion of time is really an objection to the immanentization of time's meaning—a meaning that must be fictional if it is to be alluring. Without a transcendent lodestar, we focus on the things that we wish would define our lives, and the stories we tell about them sustain us.

Yet, because our daily life in time is often made up of banal tasks too, there is often a disjunct between our stories and our actual lives. When good things arise, we are buoyed up by them, but knowledge of their contingency, paired with the slog of the everyday can easily weigh us down, and our hope for a better future can eventually erode. Engrossed in the hustle and bustle of life, however, it is difficult to notice that we have been sapped of this hope—that is, until we sit in silence. Then we feel our restlessness acutely. Augustine, in other words, helps us see that, without a strong sense of the transcendent meaning of time, daily life stands in danger of becoming a distraction against itself. Diving headlong into the errands of life, we now see, is part of this escape because it draws our attention away from ourselves and our state. The other means of escape is entertainment. Since we cannot fill our whole lives with attention-occupying activities, and, in reality, we would not want to, for they are tiring, monotonous and tedious, we must find some form of escape that involves rest.

Yet, plunged into alienated time, we have a hard time distinguishing between true rest and parodic rest. Because true rest requires more of us—it requires that we be present to ourselves and allow God to do the slow, purgative work of reorienting us to that which alone can satisfy—the sort of rest that comes with screen time is an attractive alternative. Just as Augustine laments his perpetual tendency to find comfort in the easy pleasures of life, we, today, seek comfort in the easy pleasures of our screens: they provide an escape wherein no activity is required of us. We simply consume. Yet, just as with the pleasures of Augustine's own day, we often emerge from screen time without having found what we were truly looking for—and this is truer the longer we spend in it. Alienated time, with all its pressures and disappointments, primes us to seek an escape, but prevents us from knowing what we can truly rest in.

Just as Augustine's ancient interlocutors suffered from a failure of imagination, substituting a "really long time" for true eternity, we today have created virtual eternities with the same defect. Theoretically, we could scroll down our Facebook newsfeed forever. CNN similarly never shuts off, and Netflix famously proceeds to the next episode automatically. These are worlds where the normal rules of time are suspended, and no one is prodding us to get to the next task. Screen time is atemporal; in it, the *distentio* that Augustine so laments is little felt. We are, for one prolonged moment, engrossed, but through anesthetization—we consume but are not nourished, remembering little of the time lost to our screens. Checking out, we escape time, but do not find the solace of eternity.

Ultimately, Augustine explains to us, this is because the good things of this world cannot be rested in, even if they can be delighted in. That is to say, screens are not evil, but insofar as we flee into them *instead of* reaching out to God, we use them as a tragic substitute for the deepest longings of our being. Temporal life is, on its own terms, dissatisfying—even as it can be filled with great joy. Indeed, it may well be that dissatisfaction is simply the human response to time's failure to already be eternity—our true home. Separating the world's incompleteness from its sin and pain, we can imagine how our first parents' need to wait for knowledge of good and evil could have been be transfigured into a kind of holy longing for the Day of Consummation. Such wild speculations aside, it is at least clear that, for Augustine, this holy longing is what constitutes the pilgrim life. Constantly returning to the stance of *extentio,* of reaching out to God, the pilgrim endures the wait of time whilst longing for eternity as something distinctively better. Although eternal rest remains an object of future hope, it is a hope that nourishes in the present. It is, in this way then, that we can speak about the redemption of time through *sacramental* rest.

In the title of this chapter, I have presented sacramental time as an antidote to the urge to escape into the never-ending newsfeed. This is not to suggest that we can overcome the experience of *distentio*—and thus, to escape the desire to escape—through *extentio*. Instead, as Augustine's own confessions attest, *distentio* and the pull of created things are irrevocably part of our life in time. Nevertheless, I do think that we can be lifted out of *alienated* time through *extentio,* so that daily life becomes more and more imbued with eternity—not as something far off, but as something that holds creation in being. Here, then, we come to the question of how we can sit still, given the constant and competing demands on our attention.

In my best judgment, Augustine's answer to this question would probably be, "How can we not?" This brings us back to the very paradigm shift we have watched him effect through book 11. If it is true that eternity is not a nebulous realm that we will arrive at a long way in the future, but the eternal present to which the temporal present always points, then time and eternity are much more intimately connected then we think. Showing us that the present moment is always the touching point of eternity, Augustine gives us a reason to *want* to sit still. God, he shows us, continually comes to meet us in the present, visiting us with His light and His truth. In reflecting on his own life, Augustine sees that God has not only already begun the process of gathering his life back together by giving it a purpose and a goal, He has also given Augustine the desire to contemplate—the desire to sit still and be with Him. In these moments of communion, Augustine builds up his storehouse with fodder for recollection, so that he can go back out into the world and see God's fingerprints in it.

To illustrate this, I would like to end by turning briefly to the journals of Russian Orthodox priest and theologian Alexander Schmemann. Often in his diaries, we see Schmemann lament what he calls the hustle and bustle of everyday life. Yet, we also see him cherishing aspects of everyday life—the winter snow, a beautiful sunrise, time with his grandchildren. It is evident that there is a connection between moments of liturgical prayer and his ability to see these blessings. Significantly, he writes about "liturgy as the filling of time with eternity," and, in one more than one entry, recalls how the light he received there flowed out into the rest of his day, shaping how he saw it. Here, I think, is the most significant passage on this topic. He writes:

> This morning during Matins I had a "jolt of happiness," of fullness of life, and at the same time the thought: I will have to die! But in such a fleeting breath of happiness, time usually "gathers" itself. In an instant, not only are all such breaths of happiness remembered but they are present and alive—that Holy Saturday in Paris when I was a very young man—and many such "breaks." It seems to me that eternity might not be the stopping of time, but precisely its resurrection and gathering. The fragmentation of time, its division, is the fall of eternity . . . The thirst for solitude, peace, freedom, is thirst for the liberation of time from cumbersome dead bodies, from hustle; thirst for the transformation of time into what it should be—the receptacle, the chalice of eternity. Liturgy is the conversion of time, its filling with eternity. There are two irreconcilable types of spirituality: one that strives to liberate man from time (Buddhism, Hinduism, Nirvana, etc.); the other that strives to liberate time. In genuine eternity all is alive. The limit and the fulness: the whole of time, the whole of life is in each moment.[17]

17. Alexander Schmemann, *The Journals of Father Alexander Schmemann, 1973–1983*, trans. and ed. Juliana Schmemann (Crestwood, NY: St. Vladimir Seminary Press, 2000), 78.

In this passage, we see what Augustine's reframing of time in light of eternity really means: it is the ability to see time sacramentally—as something that points to eternity. We can still lament what temporal life is not, to be sure, but we must also let God show us the degree to which it is already filled with eternity—the degree to which the world is imbued with His presence. Coming to see time sacramentally, we learn to long for time's liberation, rather than striving to simply escape it through our screens.

In conclusion, Augustine's meditations on time in book 11 are designed to enliven our desire to sit still, showing us that when we do so, either during liturgy or contemplative prayer, our knowledge and love of God grows so that we begin to see how the things around us point to Him.[18] In this way, our temporal life is liberated from alienation because we can see God's presence in it, even as we await its final liberation from *distentio* in eternity. In the meantime, it is for us to recollect the importance of sitting still, and so be liberated from the desire to escape time—or, at least, to long for that liberation, with arms raised in a gesture of *extentio*.

18. Though Augustine does not discuss the liturgy in book 11 of *The Confessions*, it is clear that he, too, thinks of it as an access-point to eternity. Consider, for example, the passage in *City of God* 10.6 (Augustine, *City of God*, trans. Henry Bettenson [London: Penguin Books, 1972], 380), where he describes the Mass:

The whole redeemed community, that is to say, the congregation and fellowship of the saints, is offered to God as a universal sacrifice, through the great Priest who offered himself in his suffering for us—so that we might be the body of so great a head. . . . This is the sacrifice which the Church continually celebrates in the sacrament of the altar, a sacrament well-known to the faithful where it shown to the Church that she herself is offered in the offering which she presents to God.

Augustinian Contemplation and Centering Prayer

Margaret Blume Freddoso

In his *Retractions*, Augustine provides a structural division of the thirteen books of the *Confessions*: the first ten are about himself and the last three are about sacred Scripture, from the words, "In the Beginning God made heaven and earth" (Gen 1:1) up to the Sabbath rest.[1] Although this division is helpful, it can also obscure the essential unity of Augustine's work. The whole of the *Confessions* is Scriptural exegesis, I would contend, and in the first ten books, Augustine is using his life to interpret Scripture, and allowing Scripture to illuminate his life. In the last three books, Augustine reflects more systematically on the first lines of Genesis in order to understand what is universal about his own experience.[2] As John Peter Kenney puts it, "even the more theologically ramified aspects of the [*Confessions*], for example the account of the *caelum caeli* from book 12, are rooted in Augustine's account of his spiritual life and emerge from reflection on that experience in light of the Scriptures."[3]

---

1. Cf. Genesis 2:2. Augustine, *The Retractions* 2.32.1, trans. Mary Inez Bogan (Washington, DC: Catholic University of America Press, 1968), 130. Maria Boulding's translation of Augustine's citations of Scripture in *Confessions* will be used throughout this chapter.

2. According to Roland Teske, the last four books of the *Confessions* are unified by "an extensive use of Neoplatonic philosophy as a means for coming to understand what the Christian faith teaches about the origin, present state, and destiny" of human beings; see Roland Teske, "The Heaven of Heaven and the Unity of St. Augustine's *Confessions*," *American Catholic Philosophical Quarterly* 74, no. 1 (2000): 44.

3. John Peter Kenney, *The Mysticism of Saint Augustine: Rereading the* Confessions (New York: Routledge, 2005), 139.

Indeed, in book 12, Augustine gives a metaphysical account of the created universe that invisibly undergirds his preceding narrative of confession, conversion, and contemplation. Central to this account are two orders of created being: formless matter and heaven's heaven. In the first part of this essay, I will develop Augustine's ontological understanding of contemplation. His description in book 9 of his experience with Monica at Ostia embodies the metaphysical principles set forth in book 12. Contemplation is not some state of absorption into the divine, but rather a soul's anticipatory participation in the realm of the blessed, who freely and perpetually gaze upon eternal Wisdom, sharing in God's eternity. They are joined to God perfectly, but they remain distinct as human creatures.

In the second part of this essay, I will show that on Augustine's account, given not only in book 12 but throughout the *Confessions*, contemplation cannot be achieved by intellectual or psychological techniques. The way to contemplation is the way of a penitent pilgrim who continually confesses his sin, his misery, and his longing to return home, as well as his faith, love, and trust in the Savior who will bring him there. It is a human way of daily incorporation into Christ's Body through the sacraments and meditation upon Scripture in communion with the Church, which bears fruit in works of charity. As Augustine and Monica's vision at Ostia demonstrates, temporal contemplation is a transcendent encounter between God and an ecclesial soul, bestowed by God as the flowering of a holy life, and a fleeting promise of what is to come. Moments such as Ostia are privileged in their likeness to heaven's heaven, but by God's grace, the whole pilgrimage is a preparation and growing participation in the soul's promised and perfect worship of her Creator and Redeemer.

In the final part of this essay, I shall examine the relationship between Augustinian contemplation and the popular contemporary practice of Centering Prayer. Although Centering Prayer is presented as traditional Christian contemplation transposed into a modern key, the practice itself is quite different from the practices that constitute the way to heaven's heaven, according to Augustine. Indeed, in practice, Centering Prayer is most closely linked to Transcendental Meditation, which has its roots in a metaphysics directly contrary to that which Augustine sets forth in book 12. From Augustine's perspective, I will propose, Centering Prayer should not be identified as prayer.

1. The Metaphysics of Contemplation

In book 12 of the *Confessions*, Augustine continues the exegesis of Genesis 1:1 ("In the Beginning, God made heaven and earth") that he began in book 11, focusing on the words "heaven and earth." For Augustine, to read Scripture literally does not mean to discover the intention of the author but rather to take the words precisely as they sound without appealing to ordinary figures of speech, even punctuation.[4] Since Genesis 1:6 speaks of God creating a vault that separates the waters below from the waters above, the heaven that God creates "in the Beginning" does not signify the corporeal heaven, but rather the "heaven's heaven" referred to in the Psalms: "The heaven's heaven is for the Lord; but he has assigned the earth to humankind" (Ps 115:16). The heaven and earth of Genesis 1 are made before any mention of days, and before the creation of the corporeal world. Both "heaven" and "earth," Augustine concludes, signify realities that are neither visible nor subject to time. However, they are not coeternal with God, but rather the first creatures that he makes.

According to Eugene TeSelle, book 12 of the *Confessions* presents one of the fullest expositions of Augustine's metaphysics, which the author begins to systematically work out during his first years as the Bishop of Hippo. In TeSelle's estimation, "the most important insight, and one which came only in this period, is that the same set of concepts can be applied to material and immaterial being."[5] Augustine first articulates this doctrine in his unfinished commentary on Genesis.[6] He draws upon Plotinus, who takes up Aristotle's correlation of matter and form with potency and act, and applies this essential distinction to the spiritual as well as the material realm. Even when, in the case of the divine hypostases, the mind's capacity to know is ceaselessly actualized, the material principle of potentiality and contingency remains present. The mind is constantly dependent upon the object of knowledge and must cling to it.[7] The principles of potency and act are found in both spiritual and corporeal creation.

In Genesis 1:1, Augustine finds signified both the highest and lowest created realities. Although heaven signifies that to which God alone is superior, and earth signifies that than which nothing is lower, Augustine underscores that both are made not from God's substance but from nothing, and both are good because they spring from God's omnipotence and goodness (12.7.7). The essential metaphysical distinctions are between God, his creation, and

---

4. See Augustine, *On Genesis: Two Books on Genesis Against the Manichees* 2.2.3, trans. Roland Teske, (Washington, D.C.: Catholic University of America Press, 1991), 95.

5. Eugene TeSelle, *Augustine the Theologian* (Oregon: Wipf and Stock Publishers, 1970), 137.

6. See Augustine, *On Genesis: Unfinished Literary Commentary on Genesis* 8.29, trans. Edmund Hill, WOSA vol. I/13 (New York: New City Press, 2002).

7. See TeSelle, *Augustine the Theologian*, 137.

nothingness, which does not signify something that exists, but rather that from which God is totally absent. All of reality apart from God is created by him and discloses him, but it must turn toward God and cling to him, or it will fall toward the nothingness out of which it was created.

For Augustine, the heaven of Genesis 1 points to the created reality which, through its perfect clinging to God, is most fully actualized. It signifies "the mind of all the citizens of [God's] holy city in that heaven above the heavens we see" (12.11.12). It is not the Wisdom who is the Son, but a created wisdom, "the intellectual order of being which by contemplating the Light becomes light itself" (12.15.20). In itself it would be dark and cold, but because it looks upon God's face always, clinging to him with immense love, it "shines with his light like noonday never dimmed, and burns with his fire" (12.15.21). This "pure mind," Augustine writes, "builds up your family of holy, spiritual beings, united in perfect concord on the foundation of peace" (12.11.12).

Heaven's heaven is the order of creation closest to God; God alone is superior to it (12.7.7). It is the most formal or actualized of creatures. Earth, by contrast, signifies that which is most remote from God, bordering on nothingness. Genesis 1:2 adds that "darkness loured over the abyss, and the earth was invisible and unorganized." Reflecting on these words, Augustine posits that earth signifies the matter that underlies all forms, but itself is utterly formless (12.8.8). It was made from nothing at all, and it is almost nothing at all. Unlike heaven's heaven it is an abstraction, for it never exists without some form. It refers to the "mutability of mutable things which gives them their potential to receive all those forms into which mutable things can be changed" (12.6.6). Formless matter is a "nothing-something," an absolute privation of all form, which nevertheless has some kind of being, namely, the capacity to receive the visible and organized forms that constitute every creature. It provides the principle of potency in every created thing. Like heaven's heaven, formless matter is unimaginable, and not subject to time. With his conception of formless matter, Augustine metaphysically affirms that everything created is good, even that which is closest to nothing.

In his creative exegesis of heaven's heaven, Augustine is perhaps influenced by Origen's suggestion in his first homily on Genesis that the heavens in verse 1 designate the angels.[8] Although his account is rooted in Scripture and the Christian faith, he is certainly indebted to Plotinus' *Enneads*. As Hilary Armstrong writes,

---

8. Berthold Altaner, "Augustinus und Origenes. Eine Quellenkritische Untersuchung," *Historisches Jahrbuch* 70 (1951): 23–25.

Who except a Christian steeped in the thought of Plotinus would pass so naturally, in a single sentence, from speaking of the *spiritalis creatura*, the company of angels, as *coelum* and *domus dei* to speaking of it as *mens*; and where else except in Plotinus can we find the conception of a Mind transcending the material world which is both one and many, a community of minds or spirits formed by and united in a single contemplation?[9]

Because of their profound unity, the heavenly citizens' contemplation of God is described as a single creature. It is the highest order of created being, not subject to change and so not subject to time, participating in God's eternity.

Although Augustine borrows a great deal from the Neoplatonists, his account of contemplation differs profoundly from theirs. In Plotinus, John Peter Kenney explains, the One's transcendence of the finite universe is understood according to its ineffability.[10] The One constitutes a separate and infinite mode of reality, although it emanates into existence the multiplicity of the finite world. The One is thus omnipresent within the finite world, but it cannot be described in finite terms. Moreover, although the One is always present to the soul through the very fact of its existence, it cannot enter into any direct relations with the soul, and it cannot be said to love the soul (or to not love the soul). "The One," Kenney writes, "is therefore a mysterious power at the root of reality, but barely within the frame of human reference. All the more reason for it to be accessible only by an interior journey in which the self strips off finitude and seeks the presence of the One through *theoria*."[11] For Plotinus, contemplation is the fruit of a soul's efforts to ascend from the material world through progressive intellectual levels of predicative removal, until it is united to the One beyond all description.

For Augustine, by contrast, God's omnipresence entails the personal, loving activity of the Creator of all things, holding each in being and redeeming humankind. "O Truth," Augustine prays, "illumination of my heart, let not my own darkness speak to me! . . . Let me not be my own life: evil was the life I lived of myself; I was death to me; but in you I begin to live again" (12.10.10). The soul cannot ascend to God's transcendence by an intellective dialectic of negation and abstraction from created things, and a flight from finitude. Rather, the infinite God must lovingly condescend to his creature, lifting her up through created things to gaze upon God's glorious Truth.

---

9. Hilary A. Armstrong, "Spiritual or Intelligible Matter in Plotinus and St. Augustine," *Augustinus Magister* I (Paris: Etudes Augustiniennes, 1954), 280.

10. Kenney, *The Mysticism of St. Augustine*, 124.

11. Kenney, *The Mysticism of St. Augustine*, 127.

Thus, Kenney observes, "Both unmediated presence and direct association are thus part of the eschatological state of the soul. But neither complete union nor absorption into eternal Wisdom are indicated, only contact with divine Wisdom."[12] The separation between uncreated Wisdom and the soul is breached by God's initiative to grant contact between the Creator and his creature, but it is never destroyed.

Furthermore, Augustine, unlike Plotinus, is deeply aware of created freedom. Although human beings live truly only by turning to their Creator, heaven's heaven is not a necessary state of universal return to the One. Rather, Augustine confesses to God, "drinking deeply from you in unswerving fidelity," heaven's heaven is "bound fast by the whole strength of its love to you, who are always present to it" (12.11.12). It is the household of the Lord, "which contemplates [his] entrancing beauty, never tiring, never turning aside to any other joy" (12.11.12). Heaven's citizens never waver in their gaze, but their attention is given to God in perfect freedom. In their willed beholding, they attain to the full measure of integrity and formedness, but this is not inevitable. They would have fallen away into formlessness, if they had not chosen to attend to God.

2. The Temporal Way of Contemplation

The metaphysics that Augustine offers in book 12, moreover, is not simply an account of the principles of act and potency that constitute each created thing, distinguishing it from God and from nothingness. Through his understanding of the heaven and earth that lie outside of temporal succession, Augustine also provides a dynamic vision of creation as the temporal development of each creature from formless matter toward the formedness of heaven's heaven. He explains it thus:

> From this formlessness were to be made another heaven and the visible, organized earth, and the beauty of fully formed water, and whatever else would thereafter constitute our world. In the making of this world a succession of days is mentioned, because the nature of these things is such that temporal succession is needed in their case to bring about ordered modifications of motion or form. (12.12.15)

Augustine is presenting the temporal life of each creature as its gradual, ordered process of formation.

Furthermore, Augustine draws from the Neoplatonic scheme of *exitus* and

---

12. Kenney, *The Mysticism of St. Augustine*, 116.

reditus to set forth a Christian doctrine of creation *ex nihilo*, grounded in Genesis, which recognizes that the creation of things is completed as they turn toward the One who made them, each according to its nature. As Augustine writes:

> You made them all, not from your own substance, in that Image of yourself that gives form to all things, but out of nothing, as formless matter quite unlike yourself, which was yet destined to be formed through your image by returning to you, the One, in proportion to the capacity of each, as imparted to it according to its kind. Thus they would become exceedingly good, whether they remained closely grouped about you or, arrayed in ever-widening circles through time and space, they bring about changes or themselves beautifully evolve. (12.28.38)

The cosmos is not made from God's substance, because then it would be coeternal and equal to God. God creates formless matter, which comes from nothing and is almost nothing, but nevertheless is good because it springs from God's omnipotence and goodness. But he also forms this into the wondrous multiplicity of created things, from the least inanimate thing all the way to the sublime heaven's heaven, and he allows creatures to participate in this formation through their *reditus* to their Creator, the One, which unifies them and gives them their fullest identity. Every creature is always constituted by a principle of form and a principle of formlessness, but it becomes more and more formed and integrated as it moves toward God, and away from nothingness.

Sin, however, is always a fall toward nothingness and a movement toward formlessness. Fallen human beings are dramatically poised between heaven's heaven and the abyss, tending toward disintegration because of the sin of their first parents, but also desiring, at the deepest level, to enter into the heavenly citizens' blessed contemplation of God. Augustine concludes his account of heaven's heaven with a beautiful prayer to be raised by God into its glorious formedness:

> Let me not waver from my course before you have gathered all that I am, my whole disintegrated and deformed self, into that dearly-loved mother's peace, where are lodged the first-fruits of my spirit, and whence I draw my present certainty, so that you may reshape me to new form, new firmness, for eternity, O my God, my mercy. (12.16.23)

For Augustine, the "pure mind" of the citizens of God's holy city is also "Jerusalem my homeland, Jerusalem my mother" (12.16.23). It is the metaphysical realm to which temporal human beings are ultimately called. Heaven's heaven is "God's house, neither terrestrial nor some massive celestial building, but a spiritual structure which shares your eternity, and is unstained forever"

(12.15.19). Every human being seeks, consciously or unconsciously, to enter this realm and find both the vision of God, and her ontological perfection. By unswervingly contemplating their glorious Creator, the saints attain the full measure of their capacity for being. The Jerusalem for which the faithful long is their entrance into this realm of perfect actuality and integrity, the fruit of their unceasing beholding of God in love.

In his account of the vision at Ostia in book 9, Augustine depicts his and Monica's contemplative experience as an ascent through "all bodily creatures and heaven itself," even through "the summit of [their] own minds," until they "touch that land of never-failing plenty where [God] pasture[s] Israel for ever with the food of truth" (9.10.24). Then he describes this region in language that clearly corresponds to his account of heaven's heaven:

> Life there is the Wisdom through whom all these things are made, and all others that have ever been or ever will be; but Wisdom herself is not made: she is as she always has been and will be forever. Rather should we say that in her there is no "has been" or "will be," but only being, for she is eternal, but past and future do not belong to eternity. And as we talked and panted for it, we just touched the edge of it by the utmost leap of our hearts: then, sighing and unsatisfied, we left the first-fruits of our spirit captive there, and returned to the noise of articulate speech, where a word has a beginning and an end. (9.10.24)

As Kenney notes, Augustine explicitly connects Ostia's vision to heaven's heaven through his reference to the firstfruits of the spirit from Rom 8:23. In book 12, Augustine gives a metaphysical interpretation of the experience at Ostia. Monica and Augustine are, for a moment, lifted through the temporal world to its ultimate fulfillment: a higher, unchanging, perfectly actualized order of reality. This is the realm of the saints' eternal, unmediated, loving contemplation of God. In their temporal contemplation at Ostia, Monica and Augustine receive an anticipatory participation in this heavenly activity by God's grace. As Kenney writes, "Monica's soul can thus be seen to participate in the inner life of this region, this transcendent and heavenly hypostasis. Her soul has . . . no native place in the transcendent, so it can only mark its place of hope."[13]

In his second description of the vision at Ostia, Augustine illustrates more precisely the ontology of contemplation:

> If . . . then he alone were to speak, not through things that are made, but of himself, that we might hear his Word, not through fleshly tongue nor angel's

13. Kenney, *The Mysticism of St. Augustine*, 116.

voice, nor thundercloud, nor any riddling parable, hear him unmediated, whom we love in all these things, hear him without them, as now we stretch out and in a flash of thought touch that eternal Wisdom who abides above all things; if this could last, and all other visions, so far inferior, be taken away, and this sight alone could ravish him who saw it, and engulf him and hide him away, kept for inward joys, so that this moment of knowledge—this passing moment that left us aching for more—should there be life eternal, would not *Enter into the joy of your Lord* be this, and this alone? And when, when will this be? When we all rise again, but not all are changed? (9.10.25)

Contemplation in this life is a brief taste of the blessed contemplative destiny to which human beings are called. The vision at Ostia reveals to Monica and Augustine the glory of this destiny, and it leaves them with ardent hope. Participation in the "pure mind" of heaven's heaven is an unmediated "moment of knowledge." In that moment, the finite, sinful soul crosses the gap separating her from her Creator by God's grace and makes contact with him by lovingly beholding him in communion with others. Heaven's contemplation is this moment of knowledge made eternal at the final resurrection.

By explicitly connecting the vision at Ostia to his account of heaven's heaven, Augustine shows the likeness between the contemplation of the pilgrim and the saint. As Kenney writes, "throughout his long career, Augustine held that momentary contemplation of God is possible for the soul through divine grace."[14] He and Monica were given this at Ostia, and Augustine found Christianity's metaphysical account of the universe to confirm and elucidate his experience. Moreover, as the *Confessions* as a whole demonstrates, God is always present to the human soul, bestowing various degrees of spiritual contact with himself through his grace. Even before the vision at Ostia, the first-fruits of Augustine's spirit are lodged in heaven's heaven by his Baptism. Augustine and Monica's experience at Ostia represents a form of temporal contemplation that is most similar to a person's eschatological destiny, but Augustine understands that a person's whole life in grace is a way of growth in contemplation. The entire way of return is illuminated by its goal: the perfection of contemplation in heaven's heaven.

Just as the saint's spiritual contact with her Creator and Redeemer is totally the gift of the infinitely merciful God to a finite, sinful creature, so too, the temporal way of contemplation is a way of confession and conversion. Contemplation begins as a soul's confession of her misery and poverty, her desire for God, and her trust in God's infinite mercy. As he describes heaven's heaven in

---

14. Kenney, *The Mysticism of St. Augustine*, 130.

book 12, Augustine gives beautiful witness to the central role of confession in a person's spiritual contact with God. Even after Ostia, confession remains the indispensable origin of contemplation. The soul who has glimpsed the glory of the Lord is on fire with desire, humility, and trust:

> O lightsome house, so fair of form, I have fallen in love with your beauty, loved you as the place where dwells the glory of my Lord, who fashioned you and claims you as his own. My pilgrim-soul sighs for you, and I pray him who made you to claim me also as his own within you, for he made me too. Like a lost sheep I have gone astray, but on the shoulders of my shepherd, your builder, I hope to be carried back to you. (12.15.21)

Through confessions such as this one, Augustine turns toward God and away from the abyss, and gradually receives the holy integration of the saints. As he advances on the way of contemplation, his scattered self is gathered, little by little, into a single longing for God, awareness of his weakness, and trust in God's mercy. His heart and attention are more and more concentrated on his Creator and Redeemer, and thus brought into unity.

Confession and conversion, moreover, are focused on Christ. Christ is the Shepherd on whose shoulders Augustine hopes to be carried back to his heavenly homeland. It is in the Incarnation that the transcendent God condescends to his creatures, overcoming the gap created by finitude and sin, and reconciling man to himself. The entire *reditus*, therefore, is Christoform. Throughout the *Confessions,* Augustine insists that there is no way to the goal apart from sacramental participation in Christ's saving work. Augustine illuminates this when he describes Monica's life in Book 9:

> She desired only to be remembered at your altar, where she had served you with never a day's absence. From that altar, as she knew, the holy Victim is made available to us, he through whom the record of debt that stood against us was annulled. He has triumphed over an enemy who does keep a tally of our faults and looks for anything to lay to our charge, but finds no case against him. In him we win our victory. Who will reimburse him for that innocent blood? Who will pay back to him the price he paid to purchase us, as though to snatch us back from him? To the sacrament of that ransom-price your handmaid made fast her soul with the bonds of faith. Let no one wrench her away from your protection. (9.13.36)

The way of contemplation is founded upon a person's sacramental incorporation into Christ's body. Through her practiced faith in the sacraments, especially the Eucharist, a person confesses her poverty and trust in God's mercy, receives spiritual contact with God, and is joined to her brothers and sisters in the Church by works of charity. Augustine eloquently makes this explicit at the end of book 10:

Filled with terror by my sins and my load of misery, I had been turning over in my mind a plan to flee into solitude, but you forbade me, and strengthened me by your words. To this end Christ died for all, you reminded me, that they who are alive may live not for themselves, but for him who died for them. See, then, Lord: I cast my care upon you that I may live, and I will contemplate the wonders you have revealed. You know how stupid and weak I am: teach me and heal me. Your only Son, in whom are hidden all treasures of wisdom and knowledge, has redeemed me with his blood. Let not the proud disparage me, for I am mindful of my ransom. I eat it, I drink it, I dispense it to others, and as a poor man I long to be filled with it among those who are fed and feasted. And then do those who seek him praise the Lord. (10.43.70)

In offering the Eucharistic sacrifice and receiving Christ's body and blood, Augustine is ever mindful both of his wretchedness, and the ransom by which he has been saved. As he is fed, he feeds others, and his longing for Christ grows. In the Eucharist, Augustine's seeking bears fruit in charity and worship. This is the way of contemplation set forth in the *Confessions,* and it is an imperfect, temporal participation in the eternal worship of heaven's citizens.

Human beings are lifted to heavenly contemplation not only by faith in the Church's sacraments, but also by faith in Scripture. In book 7, Augustine explains that the Scriptures contain all the wisdom that he originally found in the Platonists. Moreover, unlike the Platonic books they also contain God's grace, so that all those who learn from the Scriptures recognize their ignorance, and utter dependence on the wisdom of Christ. The difference, Augustine explains, is "between presumption and confession, between those who see the goal but not the way to it, and the Way to our beatific homeland, a homeland to be not merely descried but lived in" (7.20.26). The fruit of sustained meditation upon Scripture is not only illumination, but also humility and charity, so that the wisdom attained is life as well as light. By reading Scripture, Christians are healed of their pride and shame, so that they can be brought into spiritual contact with the divine Trinity. As Augustine describes vividly:

It is one thing to survey our peaceful homeland from a wooded height but fail to find the way there, and make vain attempts to travel through impassable terrain, while fugitive deserters marshaled by the lion and the dragon obstruct and lurk in ambush; and quite another to walk steadily in the way that leads there, along the well-built road opened up by the heavenly emperor, where no deserters from the celestial army dare commit robbery, for they avoid that way like torment. (7.21.27)

The sinful, finite human being might be able to dimly see the shape of the eternal destiny for which he longs, but it is impossible for him to reach this on his own. If he tries, he will quickly fall prey to evil spirits, and fall back toward the abyss of formlessness. The only way to the goal is to imitate the humility of Christ and be carried to heaven's heaven on the shoulders of the Shepherd.

Moreover, by incorporating human beings into the humanity of Christ through their faith in Scripture and the sacraments, God raises them to contemplate his transcendent divine being without doing violence to their humanity. As Augustine brilliantly demonstrates in book 12, faith in Scripture necessarily includes the use of human reason. "The words of Scripture knock at the door of my heart," Augustine writes at the beginning of the book, "and in this poverty-stricken life of mine my heart is busy about many things concerning them" (12.1.1). Augustine's use of Neoplatonist ideas in book 12 shows that human philosophy and learning can help the faithful to perceive what God has revealed. Contemplation begins as an interior conversation with God that is rooted in God's words to the soul through Scripture, and proceeds by a search for understanding.

In the second part of book 12, Augustine engages in an extensive discussion of the practice of Scriptural exegesis, defending his interpretation of Genesis against certain opponents who think it too speculative. In addition, he illuminates that meditation upon Scripture must be practiced in communion with the Church, if it is to advance a person along the way of contemplation. Because of the infinite glory of Truth himself, Augustine explains, and the penury of human understanding, "a great variety of interpretations, many of them legitimate, confronts [human] exploring minds" as they search among the words of Scripture to discover God's will (12.24.33). Augustine compares the words of the Bible to "a spring welling up in quite a small space, yet by means of its branching streams it is a source of richer fertility, and waters wide tracts of countryside" (12.27.37). Scripture invites many interpretations and modes of exegesis, so that truths confessed by each member of the body of Christ may build up to better manifest the Truth himself. The Lord invites his people to "feed on [his] truth in the wide pastures of charity," and to delight in this together (12.23.32). Through the manifold confessions of the faithful over the course of the Church's history, each human being is prepared to enter into the communal contemplation of the citizens of heaven, united by the One upon whom they gaze in love.

In the autobiographical books of the *Confessions,* book 12's universal account of the *reditus* to God through Christ is incarnated in Augustine's life. Like every human being, Augustine is dramatically poised between heaven's heaven and the abyss, and his individual choices either move him towards integrity and happiness, or toward formlessness and misery. In book 3, Augustine marks his reading of Cicero's *Hortensius* as a turning point in his life. Through reading Cicero's book, Augustine becomes enflamed by a desire for wisdom, and writes that "he began to rise up, in order to return to [God]" (book 3.4.7).

This desire for an abstract wisdom, however, is not enough. Augustine turns his attention to the Scriptures, but his "swollen pride recoiled from its style and [his] intelligence failed to penetrate to its inner meaning" (3.5.9). He falls prey to the lies of the Manicheans and cannot conceive of an immaterial reality. "Throughout those nine years," Augustine writes, "from my nineteenth to twenty-eighth year, I and others like me were seduced and seducers, deceived ourselves and deceivers of others, among a welter of desires: publicly through the arts reputed "liberal," and secretly under the false name of religion" (4.1.1). In this time, Augustine is estranged from himself, especially the death of his unnamed friend dies in Thagaste plunges him into misery. "I remained to myself an unhappy place where I could not live," he confesses (4.7.12), "but from which I could not escape. Whither could my heart flee to escape itself? Where could I go and leave myself behind? Was there any place of refuge where I would not be followed by my own self?"

Frederick Crossan suggests that the overall movement in books 2, 3, and 4 is Augustine's descent towards alienation from God, other human beings, and himself, whereas books 6, 7, and 8 mark successive stages of his ascent to God and the community of the heavenly Jerusalem.[15] The turning point comes when Augustine encounters Faustus in book 5 and begins to recognize the errors of Manicheanism. "Thus it came about that this Faustus, who was a death-trap for many, unwittingly and without intending it began to spring the trap in which I was caught, for thanks to your hidden providence, O God, your hands did not let go of my soul" (5.7.13). In book 6, which begins with the image of the widow's son raised from death, Augustine becomes more and more dissatisfied with his professional success, and he is drawn toward Epicureanism, which scorns worldly ambitions. In book 7, he reads the books of the Platonists, and comes to see that God is incorporeal, and that evil is not a substance, as Mani had taught. At the end of book 7, he discovers the writings of St. Paul, and finds

---

15. Frederick Crossan, "Structure and Meaning in Augustine's *Confessions,*" Proceedings of the American Catholic Philosophical Association 63 (1989): 84–97.

the truths he has already recognized together with the truth of his own misery, and God's wondrous gift of grace.

Book 8, which is the only book to begin with the word "Deus," opens with a song of thanksgiving to God for implanting his words firmly in Augustine's heart. What Augustine now longs for is not greater certainty about the Truth, but a more steadfast abiding in Truth. "I was attracted to the Way," he writes, "which is our Savior himself, but the narrowness of the path daunted me, and I still could not walk in it" (8.1.1). He is finally liberated from the weight of his sinful habits by hearing the word of God addressing him in Alypius' garden, telling him to "put on the Lord Jesus Christ," instead of losing himself in "dissipation and drunkenness, debauchery and lewdness, arguing and jealousy" (8.12.29; Rom 13:13–14).

In book 9, Augustine addresses Christ directly for the first time since book 1. He reads the Psalms and is baptized, and in Ostia he is given, with Monica, a brief participation in the contemplation of heaven's heaven. Shortly after, Monica dies. Augustine is 33, and the radical difference between Augustine's grief over his mother's death, and his misery when his unnamed friend dies at the end of book 4, illuminates how far Augustine has advanced along the way of contemplation. He is sorrowful, but he and his friends sing psalms, and "with this salve of truth [he] soothed the agony that was known only to God" (9.12.30). He does not repress his sadness, "even if he is guilty of some carnal affection," but finds comfort in weeping before God "about his mother and for her, about himself and for himself." When his heart is healed of this wound, he pours out tears of penitence and holy fear, begging the Lord to forgive his mother for her sins and asking prayers from all whom he aims to serve through his confessions (9.13.34). In book 4, grief reveals the instability of his identity; in book 9, grief manifests his true integrity in depending totally on Christ.

In book 10, Augustine writes that he will confess to God and to his neighbors not what he has been, but what he still is. He then immediately embarks on a quest to see God, for God has pierced Augustine's heart with his word, and Augustine has fallen in love with him.[16] Augustine also confesses that he still struggles with concupiscence of the flesh, concupiscence of the eyes, and worldly pride. He has seen Truth's blazing splendor, but fallen back because of his disordered loves, and so he remains an enigma to himself" (10.33.50). God continues to lead Augustine to contemplation through an ecclesial life, teaching that wisdom is found not by fleeing into solitude, but by accepting his poverty and living for Christ who died for him, as Paul teaches (10.43.70).

---

16. See *conf.* 10.6.8.

By reflecting upon Scripture, his own experience, and the metaphysics of creation, Augustine perceives that human beings are always tempted to fall back toward formlessness until their gaze is unfailingly fixed on God in the eternal contemplation of heaven's heaven. And yet, God in his loving mercy is always present to the soul, revealing her misery, recalling her to himself, and leading her toward the luminous integrity and communion for which she has been created. The way to heaven's heaven is confession, conversion, sacramental incorporation into Christ's body, and meditation upon Scripture in communion with the Church. Graced conformation to Christ lodges the firstfruits of a person's spirit in her eternal destiny, and infallibly produces love for her neighbor. Through the Incarnation, the way is an increasingly closer participation in the end: the soul's unfailing adherence to her Creator and Redeemer, gazing upon his face and sharing in his eternity without losing her humanity, united with all of heaven's citizens in her love for the divine Trinity.

3. Centering Prayer and The Augustinian Way of Contemplation

Many Christians in contemporary society identify contemplation with a practice called centering prayer. This practice was developed in the 1960s and '70s by three Trappist monks at St. Joseph's Abbey in Spencer, Massachusetts: William Meninger, Basil Pennington, and Thomas Keating. According to Keating, "this was during the time of the first wave of the renewal of religious life after the Second Vatican Council, when many questions were raised for the first time and interreligious dialogue was encouraged by the Holy See."[17]

Meninger, Pennington, and Keating invited several local teachers from the Eastern religions to instruct the monastery in their spiritual practices. One of these teachers introduced the monks to Transcendental Meditation, a practice that has its roots in ancient Hinduism.[18] The example and message of these spiritual teachers raised questions among the Trappist monks. As Keating writes, "why were the young disciples of Eastern gurus, Zen roshis, and teachers of Transcendental Meditation, who were coming to the abbey in the 1970s for dialogue, experiencing significant spiritual experiences without having gone through the penitential exercises that the Trappist order required?"[19]

Meninger, Pennington, and Keating therefore decided to use Eastern spiritualities to develop a form of Christian contemplation that would be

17. Thomas Keating, *Intimacy with God* (New York: Crossroad Publishing, 1994), 11.
18. Keating, *Intimacy with God*, 12.
19. Keating, *Intimacy with God*, 13.

attractive to modern Christians. Keating writes that he simply asked the question: "Could we put the Christian tradition into a form that would be accessible to people in the active ministry today and to young people who have been instructed in an Eastern technique and might be inspired to return to their Christian roots if they knew there was something similar in the Christian tradition?"[20] Meninger developed a method called "Prayer of the Cloud," in which a single word such as "God" or "Love" is simply repeated over and over again, expressing a person's "naked intent direct to God."[21] Pennington gave a retreat based on this method to a group of provincials from various religious congregations in Connecticut, and they suggested to use the term "Centering Prayer" to describe the practice, which likely came from Thomas Merton's use of the phrase in his writings.[22]

In the summer of 1982, Keating visited the Lama Foundation in New Mexico, an "ecumenical community of spiritual seekers" that included Catholics and Jews. According to Keating, "many of the Catholics were disaffected from the religion of their youth because of the legalistic and overmoralistic teaching that many had received in their local parishes and Catholic schools; they now felt spiritually enriched by their experiences in Buddhism and Hinduism."[23]

In 1983, Keating returned to Lama and put together a Christian contemplative retreat that included a significant amount of time for Centering Prayer. Later that year, he was invited to form an organization that would teach Centering Prayer in parishes. After a warm response at St. Ignatius Loyola Church in New York City, and the encouragement of the Columbia University chaplain, the Trappist monks met with a number of religious figures from the metropolitan New York area to form an organization called Contemplative Outreach.[24] Their goals were to offer Centering Prayer in parish and diocesan contexts, to train facilitators and teachers, and to develop materials.[25]

Today, Contemplative Outreach supports over 90 contemplative chapters in 39 countries, serving over 40,000 people.[26] According to Contemplative Outreach's website, Centering Prayer is "a receptive method of Christian silent prayer that prepares us to receive the gift of contemplative prayer, or prayer in which we experience God's presence within us, closer than breathing, closer

---

20. Keating, *Intimacy with God*, 15.
21. Keating, *Intimacy with God*, 15.
22. Keating, *Intimacy with God*, 16.
23. Keating, *Intimacy with God*, 17.
24. Keating, *Intimacy with God*, 19.
25. Keating, *Intimacy with God*, 20.
26. Contemplative Outreach, "About Us," at www.contemplativeoutreach.org/about-us-0.

than thinking, closer than consciousness itself."[27] Contemplative Outreach presents Centering Prayer as a practice that is deeply rooted in the Christian tradition of contemplation:

> Centering Prayer is drawn from the ancient practices of the Christian contemplative heritage, notably the traditional monastic practice of Lectio Divina and the practices described in the anonymous fourteenth century classic *The Cloud of Unknowing* and in the writings of Christian mystics such as John Cassian, Francis de Sales, Teresa of Avila, John of the Cross, Therese of Lisieux, and Thomas Merton. Most importantly, Centering Prayer is based on the wisdom saying of Jesus in the Sermon on the Mount: . . . when *you pray, go to your inner room, close the door and pray to your Father in secret. And your Father, who sees in secret, will repay you.* (Matt 6:6 NAB)[28]

Contemplative Outreach also mentions Augustine as a primary figure in the Christian tradition of contemplative prayer, and thus a source for the development of Centering Prayer.[29]

In practice, however, Centering Prayer is almost identical to Transcendental Meditation. This technique was first taught by the Hindu monk Swami Brahmananda Saraswati, who died in 1953, but its roots lie in the tradition of the Vedic Rishis of ancient India.[30] From the late 1950s onward, the practice was promoted internationally by one of Guru Dev's disciples, the Maharishi Mahesh Yogi.[31] Today, Transcendental Meditation is a global movement that has been taught to millions of people.[32] In both Transcendental Meditation and Centering Prayer, a person sits in a comfortable position with eyes closed, and silently repeats a word or a phrase that is used to empty her mind of thoughts, desires, sensations, and feelings. Whenever she becomes aware of a thought or desire, she gently lets it go, using her chosen word to do this. She does this for at least twenty minutes, ideally twice a day.[33] The central difference between

27. Contemplative Outreach, "Centering Prayer," at www.contemplativeoutreach.org /centering-prayer-1.

28. Contemplative Outreach, "History of Centering Prayer," at www.contemplativeout reach.org/history-centering-prayer.

29. Contemplative Outreach, "History of Centering Prayer."

30. John Gordon Melton, "Transcendental Meditation," Encyclopaedia Brittanica Online, at www.britannica.com/topic/Transcendental-Meditation.

31. Melton, "Transcendental Meditation."

32. Melton, "Transcendental Meditation."

33. The Meditation Trust, "Transcendental Meditation Frequently Asked Questions," at www.meditationtrust.com/transcendental-meditation-frequently-asked-questions/; Contemplative Outreach, "Centering Prayer," at www.contemplativeoutreach.org/centering-prayer-1.

the two practices is that in Transcendental Meditation, a person uses a secret mantra, given by a trained teacher, which is a Sanskrit sound that is meaningless and close to the primordial hum (Om).[34] In Centering Prayer, a person uses a sacred word that either has to do with God, or a state of the soul (love, peace, joy, etc).[35]

Contemporary Transcendental Meditation is typically presented as a nonreligious practice that simply aims to bring about a state of altered consciousness in which a person's thoughts are quieted, and she is free from cares and worries, stress and strain. On a popular website aimed at marketing Transcendental Meditation, it is presented as a technique for transcending the conscious level of thought to experience its source, silence or pure consciousness, which is happiness. From here, a person "spontaneously returns to activity with the dynamic power of nature's silent, restful alertness which then supports all [his] thought, speech and action (experienced briefly as the "zone" in sport) and thereby produces a potentially much greater range of mental, physical and spiritual benefits."[36]

Although Transcendental Meditation is presented as a spiritual or psychological technique that can be detached from a religious framework, it has its origins in Hinduism. Maharishi Mahesh Yogi lays out the basic metaphysical principles that undergird the practice. First, he points to the existence of Being:

> Underneath the subtlest layer of all that exists in the relative field is the abstract, absolute field of pure Being, which is unmanifested and transcendental. It is neither matter nor energy . . . This state of pure existence underlies all that exists. Everything is the expression of this pure existence or absolute Being which is the essential constituent of all relative life. The one eternal unmanifested, absolute Being manifests itself in many forms of lives and existences in creation.[37]

The Maharishi explicitly draws from the oldest records of Indian thought: "The eternal texts of the Vedas, crowned with the philosophy of the Upanishads, reveal the relative and Absolute as two aspects of the one reality, Brahman,

34. The Meditation Trust, "Transcendental Meditation Mantras," at www.meditationtrust.com/transcendental-meditation-mantras/.

35. The Contemplative Society, "Centering Prayer," at www.contemplative.org/contemplative-practice/centering-prayer/.

36. The Meditation Trust, "How is Transcendental Meditation Different?," at www.meditationtrust.com/how-is-transcendental-meditation-different.

37. Maharishi Mahesh Yogi, *The Science of Being and the Art of Living* (London: International SRM Publications, 1966), 27.

absolute Being, which, although unmanifest in Its essential nature, manifests as relative creation."[38]

On this account, Being is omnipresent, and permeates everything. It is the essential, basic nature of the mind. The Maharishi writes that "the great words of enlightenment found in the Vedas express Being as the ultimate reality, and they find It within man as his own inseparable Self."[39] However, many minds are ignorant of it. "Since the mind ordinarily remains attuned to the sense, projecting outwards towards the manifested realms of creation," the Maharishi writes, "it misses or fails to appreciate its own essential nature, just as the eyes are unable to see themselves . . . It is not obvious even though it underlies all creation."[40] The essential nature of Being, however, "is absolute bliss-consciousness."[41] Without knowledge of absolute bliss-consciousness, the Maharishi continues, life is like "a ship without a rudder, ever at the mercy of the tossing sea . . . the life of the individual without the realization of Being is baseless, meaningless, and fruitless."[42]

That which is opposed to Being is karma, or action.[43] Karma transforms the pure consciousness of Being into the individual conscious mind. "By the process of karma, all creation must move continuously through the eternal cycle of birth and death, creation, evolution, and dissolution."[44] Any process that brings karma to an end brings about the state of Being. According to the Maharishi, Transcendental Meditation is the most universally available, peaceful, and easy way to attain the state of eternal Being and avoid the grip of karma. He describes the reason for its effectiveness thus:

> Perception in the outward direction is the result of a progressive increase of activity in the nervous system; perception in the inward direction is the result of diminishing activity until the nervous system ceases to function and reaches a state of stillness, a state of restful alertness. This is the state described in the words: Be still and know that I am God. This stillness is achieved ideally when activity in the nervous system is brought to that state of restful alertness where even the mind's activity is reduced to nil, where the thinking process has been reduced to a point at the source of thinking. At this point perception remains in a state of absolute consciousness, the state of enlightenment is gained and absolute transcendental Being comes

38. Mahesh Yogi, *The Science of Being and the Art of Living*, 36.
39. Mahesh Yogi, *The Science of Being and the Art of Living*, 36.
40. Mahesh Yogi, *The Science of Being and the Art of Living*, 30.
41. Mahesh Yogi, *The Science of Being and the Art of Living*, 28.
42. Mahesh Yogi, *The Science of Being and the Art of Living*, 29.
43. Mahesh Yogi, *The Science of Being and the Art of Living*, 46.
44. Mahesh Yogi, *The Science of Being and the Art of Living*, 46.

to be on the conscious level of life; or the conscious level of the mind reaches the transcendental level of Being.[45]

According to Maharishi, Transcendental Meditation is a "mechanical path to God-realization,"[46] meaning that it does not require intellectual or emotional assistance. Therefore, any person is capable "of realizing God by this path, irrespective of his intellectual or emotional state of development."[47] When the mind moves outward after reaching the transcendental level of Being, "its activity brings the light of transcendental, absolute Being into the outer world, thereby increasing the intensity of bliss in the perception of the gross, manifested fields of creation."[48]

The Maharishi views the practice of Transcendental Meditation as the great secret of human happiness. In the introduction to his book, he explicitly describes it as a practice that "deals with the fundamentals of all problems of life and suggests one solution *to eradicate all suffering* (emphasis mine)."[49] Indeed, Transcendental Meditation "offers the principle of a practical technique to enable all men to harmonize their inner spiritual content with the glories of the outer material life and *to find their God within themselves* (emphasis mine)."[50] Needless to say, this metaphysics is in fundamental contradiction with Augustine's understanding of created reality.

Keating adamantly insists that Centering Prayer is an authentic form of Christian contemplation that is grounded in the Christian tradition of prayer.[51] He writes that Centering Prayer arises from the Trinity dwelling within all baptized Christians, and is rooted in God's life within their souls.[52] Indeed, Keating claims that "Centering Prayer is focused on the heart of the Christian mystery, which is Christ's passion, death, and resurrection."[53] He links Centering Prayer to the prayer of quiet described by Teresa of Avila and John of the Cross, when souls simply wait upon God with loving attentiveness. "Since *the love of God is poured into our hearts by the Holy Spirit* (Rom. 5:5), as St. Paul says," Keating writes, "we, too, as contemplative prayer grows, participate more fully in this movement of grace. The divine presence becomes a fullness that no longer

---

45. Mahesh Yogi, *The Science of Being and the Art of Living*, 302.

46. Mahesh Yogi, *The Science of Being and the Art of Living*, 303.

47. Mahesh Yogi, *The Science of Being and the Art of Living*, 303.

48. Mahesh Yogi, *The Science of Being and the Art of Living*, 303.

49. Mahesh Yogi, *The Science of Being and the Art of Living*, 29.

50. Mahesh Yogi, *The Science of Being and the Art of Living*, 19.

51. Keating, *Intimacy with God*, 11.

52. Keating, *Intimacy with God*, 32.

53. Keating, *Intimacy with God*, 35.

requires the stepping-stones of thoughts, feelings, and particular acts, at least not habitually."[54]

Centering Prayer is not an exercise of attention that requires concentration. Rather, Keating explains, it is an exercise of intention. "It is our will, our faculty of choice, that we are cultivating. . . . It is an acceptance not only of God's presence, but also of God's action."[55]

Keating recognizes that contemplative prayer must be given by God, and so he explains that Centering Prayer is not precisely contemplation, but rather a preparation for it. He explains,

> In the broad sense of the term, it might be called the first step on the ladder of contemplative prayer. We only know that we are moving in this direction through our practice, and that the Spirit is moving toward us. As our practice becomes more habitual, the action of the Spirit's gifts of wisdom and understanding become more powerful and gradually take over our prayer, enabling us to rest habitually in the presence of God.[56]

Centering Prayer is presented as one of the most effective ways to habitually practice the presence of God, which, as Augustine would agree, is essential to the life of every Christian.

There remains a question, however, as to whether a practice that is so deeply tied to a metaphysics antithetical to Christianity truly leads a baptized person to communion with the Trinity dwelling within her. Augustine's metaphysical understanding of contemplation in book 12, and his corresponding account of the temporal way of contemplation, helpfully illuminates this question.

As we have seen, Augustine recognizes that God is eternal, absolute being, goodness, and perfection. The human being, by contrast, is intrinsically finite and subject to change. She is also in a state of misery because of her inclination to move away from God toward nothingness. In the Incarnation, however, the transcendent God mercifully condescends to dwell with a human being in her creatureliness and sinfulness, graciously lifting her up into spiritual contact with Himself, but never erasing the holy distance between Creator and created. The person is never absorbed into God at the expense of her humanity, nor does she ever forget God's gratuitous goodness to her. In the perfect contemplation of heaven's heaven, she lovingly beholds God's glorious eternity in communion with all the saints and angels, unfailingly concentrating her heart and attention on the divine Trinity. She eternally worships God in gratitude for his

54. Keating, *Intimacy with God*, 43.
55. Keating, *Intimacy with God*, 57.
56. Keating, *Intimacy with God*, 55.

wondrous mercy that has saved her from her misery. Through her contemplative union with God, the redeemed person receives the unique human integrity and communion for which she has been created. God graciously conforms her to the image of his divine Son, but at no point does she become God or find her God within herself, as Maharishi proposes.

The temporal way of contemplation, as we have seen, is an imperfect yet deepening participation in the eternal contemplation of the saints and angels by gradual incorporation into Christ's sacred humanity. The goal of the Christian is never to overcome or eradicate all thought and desire in order to be absorbed into God's infinite simplicity. Rather, as Augustine recognizes so clearly, the goal is for a person's thoughts and affections to be healed by humble, practiced faith in Christ as a member of his body. Human beings are conformed to Christ through the sacraments and thoughtful meditation on Scripture in communion with the whole Church. Prayer is not a technique or activity to achieve an altered state of consciousness, but rather a conversation between an ecclesial soul and her Creator and Redeemer, made possible by the Holy Spirit's grace. Prayer always bears fruit in works of charity.

Teresa of Avila and John of the Cross's "prayer of quiet" lies outside the scope of this paper, but it has a clear place within Augustine's account of the temporal way of contemplation. Through reception of the sacraments, meditation upon Scripture, the practice of conversation with God, and growth in charity, the faithful soul learns to be habitually recollected in the presence of the divine Trinity dwelling within her by sanctifying grace. This habit of recollection, however, cannot be achieved apart from these means; it is the fruit of the soul's incorporation into Christ's body. It cannot be arrived at by a simple technique of thought-emptying. And the faithful soul practices the presence of God by attending to the Father, Son, and Spirit with her mind, even if this is habitual rather than active, and by loving Christ and his members with her will.

On Augustine's account, moreover, conformation to Christ centers upon a person's participation in the mysteries of his death and resurrection. This happens through the Eucharist, and through a person's dying to self that she may live for God and neighbor. Keating claims that Centering Prayer is rooted in the mysteries of Christ's death and resurrection, but his understanding of this rootedness is very different from Augustine's.

"Centering Prayer," Keating writes, "is simply a humble method of trying to access [God's] infinite goodness by letting go of ourselves. Consent to God's presence and action symbolized by the sacred word is nothing else than self-surrender and trust."[57]

57. Keating, *Intimacy with God*, 35.

On Augustine's account, a person dies to herself by confessing her weakness and misery, abandoning herself to God's mercy, and allowing grace to gradually purify her from sin and bring about growth in virtue. She imitates Christ's obedience and humility by humbly submitting her mind and will to God's word and law within the community of the Church. She participates in his Passion by performing acts of love for God and neighbor, over and over again, at the cost of her comfort and her pride.

In Centering Prayer, by contrast, a person dies to herself simply by emptying all of her thoughts and altering her state of consciousness. It is unclear how this involves any sort of suffering, which lies at the heart of the Christian way of contemplation. Indeed, as Maharishi makes explicit, the goal of Transcendental Meditation is the elimination of suffering.

For Augustine, both Transcendental Meditation and Centering Prayer would represent the same temptation as Neoplatonism. The way to intimacy with God is not to ignore the pain of one's misery and abstract from everything that is human and finite, but rather to ascend to Christ's divinity through conformation to his suffering humanity, by the grace of God.

On Augustine's account, therefore, a person is not actually making spiritual contact with God through the practice of Centering Prayer. For Augustine, this practice would not be prayer at all; calling it "prayer," and even identifying it as contemplation, would be very dangerous. For if a person were to practice Centering Prayer as a replacement for the true way of contemplation, then she would never turn to God, and grow in integrity and wisdom. Rather, by remaining imprisoned within herself and disengaging from her human experience, she would fall further into formlessness and disintegration. This is a real risk for many contemporary Christians.

4. Conclusion

In book 12 of the *Confessions*, Augustine articulates a metaphysical understanding of the created cosmos that corresponds to his personal experience of confession, conversion, and contemplation. In his goodness, God allows human beings to participate in their creation and grow in integrity and formedness, until they attain the unique identity and communion for which they have been created. They move toward their destiny by lovingly turning to the One who made them. Because of the fall of the first human parents, however, each person is dramatically poised between the formedness of heaven's heaven, and the formlessness of separation from God. Each person has a sinful tendency toward this abyss, but her fundamental desire is to contemplate God. The human being's way to the blessed contemplation of heaven's heaven is not to reject her finitude and sinfulness, but rather to confess her misery and need for the Holy Spirit's grace. The way is to allow the Holy Spirit to gradually incorporate her into the sacred humanity of Christ through her reception of the sacraments and meditation upon Scripture and the Church's tradition.

The popular contemporary practice of Centering Prayer claims to be a modern form of contemplation that is rooted in the Christian tradition, including the doctrine of Augustine. The practice itself, however, developed from a metaphysics directly contrary to that which Augustine sets forth in book 12. The technique originally aims to lift a person out of her particular, temporal experience so that she may be absorbed into a pure, unchanging, divine consciousness that is her true identity. By emptying her thoughts, the human being hopes to overcome the experience of suffering. The leaders of the Centering Prayer movement may identify it as the traditional Christian prayer of quiet or recollection, but unlike this prayer, Centering Prayer is not the natural flowering of a penitential, sacramental life, regular conversation with God rooted in Scripture, and works of charity. On Augustine's account, Centering Prayer is not prayer at all, and should not be practiced as a substitute for the Christian way of contemplation.

Even if Centering Prayer can legitimately be used as a psychological technique to combat anxiety, for Augustine, the goal of the Christian must never be to simply detach from her thoughts and emotions. Rather, by accepting her suffering and casting herself into the merciful arms of Christ, a person's mind and heart can be conformed to his through the practices of his Church. In this way, instead of becoming detached from all things, including herself, she will be securely attached to the divine Trinity, and to all her brothers and sisters who have been ransomed by Christ's blood. True contemplation does not erase a person's human identity, but rather brings her to the luminous, unique integrity for which she has been created, found in communion with Father, Son, and Spirit, and all the saints and angels.

BOOK 13

The Heart Finds Rest through the Church

Joseph Grone

> "'Then who is she?' I said. 'The church,' he replied. I said to him, 'Why, then is she elderly?' 'Because,' he said, 'she was created before all things; therefore she is elderly, and for her sake the world was formed.'"
>
> THE SHEPHERD OF HERMAS 1.2.4[1]

Much has been said in recent years about the rise of the "Nones," that is, those who identify as atheist or agnostic or who simply do not identify with any religious community. In 2019, surveys from the Pew Research Center found that 26 percent of U.S. adults identified as religiously unaffiliated in one way or another, up from 17 percent in 2009, while those who identified as Christian fell from 77 percent to 65 percent.[2] There are, undoubtedly, a number of reasons for such a development, but certainly among them is the stark sense of individualism that has long pervaded the modern West. In the United States, especially, an individual's freedom is often understood to depend upon autonomy from the influence of others. Any external demands upon a person, including those of the common good, are judged to be acceptable only to the point that the person's own individual will is not obstructed. Indeed, even as loneliness and social isolation have been found to be on the rise,[3] it never-

---

1. *The Shepherd of Hermas* 1.2.4, in Michael W. Holmes, trans., *The Apostolic Fathers in English*, 3rd ed. (Grand Rapids, MI: Baker Academic, 2006), 211.

2. "In U.S., Decline of Christianity Continues at Rapid Pace," Pew Research Center (October 17, 2019), at www.pewforum.org/2019/10/17/in-u-s-decline-of-christianity-continues-at-rapid-pace/.

3. See, for instance, the results of a September 2018 survey in "All the Lonely People: Loneliness Is a Serious Public-Health Problem," *The Economist* (September 1, 2018), at www

theless remains that disconnectedness from others seems to be the defining feature of the person.

For religion, this has fostered not just a pluralism in the secular societies of the West, but a radical relativism, in which an individual's own beliefs have no true relevance to those of others. The belief has more to do with personal conviction than with any objective reality. Accordingly, fostered by a naturalistic impulse that explicitly or implicitly rejects discussions of the supernatural, the churches and religious communities to which people belong have often become understood simply to be gatherings of like-minded individuals, not unlike any other man-made organization. They are perceived to be little more than social outlets, certainly a good, but chosen as a matter of personal preference, rather than for the teleology and sense of transcendence that ostensibly defines them.

For the "Nones," then, the church can easily be replaced by other forms of community in a secular environment, ones which may be more in line with one's own interests. One may even feel that a more sincere spirituality would be possible in the privacy of one's own home, rather than in a community that submits to the authority of religious leaders. In this line of thinking, a church often has little appeal, even to those who are lonely and lacking in community, since it seemingly offers little more—and potentially even less—than they might find elsewhere in the world. In the face of such an understanding, however, Augustine offers an altogether different vision in book 13 of the *Confessions*. Here, Augustine instead discusses the Church as a reality that God has prepared from the very beginning, a source of communion and rest through which God fulfills the deepest desires of every human being.

For modern readers, the concluding books of Augustine's *Confessions* are undoubtedly strange, and book 13 is especially so. The autobiographical genre of the first nine books is plenty familiar, but from the beginning of book 10, Augustine's story fades into the background. The narrative form that dominated the first nine books gives way to one that seems more suited to a philosophical or theological treatise. Book 13 grows even more distant from the autobiographical genre, as it continues the meditations in books 11 and 12 on excerpts from Genesis and evolves into a full exegesis of the first creation story. It is here, however, that the ultimate subject of Augustine's autobiography comes into light. As much as the *Confessions* is intended as an offering of Augustine's own

.economist.com/international/2018/09/01/loneliness-is-a-serious-public-health-problem. For a recent scholarly study on the subject, see Stephanie T. Child and Leora Lawton, "Loneliness and Social Isolation Among Young and Late Middle-Age Adults: Associations with personal networks and social participation." *Aging & Mental Health* 23, no. 2 (February 2019): 196–204.

life and praise to God, it was never about him alone. Rather, Augustine's own narrative of restlessness and wandering are a part of a broader narrative: the drama of humanity as a whole and its redemption through the Church.

For Augustine, as for the second-century *Shepherd of Hermas* before him, the world was created for the sake of the Church.[4] In book 13, Augustine demonstrates that every element of the first creation story not only speaks of the origins of spiritual and material beings; it also points to their redemption and illumination. For humans, that redemption is suited to their dual nature, as it is effected through the sacramental reality of the Church.

In Augustine's reading, then, the Church as it exists throughout all time is present in mystery from the foundation of the world, where it is revealed through God's creative activity. It is into this mystery that Augustine was initiated at the font in Milan, like all others who have been immersed in the waters of baptism. In this sense, as book 13 reflects upon the Church, it fulfills what Augustine had begun in book 9. There, Augustine described his entrance into the Church seemingly without any significant theological reflection, writing, "And so we were baptized, and all our dread about our earlier lives dropped away from us. During the days that followed I could not get enough of the wonderful sweetness that filled me as I meditated upon your deep design for the salvation of the human race" (9.6.14). It is in book 13 that Augustine's meditations bear fruit. Here, the depths of the baptismal font are finally explored, as his own baptismal restoration is cast in the broader context of the salvation of humanity.

By his baptism, Augustine's own story has been joined to those of many others, who themselves have been drawn out of darkness and wandering and incorporated into the communion of light and rest. Far more than a society of individuals, then, the Church is a community prepared from the beginning, a place through which God restores his people who have gone astray. Through God's activity in the Church, the loneliness and restlessness of each individual are sated, as each one is made alive again through grace and ultimately remade according to the image of God who created them.

1. Creation and Illumination (13.1–11)

As with each book of the *Confessions*, Augustine begins book 13 in prayer. In this instance, he offers praise for his unmerited creation according to nature

---

4. This phrasing echoes that used in the *Catechism of the Catholic Church* §760. The quotation itself may be found above, in the epigraph.

and for his unmerited re-creation according to grace. God created him, Augustine acknowledges, not that he might cultivate God as the pagans strive to do for their gods, but that God might cultivate him. When God creates, he not only wills the creatures' being (*esse*), but also their well-being (*bene esse*), which comes about only through right relationship with God.[5] By this prayer, Augustine provides a framework for the upcoming book, in which he shows God's providential care for his creatures to be revealed even from the moment they were created. In the very act of bringing creatures into being, God intended and prepared their well-being, which, for the rational creature, is found in loving, serving, and worshiping God (13.1.1). Augustine here recalls, then, a theme that has echoed since the very beginning of the *Confessions*, where he wrote, "And so we humans, who are a due part of your creation, long to praise you. . . . You stir us so that praising you may bring us joy" (1.1.1).

From here, Augustine reflects upon the relationship between God and his creations, beginning with a discussion of the contingency of created things. No creature, whether among the higher spiritual beings or the lower corporeal beings, has an intrinsic right to existence; rather, all came to be through God's free and abundant goodness. Likewise, creatures have no goodness that is of their own accord, though they are nevertheless "exceedingly good because they are from you, the one supreme Good" (13.2.2). All things came to be through the Word of God, and so too are all things illuminated through the Word. For this reason, Augustine suggests, when God speaks, "Let there be light" (Gen 1:3), it does not reveal a material act of creation alone, but also a spiritual one. Just as all of creation was without form until it was enlightened by the Word, so too are spiritual creatures—namely, angels and humans—unformed and without the light of goodness, righteousness, and wisdom unless they hold fast to the Word (13.2.3). Augustine thus continues, acknowledging that although spiritual creatures are, by their nature, capable of receiving illumination, they are not radiant in blessedness by nature. In his simplicity, God alone lives in blessedness (*beate*) by nature, for he is beatitude (*beatitudo*) itself (13.3.4). The radiance of blessedness only comes about in the creature at God's command, so in order for the spiritual creature to share in the radiance of the Light, it must contemplate the Light and receive its radiance as freely given.

It is for this reason, Augustine explains, that the Spirit rests upon the waters

---

5. "No, you command me to serve you and worship you that it may be well with me of your bounty, who have granted me first to exist, that I may enjoy well-being [*ut de te mihi bene sit, a quo mihi est, ut sim, cui bene sit*]" (13.1.1). All Latin citations from L. Verheijen (ed.), *Augustinus: Confessionum libri XIII*, CCL 27 (Turnhout, Belgium: Brepols, 1981).

in Gen 1:2. The Spirit's resting is not a reflection of his dependence upon the waters or upon creation at large, but rather of creation's dependence upon God. God has no need or lack that creation might satisfy; rather, God pours out his goodness upon the needs of his creatures so that they might rest in him. It is only by abiding in God's grace, living "more and more fully on the fount of life" (13.4.5), that spiritual creatures are perfected, illumined, and beatified. It is in this way that "heaven's heaven" (13.5.6; cf. Ps 113:24 [115:16]) is said to be brought from darkness into light, as spiritual beings are converted to him who grants them his blessedness. This effect of conversion is, he further explains, a thoroughly Trinitarian act, as all three persons are revealed by the end of the second verse of Genesis: the Father ("God") made the heavens and the earth in the Son ("Beginning"), as the Spirit rested above the waters (13.5.6).

The operation of the Trinity serves as Augustine's primary focus through-out Chapters 6–11, as he considers the Spirit's seemingly late arrival in the story of creation. Augustine observes that the Spirit is said to rest above the waters only after the Father, the Son, the heavens, the earth, and even the darkness over the deep have been described. Begging for an explanation from the truth and charity that come from the Spirit alone (13.8.9),[6] Augustine suggests that this was written so that we might understand the Spirit's role in the divine econ-omy. He is stationed above the waters of this world so that he might pour his love into our hearts (cf. Rom 5:5) and thereby draw us upward to God (13.6.7–7.8).[7] For just as bodies are drawn to where their weight lies, so too does the Spirit's love draw the creature to himself, as Augustine writes, "My weight is my love, and wherever I am carried, it is this weight that carries me. Your Gift sets us afire and we are borne upward" (13.9.10). With the Spirit's gift of love, we are drawn away from the love of this world and from the uncleanness of our own spirit, and we instead begin to love the holiness of God's Spirit (13.7.8). As with Augustine himself, the creature is led by the Spirit out of darkness and into the light of God (13.8.9). Filled with the love of the Spirit and singing the Songs of Ascent, he advances ever upward into union with God (13.9.10).

Augustine is quick to note, however, that such conversion is wrought by the Spirit among humans alone, not among angels. Since angels are timeless,

6. Cf. John M. Quinn, *A Companion to the Confessions of St. Augustine* (New York: Peter Lang, 2002), 813.

7. As Augustine will demonstrate in his exegesis on the third day of creation, the waters of the sea represent this world, and those who dwell within the sea are those whose love is for this world alone. Thus, as he speaks of the Spirit's pouring out of love as he hovers over the waters, Augustine also points to the movement he describes later in the commentary, in which the Holy Spirit draws us out of the waters of the sea and onto the dry land of the Church.

they have never had the experience of wandering from God as humans do, so the movement from darkness into light is merely said of the good angels in order to demonstrate that they could have been in darkness, but by God's grace and by the turn of their will, they instead abide in the light (13.10.11). Humans, on the other hand, are distant from the Trinity by the effects of sin, yet through the Gift of the Spirit they may begin their return to God by contemplating the image of the Trinity within themselves. Thus, beginning a lifelong quest that appears most famously in books 8–10 of *De Trinitate*, Augustine seeks to define what that image is within the person. Here in the *Confessions*, he suggests that the image of the Trinitarian God lies in the person's being, knowledge, and will, three elements of the human person that are inseparable from one another yet still distinct (13.11.12). It is through this image, he suggests, that the person is drawn up by the love of the Spirit into the unity of the Trinity itself, but by no means is this accomplished apart from others. In fact, it is through the Church that one receives the faith to recognize that image.

2. The Church in the Six Days of Creation

Having contemplated the manner in which spiritual beings are illuminated by the Spirit of God, Augustine turns to the manner in which that illumination takes place, as it is revealed through the six days of creation. Commentaries on the Hexaemeron (Greek for "Six Days") were quite common in late antiquity, but the six days of creation would prove to be especially fruitful for Augustine's writings. Reflecting his understanding of the multivalence of Scripture, Augustine returns often to the Hexaemeron in his writings and he approaches it through a variety of lenses.[8] What he presents in the *Confessions*, however, is quite distinct from the others, as he utilizes the allegorical method he gleaned from Ambrose to great effect (see 6.4.6). Here, Augustine reads the creation story for what it reveals about the redemption of humanity throughout time,

---

8. Even beyond his three works explicitly framed as commentaries on Genesis, Augustine also comments upon the six days of creation extensively in book 11 of the *City of God* and uses them as an outline for presenting salvation history to catechumens in his *Instructing Beginners in the Faith* (*De catechizandis rudibus*). Regarding the multivalence of Scripture, especially of the verses of Genesis, Augustine writes in book 12 of the *Confessions*,

> A spring wells up in quite a small space, yet by means of its branching streams it is a source of richer fertility, and waters wider tracts of countryside, than can any one of the derivative streams alone, far though this may flow from its parent fount. So too the steward you entrusted with the telling of your story confined his message within a small compass, yet this narrative, destined to supply a theme for many messengers of the word, is a spring whence rivers of limpid truth gush forth. (12.27.37)

so that each creative act reveals a different facet of the Church through which humanity comes to share in the radiance of divine light.

The First Day: The Church Illumined by Faith (13.12.13–13.14.15)

Augustine begins his analysis of the Hexaemeron with the creation and illumination of two groups within the Church. As he explains, the Trinitarian God, in whose name we are baptized and in whose name we baptize others (13.12.13, p. 419; cf. 1 Cor 1:15, Matt 28:19), "creates the heavens and the earth" as he establishes those who are spiritual (*spiritales*) and those who are carnal (*carnales*) among the people of his Church (13.12.13).[9] Augustine's distinction here arises from 1 Corinthians, where Paul compares the spiritual to the mature who can handle solid food, and the carnal to children who still require milk (1 Cor 3:1–3). For Augustine, the spiritual are those who have spiritual vision, able to see rightly and with true understanding in the light of the Spirit of God. The carnal, on the other hand, are still worldly and rely upon their corporeal senses, not yet possessing full understanding but nevertheless living by faith (cf. 13.18.23 and 13.23.33). Both, however, are illumined by God's command of "Let there be light" (Gen 1:3), as the light of faith bestowed in baptism is offered to the spiritual and carnal alike (13.12.13).

Although by this gift of illumination the members of the Church on earth have been given a share in God's light, they do not yet see the light face-to-face, nor are they yet at rest in the light. Though they indeed receive salvation through the gifts of faith and hope, the earthly Church has not yet attained that salvation in its fullness. As Augustine notes, even Paul, who acted as an intermediary between Christ and his bride the Church and even spoke on Christ's behalf to those who were still in the unformed abyss of faithlessness, did not yet consider himself to have attained salvation. Therefore, like Paul, the members of the earthly Church also long for their heavenly home (13.13.14). They progress through this world as pilgrims, journeying with joy toward eternal union with God, but remaining always in flux until the end: "I find a little respite in you when I pour out my soul in rising above myself with a shout of joy and praise, the clamor of a pilgrim keeping festival. Yet still my soul is sad, because it slips back and becomes an abyss once more, or rather, it feels itself to be still in the depths" (13.14.15). Even as the pilgrim falls amid the darkness of his journey, he is nevertheless a child of light and is only truly at home in the light

---

9. This binary, it should be noted, does not correspond to Augustine's two cities formed by two loves, as described in *De civitate Dei 14.28*. Augustine does, however, provide a parallel to this in his commentary on the third day.

of day. Yet it is only at the end that God finally distinguishes between the night and the day, separating those who are truly children of light from those who remain children of darkness.

The Second Day: The Vault of Scripture (13.15.16–13.16.19)

Turning his attention to the second day of creation, Augustine identifies the vault placed in the heavens, which separates the waters above from the waters below, as a symbol for Scripture. As the sky is stretched out above the earth like a tent (cf. Ps 103[104]:2), so has Scripture spread over the whole world through the ministry of men and women, and it likewise divides those above from those below (13.15.16). Those in the heavens above the vault have no need of Scripture, since they behold God unceasingly, reading and loving his unchangeable will in eternity. But for those on the earth below, Scripture provides a covering for their sin (cf. Gen 3:21). It is a gift that humbles them in their pride and invites them instead to turn their gaze toward heaven. As Augustine writes, "Nowhere else, Lord, indeed nowhere else do I know such chaste words, words with such efficacy to persuade me to confession, to gentle my neck beneath your kindly yoke and invite me to worship you without thought of reward" (13.15.17). Scripture guides human beings toward their created intent, forming them in right relationship with God, even though the words of Scripture themselves remain somewhat obscure in this life. The apostles and prophets, who preach the Word through Scripture, act as clouds that rain God's revelation upon the earth below, but like the obscurity of the clouds themselves, that revelation is always offered in the mystery. In order, then, to receive God's revelation rightly and thereby see God in the midst of the clouds, those on earth depend upon the Spirit's gift of understanding (13.15.17).

However, Scripture's revelatory function is not to remain forever. Just as the skies will be rolled up like a scroll at the end of time (cf. Rev 6:14), so too will Scripture no longer be required in eternity (13.15.16). Scripture is intended for those who still journey through this world, depending upon faith to help them see God in the midst of darkness and obscurity, but at the end they will look clearly upon the Word himself. Already enkindled in love for God now through the Scriptures, there they shall be like him and see him as he is, not simply as he reveals himself in Scripture (13.15.18). After all, those who are earthly and mutable can only come to know the transcendent, immutable God by the gift of illumination and by his condescension to our state. While humans indeed image God by their being, knowing, and willing, God is, knows, and wills unchangeably, and humans therefore cannot know God as he knows himself on this side of eternity, not even through revelation (13.16.19).

The Third Day: Bitter Sea and Dry Land as the Two Loves (13.17.20–21)
Under the vault of Scripture, Augustine finds two societies of people signified by the separation of the sea and the dry land on the third day of creation. Unlike his description of the spiritual and carnal peoples in the Church, Augustine presents in Chapter 17 an allegorical parallel to his common image of the two cities formed by two loves.[10] For Augustine, the bitter, turbulent waters of the sea represent the mass of those who journey through this life without the sweetness of love. Gathered "into a single mass [*in societatem unam*]" (13.17.20; cf. Gen 1:9), these are enveloped by the cares of the world and tossed about like the waves of the sea as they perpetually seek after temporal happiness. Never finding respite for themselves, they continually surge with violence against the dry land, so that it is only by God's imposing of order upon his creation that the sea remains separate from the land.

The dry land, on the other hand, represents the "*animas sitientes tibi*" (13.17.21), all those souls who thirst not for the bitter waters of the sea, but for the sweet waters that God alone provides. They are the members of the Church, who stand apart from the cares of the world and rely only upon God. As good earth they receive the waters of God's grace and are thus able to bear fruit through the love of neighbor.[11] Having learned compassion through their own weakness and through their own dependence upon the love of God, they themselves turn outward in love through the performance of the corporal works of mercy. And just as a diversity of plants bursts forth from the earth, so too do these acts of love proliferate in a variety of forms both small and great. As Augustine explains, such acts may be shown either through the light provisions of grass or the stout protections of a tree "which in its benign strength can lift an injured person clear of the grasp of a powerful oppressor, and furnish protective shade by the unshakable firmness of just judgment" (13.17.21). Through the bearing of fruit through works of justice and mercy, the Church shows forth to the world the love that they themselves have received from God. As such, they are empowered to remain apart from the cares of this world and instead begin to transform it according to the love of God.

---

10. *ciu. Dei* 14.28.

11. Augustine seems also to have in mind the Parable of the Sower found in Matthew 13:1–23, Mark 4:1–20, and Luke 8:4–15.

The Fourth Day: Luminaries in the Firmament as the Spiritual Gifts (13.18.22–13.19.25)

Turning to the fourth day of creation, in which luminaries are placed in the firmament to mark day from night, Augustine again invokes the distinction between the spiritual and carnal members of the Church. The spiritual members, he explains, have indeed borne fruit through the works of mercy, but they have also turned toward the Word above in contemplation. In so doing, they have begun to share in the light of the divine Word and thereby to shine as luminaries for the rest of the Church. Schooled in the vault of Scripture, they are God's spiritual children, doing by grace that which God himself does by nature. Just as God in his judgment separates the light from the darkness, so too do the spiritual members in their own way "mark the distinction between realities of the mind and sensible things, as between day of night, or between souls devoted to the life of the mind and others preoccupied with sensible matters" (13.18.22).

But God does not bestow such a gift in the same way to all and at all times. While the spiritual members are indeed endowed by the same Spirit, they exhibit a diversity of spiritual gifts (cf. 1 Cor 12:4). Just as God illuminated the earth by creating the greater light for ruling the day, the lesser light for ruling the night, and the stars to shine in the night sky (Gen 1:16–18), so too does the Spirit provide a hierarchy of gifts among the luminaries of the Church. For Augustine, the "greater light," which surpasses the other spiritual gifts, is wisdom. The spiritual person dwells in the light of day by residing in wisdom and offering it in service to others, so that they too might find joy in the truth.

However, the effulgence of wisdom is not suited to every member of the Church, and so spiritual persons also reflect the lesser spiritual gifts. With these, they help to illumine the carnal members of the Church, for the carnal dwell for now in the darkness of night, depending upon the light of the lesser luminaries as they journey toward the day. Among these, Augustine concludes, the "lesser light" is knowledge, while the stars are the other gifts of the Spirit: healing, miracles, prophecy, discernment of spirits, tongues (cf. 1 Cor 12:5–11).[12]

From here, Augustine explains in Chapter 19 how one becomes such a luminary. For this, he recalls the story of the rich young man (Matt 19:16–30; Mark 10:17–31; Luke 18:18–23). The man implores Jesus what more he must do to inherit eternal life, having observed all the commandments from his youth,

---

12. Augustine does not echo Paul's inclusion of the interpretation of tongues. Regarding this omission, Quinn simply theorizes that Augustine believes the interpretation of tongues to be implicit in the speaking of tongues; see Quinn, *A Companion*, 838–839.

but Jesus commands that he do still more: "'If you wish to be perfect, go, sell what you have and give to the poor, and you will have treasure in heaven. Then come, follow me'" (Matt 19:21).

In that story, Augustine again sees the distinction between the carnal members of the Church and those who are, by grace, the perfect, spiritual members. All must strive to do as the rich young man had already done. By his observance of the commandments, he had rid himself of the thorns of vice and had prepared himself for the waters of grace, through which he might bear fruit in love of neighbor. But those who wish to be perfect must go further, leaving behind the concerns of this world and following the Lord in the path of wisdom. The spiritual are thus conformed to the light of wisdom, so that they might shine forth their gifts for others. Like the apostles at Pentecost, they go forth to all nations, illumined with tongues of fire, offering wisdom to the spiritual and ensuring that the carnal are not overwhelmed by darkness. Augustine thus enjoins the spiritual,

> Separate the light of the mature, who yet are not angels, from the darkness of the little ones, who yet are not to be despaired of; shine over the whole earth, and let the day, radiant with its sun, tell out the word of wisdom to the day, and the night, steeped in moonlight, proclaim the word of knowledge to the night. (13.19.25)

Here, no doubt, Augustine bears in mind not only his own mission in the Church, but also the examples of others he has encountered, such as the bishop Ambrose. These share in the gifts of the Spirit, not only acting with mercy toward those in need, but also speaking words of wisdom and knowledge to the Church as luminaries for both the spiritual and the carnal members.

The Fifth Day: Sea Creatures as Sacraments and Miracles, Birds as Messengers (13.20.26–28)

In his exegesis of the fifth and sixth days, Augustine traces the journey of the one who comes to be alive in faith and thereby comes to share in the restoration of humanity to its created intent. This journey begins with God's activity in the world through his saints, represented in God's populating of the waters and the air on the fifth day.

Recalling that the sea is a symbol for the mass of people who are enveloped in the cares of the world, Augustine explains that the fish and the whales represent the saints' activities among them. The fish specifically symbolize the sacraments that the saints perform—in particular, baptism and the sacramental rites that initiate new members into the Church—whereas the saints' miracles are represented by the whales. Both of these are said to be brought forward by the sea, Augustine notes, because God's actions there are occasioned by needs of those who are tossed about by the tumult of the world (13.20.26–27).[13] As he explains, if not for the sin of Adam, "there would have been no need for the deeds performed and the words spoken by your stewards amid the pounding waves, words and deeds material and sensible, yet fraught with sacramental power" (13.20.28). Instead, God responded to the sins and needs of his people with mercy; he sought to draw them out of the tumult of the sea and onto the dry land of the Church. Through miracles, therefore, God drew people to himself, and by sacraments he effected their true transformation.

But God did still more through his saints. From the sea, he also produced birds that would fly close to the vault of Scripture and go forth over both the land and the sea. These signify the saints who, by grace, go out into the world to preach the Scriptures, not only prompting new members to first faith, but also—as he explains in the next section—encouraging its continued growth among them (13.20.26). In the sea creatures and the birds, then, Augustine sees represented the very propagation of the Church: the preaching of the Gospel, the performance of miracles to produce wonder among the peoples, and the subsequent initiation of new members from among them. Yet even if persons are baptized and initiated into the Church, they would not advance further if their soul did not continue to grow toward maturity (13.20.28), and it is this growth that he observes in the sixth day.

The Sixth Day, Part A: Living Creatures upon the Earth as the Living Soul (13.21.29–31)

In the first of two creative actions on the sixth day, God brings forth animals that crawl upon the earth, described in Augustine's text of Genesis as the creation of the *anima viva*, "the living soul" (13.21.29).[14] This living soul, for Augustine,

---

13. When comparing this statement to English translations of Genesis, this insight seems odd, at least for this day. In most English editions, Gen 1:20 is phrased something like the following: "Let the water teem with an abundance of living creatures" (NABRE), and accordingly "the water teems" (Gen 1:21) with those creatures. It is not the same with Gen 1:24, which suggests that the earth itself is responsible for the animals who come to dwell upon it: "Let the earth bring forth every kind of living creature." In the Latin of the Vulgate and in Augustine's Latin edition, both the waters and the earth are given the same kind of agency, as both commanded to produce their respective creatures: *"Producant aquae"* (Gen 1:20), *"quam produxerant aquae"* (Gen 1:21), and *"Producat terra"* (Gen 1:24).

14. Maria Boulding translates this alternately as "living creature" and "living soul" depending upon its surroundings, giving the impression that "living soul" is allegorical. Most English translations of Gen 1:24, after all, render the verse as something along the lines of "Let the earth

signifies the one who has been drawn from the waters of the world, brought to first faith, and cleansed by baptism, now dwelling fully alive upon the land of the Church. Moreover, Augustine certainly sees his own journey in this living soul, as by his own baptism in Milan, he too had found life by detaching from the cares of the world and entering into the kingdom of God.[15] As Augustine says, the living soul is "believing earth, clearly demarcated from the waves of the sea and their bitter unbelief" (13.21.29).

The soul is made alive by the faith received through baptism into the Church. No longer does the soul have need of the miracles and sacraments of the sea that introduce one to the faith, but the faithful soul does nevertheless require the continued sustenance of faith upon the land. For this reason, the birds not only fly above the waters of the sea, but they also flock upon the land. That is, the ministers of the Church who once introduced the Gospel to the faithless in the world continue also to preach the Gospel to the faithful in the Church, so that they always might be strengthened and edified by the Word (13.21.29). Moreover, Augustine adds, one of the fish of the sea is drawn from the water and placed upon a table to nourish the creatures of the land, since the sacrament of the Eucharist belongs not only to the rites of initiation but also to the continued sustenance of the faithful. It is therefore through the liturgical act, as the Gospel is preached and the Body of Christ is offered upon the altar, that the parched land continues to be watered by the Word of God who is the fount of life (13.21.29). In word and sacrament, the ministers of the Church continue to nourish the faithful, living souls, but they also go further, offering their own imitation of Christ as a model for them to emulate.

Thus, nourished by the grace of the Word and guided by his ministers, the living soul is empowered to tame the wild beasts that continue to assault it. These beasts, Augustine explains, are the soul's own impulses and desires for the things of the world, which linger from its time in the sea and continually draw it back to the sea. They tend not toward life in Christ, but toward death. Yet, by the grace of the Word, the soul restrains its impulses with reason and

---

bring forth every kind of living creature" (NABRE) or "Let the land produce living creatures according to their kinds" (NIV). Augustine's Latin text appears to be *"Producat terra animam vivam . . ."* and a similar text is reflected by the Vulgate: *"Producat terra animam viventem in genere suo . . ."* The literal reading of the verse in Latin, then, could indeed be speaking of all beings with living souls—that is, animals—but it is equally literal, if not more so, to regard it with Augustine as "living soul."

15. Augustine here describes baptism as "the means of entry into the kingdom of heaven" (13.21.29).

tames its evil desires with goodness, thereby finding the fullness of life that God alone provides.[16]

The Sixth Day, Part B: Humanity in God's Image as the Spiritual Person (13.22.32–13.23.34)

The second half of the sixth day, for Augustine, reflects again upon the spiritual person, as it reveals the elevation of the living soul to the spiritual life. Just as God created humanity in the beginning according to his image and likeness, so too does God now reform the soul according to the same. With this reformation, the living soul, still a carnal person dwelling within the Church, is nurtured to be a mature, spiritual person.

As Augustine explains, such a person no longer depends upon the ministers of the Church to understand truth, but is rather granted the grace of understanding: "A person thus made new considers your truth and understands it. He does not need some other human being to explain it to him so that he may imitate his own kind; you explain it to him, so that he can discern for himself what is your will, what is good and pleasing to you and perfect" (13.22.32; cf. Rom 12:2).

Completing the picture begun in the fourth day, in which the spiritual person was shown to reflect the gifts of the Spirit as a luminary for the Church, Augustine shows here that it is by becoming a spiritual person that one participates fully in humanity's created identity as an image of God (13.22.32).[17] Such a person, contemplating the Trinity in Unity, is thus "renewed in the knowledge of God in accordance with the image of his creator. He becomes a Spirit-filled person, fit to judge of any matters that call for judgment, though he himself is not subject to the judgment of his fellows" (13.22.32).

The spiritual person, for Augustine, is alone suited for the responsibility of judgment in the Church. This is not to say, of course, that all spiritual persons have roles of ecclesiastical authority; rather, as revealed by the creation of humanity both male and female, God brings about spiritual persons both among those with authority (allegorically, "male") and those who obey their authority ("female"). In truth, neither bodily sexuality, nor race, nor societal status, nor ecclesiastical position has anything to do with one's status as a carnal

16. Addressing the various types of animals named in Genesis, Augustine explains that the living soul must make the wild beasts gentle, the domestic animals responsive, and the snakes harmless (13.21.31).

17. For more on Augustine's understanding of the person as the image of God, see Gerald P. Boersma, *Augustine's Early Theology of Image: A Study in the Development of Pro-Nicene Theology*, OSHT (Oxford: Oxford University Press, 2016).

or spiritual person,[18] but those who are spiritual nevertheless have "dominion over the fish of the sea, the birds of the air, the tame animals, all the wild animals, and all the creatures that crawl on the earth" (Gen 1:26).

Reformed according to the very image of God, spiritual persons have the wisdom and understanding that allows right judgment over the things of the Church. They cannot judge the luminaries of wisdom and the other spiritual gifts, nor the Scriptures that serve as the vault over the earth, nor the divine law that Scripture contains; the spiritual are entirely subject to these. Neither can they judge between the spiritual and carnal peoples, nor those who are outside the Church who are "the mudbound races of this world" (13.23.33). for to judge between peoples belongs to God alone, who will separate the chaff from the wheat at the end of time (cf. Matt 3:12). But the spiritual person "can be said to exercise judgment in areas where he also has authority to correct what is wrong" (13.23.34). Those with authority over the rites of the Church and the preaching of the Church "judge and approve what they find done rightly, but condemn anything they find amiss" (13.23.34),[19] whereas the one without such authority "exercises judgment by approving what he finds proper and rebuking anything he finds amiss in the activities and conduct of the faithful" (13.23.34). The spiritual person, then, is a servant to the Church, ministering to the members in whatever way possible, so that they too may find life in the Word.

3. Additional Comments on Creation

The Dynamic of Grace in the Church: Commandments and Provisions for Creation

Having discussed the six days of creation through which God prefigured the Church, Augustine treats the commands and provisions by which God establishes the continuity of creation, beginning with God's injunction to increase and multiply (Gen 1:22, 28). However, in the Genesis account, God gives this

---

18. As Augustine says, "In respect of bodily sexuality male and female here have no significance, any more than do differences between Jew and Greek, slave and free" (13.23.33).

19. Augustine adds,

This they do through the celebration of those rites whereby people whom your mercy has sought out in the vast ocean are initiated; or at the solemn rite which makes present the fish raised up from the deep and devoutly eaten by the faithful; or by preaching, which through exegesis, discussion and argument attempts to make plain the meaning of your words, while subjecting itself always to the authority of your book as though winging its way beneath the sky; and through blessing and invoking you, so that as these sounds break from our mouths and make themselves heard, the populace may answer, "Amen." (13.23.34)

command only to humans, birds, fish, and the other sea creatures, not to the plants or to the beasts upon the land, even though the latter propagate similarly. He concludes, therefore, that this distinction must have been made in Scripture for a reason, though it must have a figurative meaning, not a literal one.

Augustine proposes two interpretations of the command, one for each group to whom it is directed. The first regards the command as it is directed to the offspring of the sea (i.e., fish, whales, and birds) in Gen 1:22. In this case, Augustine explains, God commands that material signs be multiplied in the world, so that simple truths like the love of God and neighbor might be signified in "a variety of mysterious ways" (13.24.36). Through sacraments, miracles, and the preaching of the Gospel, both words and deeds act as signs, pointing together to the same truths of the Gospel. With this command, then, God intends that the signifiers themselves be multiplied, while the realities signified remain singular. The second interpretation regards the command as given to humans in Gen 1:28, and it operates as an inverse of the first. With the command that humans be fruitful, God intends "the fecundity of our human reason" (13.24.37), through which the spiritual person might come to understand that a single statement of scripture holds a variety of meanings. In this case, the signifier remains singular, while the realities signified by it are multiplied in the person's understanding. As Augustine argues, the proliferation of meanings for a single passage is good, even intended by God himself, so long as all meanings drawn from the passage are true.

Noting that the speaking of such truth comes only from God's inspiration, Augustine moves on to discuss God's provision of food for his creatures. Here, Augustine observes that God assigns food in the Genesis account for humans, birds, snakes, and the beasts of the land (i.e., the *anima viva*),[20] but he does not make a similar statement for fish and whales. The former feed upon the fruits that come forth from the land, fruits that are, as stated above, the works of mercy by which another's physical needs are cared for.[21] These works are to be offered as food to those spiritual persons who dispense mysteries to others (human beings), to the living souls who offer an example to follow (land animals), and to the preachers who sing the word throughout the land (birds) (13.25.38).

20. While Augustine here uses the Latin *bestiis terrae*, it is clear from the section that he is referring to the *anima viva*, as he writes, "We owe [food] to them also as 'living creatures' (*animae uiuae*), in that they offer themselves as an example to be followed in every kind of self-restraint" (13.25.38).

21. See the above discussion on the third day of creation.

However, Augustine, recalling Paul—who rejoiced in the good deeds of the Philippians—argues that the fruit that comes forth from the earth is not, in fact, the action alone; the Philippians did not 'feed' Paul simply because they did good deeds. "It is not what they give that is the fruit," he writes, "but the intention with which they give" (13.26.39). The fruit is offered as food when it arises from a truly good spirit, out of love for Christ and out of a desire, for example, to care for a prophet precisely because he is a prophet, or a righteous person because he is a righteous person (cf. Matt 10:41). In this case, such an act is not merely the offering of a gift, but the offering of food for the souls of those who receive the gift (13.26.41). For this reason, Augustine argues, the people of the sea, who are still in need of the fish and the whales, cannot truly feed the servants of God, since their care for them would be done "without knowing why it should be done or what is implied" (13.27.42). That is, their acts of love are not properly ordered; rather than subordinating their love for the creature to their love for the Creator, they find the end of their love in the creature. To use terms Augustine famously adopts in *De doctrina Christiana*, rather than showing the love of use (*uti*) for the person, they are instead showing the love of enjoyment (*frui*).[22] It is for this reason, then, that the fruits of the earth are not given as food for the sea creatures, for they grow only upon the land as food for those upon the land.

From these sections, it is profoundly apparent that divine grace is constantly active in the Church and her members, as God works through his people to foster the continued growth and life of the Church. Marvelous signs, sacraments, and preaching are multiplied in the world, producing faith among the faithless. The meaning of Scripture is multiplied in the spiritual members of the Church, so that by their words and deeds, they might afford a further witness for the faithful. So too is the food that nourishes the people of God the product of grace. Through the waters of divine grace, fruit springs up among the people by the faith-filled performance of the works of mercy. Such rightly-ordered action shows true care for the needs of their brothers and sisters, while at the same time orienting that care ultimately toward the love of God. In this way, Augustine shows the Church to be a dynamic community in which all are fed by others and feed others in their constant dependence upon the font of grace.

---

22. See book 1 of *De doctrina Christiana*, especially 1.3.3–5.5 and 1.26.27–29.30.

Exceedingly Good (13.28.43–13.31.46)

Having exegeted the various elements of the creation narrative, Augustine finally takes on a question that he has explored throughout the *Confessions*: the goodness of creation. Throughout the creation narrative, things are said to be good (*bonum*) seven times (in his version of Genesis), but on an eighth occasion, things are said to be exceedingly good (*bona valde*) (13.28.43). From this it is apparent, he suggests, that every created thing is good individually, but when all things are seen as a whole, they are exceedingly good. The things of the world are at their most beautiful when they are together (13.28.43).

As somewhat of an aside, Augustine observes that while Genesis describes these statements of creation's goodness as happening at distinct times, it did not occur in this way for God himself, due to his eternality. God sees and acts timelessly, knowing every moment as if it were present, and it is out of this timelessness that God works in the distinct separations of our own time. Thus, as God identifies things in creation to be good at particular moments, he himself also sees every creature at every moment in time, within the context of the whole, and he sees the whole to be exceedingly good. A similar conclusion may thus be drawn about the Church, which creation has been shown to signify throughout book 13. The individuals who are found within the Church are indeed good individually (according to their nature), but they exhibit even greater goodness and beauty when they abide within the community of the Church. It is unity itself that grants an even higher dignity, and it is through the Holy Spirit that they are bound together in that unity.

Against the Manichees, then, it must be asserted that creation itself is good, for it came forth from God alone and reveals the redemption that God effects on behalf of his people. To assert to the contrary, that creation comes forth from a hostile intelligence, Augustine says, is simply absurd: "People who allege this are mad, because they do not contemplate your works through your Spirit, nor recognize you in them" (13.30.45). But the person who is filled with the Spirit of God is able to see creation rightly, both in its goodness and in its sacramentality. Indeed, Augustine explains, the only way in which one can recognize the goodness of creation is for God to delight in its goodness through him. It, too, is a product of grace at work in the individual.

With this understanding, then, Augustine presents three different lenses through which one might view creation, each of which he himself adopted at some time. First, one may see creation as evil and therefore to be rejected in favor of God, as the Manichees do and as Augustine once did when he was among them (5.10.20). Second, one may see creation as good, but fail to find God through creation. Such a one enjoys (*frui*) creation, rather than using (*uti*) creation to love God. As is clear from the narrative of the *Confessions*, Augustine himself was wrapped up in this kind of love as he too was tossed about in the sea of the world.[23] Finally, one may see creation as good in the way that God himself sees it. In this view, all things are understood to be good because they derive from God's own being, and they therefore lead one to love God. Such a one rightly has the love of use (*uti*) for creation and the love of enjoyment (*frui*) for God (13.31.46). It is in this third way that Augustine insists we must see creation, for in this way one recognizes not only the goodness of its origins and its nature, but also the goodness of God's redemptive action in the world.[24]

4. Summary and Rest

As Augustine concludes book 13, he offers a summary of his exegesis of the creation account. After recounting the literal events of the creation story, the author lingers upon what may be drawn from the creation of humanity as man and woman, asserting that although women are physically subordinate to men, they are nevertheless equal according to their rational mind and intelligence.[25] However, Augustine also identifies another meaning signified by the passage, one that describes the souls of both men and women. For the rightly ordered person, one's impulse to act ought to be obedient to the directions of one's rational mind (13.32.47). It is only in this way that the human being may truly live according to the created order, in which the good of all created things is achieved by their praise and love of God their Creator.[26]

23. See, for example, his famous prayer in book 10: "Late have I loved you, Beauty so ancient and so new, late have I loved you! Lo, you were within, but I outside, seeking there for you, and upon the shapely things you have made I rushed headlong, I, misshapen. You were with me, but I was not with you. They held me back far from you, those things which would have no being were they not in you" (10.27.38).

24. For more on Augustine's understanding of creation that is reflected here, see Jared Ortiz, "Creation in the *Confessions*," in David Vincent Meconi (ed.), *The Confessions*, 475–90, Ignatius Critical Editions (San Francisco: Ignatius Press, 2012).

25. Augustine's assertion that women are physically subordinate to men is not fully explained in this passage, but there is a clear implication it relates primarily to the man as head of his wife, expressed both in Gen 3:16, where God says to the woman, "Your urge shall be for your husband, and he shall rule over you," and in Eph 5:23, where Paul writes, "For the husband is head of his wife just as Christ is head of the church." It is significant, however, that as Augustine considers the literal meaning of the creation of man and woman, he lingers not on idea of subordination, but on their equality, as well as on a factor which is shared by both.

26. "Your creation sings praise to you so that we may love you, and we love you so that praise may be offered to you by your creation" (13.33.48).

After this, Augustine recounts his allegorical exegesis, presenting again the ways in which the Church and her members are signified by God's works of creation. Christ himself, he suggests, affords the transformative lens through which humanity can see created things rightly, as he writes, "In your Word, your only Son, we saw them severally as good and collectively as exceedingly good; for what we saw was heaven and earth, the Head and the body of the Church which you predestined before time began, when there was neither morning nor evening" (13.34.49).

Thus, from the first moments of creation Augustine finds revealed God's merciful actions for a lost and tumultuous people. There he sees the process of illumination, which he himself has experienced, whereby those who are lost in darkness are restored by the light of faith. And he sees that it is through the Church that the Spirit brings newness of life to those who have fallen and ultimately gives a sharing in God himself. It is therefore through the Church, signified by the six days of creation, that one finally comes to the seventh day.

In this final section, Augustine turns once again to prayer, begging that God might give the peace of repose after the labors of the six days. Just as morning and evening of each day of creation passed away and gave way to the next, so too will "this whole order of exceedingly good things, intensely beautiful as it is, . . . pass away when it has served its purpose" (13.35.50). However, unlike the six days of creation, the seventh day has no evening in the Genesis narrative. Rather, God "sanctified it that it might abide forever" (13.35.51) so that God's rest on the seventh day might signify "the Sabbath of eternal life" (13.36.51). Thus will humanity share in the eternal rest of God at the end of time, just as they share in the eternal work of God through the labors of the Church in time.[27] The seventh day, therefore, represents the very goal of the Church in the perfection of her members, as it is through the Church that God grants eternal rest for those who once were restless in the world.

It is through the Church, then, that the Spirit works to bring about the conversion of those lost in the world, as Augustine himself once was. Reflecting upon the Spirit's role in this conversion, he writes, "Once our heart had conceived by your Spirit we made a fresh start and began to act well, though at an earlier stage we had been impelled to wrongdoing and abandoned you; but you, O God undivided and good, have never ceased to act well" (13.38.53). It is therefore only by God's own good works, accomplished through the efforts of the members of his Church, that Augustine may look forward to the promise of

---

27. "And then you will rest in us, as now you work in us, and your rest will be rest through us as now those works of yours are wrought through us" (13.37.52).

the Kingdom. By God's grace, he has moved from the restlessness and wandering in the world to the peaceful labors of the Church, through which he has the hope of final rest in God. For this reason, Augustine concludes the *Confessions* by praying for the understanding that comes not from any created thing, but from God alone, expressing his continual dependence upon God, as the dry land dependent upon the font of life.[28] It is, after all, only through God's grace, operative through the Church, that any can reflect the goodness of humanity's created intent and hope one day to share eternally in him.

5. Conclusion

With book 13's exegesis of the Hexaemeron, Augustine closes the *Confessions* by focusing not on his own narrative as an individual, but on that of the Church in which all other narratives are bound together. The "I and Thou" dynamic, which has seemingly dominated the *Confessions*, is subsumed into the mystical "We" of the Church united in the eternal love of the Trinity. And it is in this meditation on the Church that many of the most prominent themes of the work as a whole reach their denouement. The restlessness that Augustine acknowledged from the very beginning is sated by the promise of perpetual rest in God (1.1.1). The Scriptures, which he once believed to be unrefined and unintelligible, are here presented in the richness and profundity that becomes visible through the lens of allegory (cf. 3.5.9 and 6.4.6). Creation, which once drew his attention away from God, and which he once believed to be the product of an evil God, is now affirmed to be exceedingly good (cf. 5.10.20 and 10.27.38). The grace that drew him out of his sinful pride is now acknowledged in gratitude, as his salvation is recognized not to be his alone, but to be a participation in the redemption of the Church as a whole. Book 13 therefore exhibits the gift of sight illumined by baptismal faith, with which he now sees creation rightly as a sacrament of the love of God.[29]

---

28. "Let us rather ask of you, seek in you, knock at your door. Only so will we receive, only so find, only so will the door be opened to us. Amen" (13.38.53).

29. John Cavadini likewise explains that this sight is brought about in the Christian through Eucharistic remembering. The charity given through the Eucharist fosters the light of faith, through which one is able to see creation rightly. The memorial of Christ's sacrifice in the Eucharist allows the faithful to see the mercy through which humans have hope of salvation. In the same way, the memory of God's work in creation allows the faithful to see God's work in the redemption of his creatures. Memory is bound to hope; the origin of the world points to its future redemption. John C. Cavadini, "Eucharistic Exegesis in Augustine's Confessions," *Augustinian Studies* 41, no. 1 (2010): 87–108.

Even more, though, Augustine's exegesis shows that from the beginning, the Church was prepared by God as the means through which humans might participate in God as their end. God's works in the creation of heaven and earth reveal his works on behalf of humanity throughout time, and it is on account of these works that all, even those who are still tossed about in the cares of the world, have cause for hope. Through the activities of the Church and her members, God continues to act on behalf of all, so that those who would be his people might come to dwell in community upon the dry land, rather than persisting in wandering through the sea. Baptized into the communion of the Church, each is restored to life by grace, and through the grace that operates in this communion, each is elevated to share in the Spirit of God.

Contrary to the insistences of the modern perspective, then, no person truly stands alone. For Augustine, the loneliness and the restlessness of humanity indeed find satisfaction in the God who created them, but this is not a journey accomplished as an individual apart from others. Rather, it is traversed through the Church, not a human institution blown about by the capricious whims of individuals, but a divine communion established by God from the beginning and for which the human person was created. Only in this communion of grace does the human heart find its true hope in the eternal rest of God.

Contributors

DR. MARGARET BLUME FREDDOSO received her doctorate in Theology from the University of Notre Dame in 2019. She has taught in Notre Dame's Program of Liberal Studies and worked for the McGrath Institute of Church Life. Presently, she is a postdoctoral teaching scholar at Notre Dame's Center for Citizenship and Constitutional Government. Her research focuses on the central role of theological hope in Thomas Aquinas's vision of the human being's journey to God, as well as Augustine's influence on Aquinas's understanding of hope.

DR. GERALD P. BOERSMA is Associate Professor of Theology at Ave Maria University, where he also serves as the Director of the MA Program in Theology. His research focuses on Patristic theology, especially fourth and fifth century Latin Christianity and the thought of Augustine. He is the author of *Augustine's Early Theology of Image* (Oxford, 2016). Currently, he is writing a book on Augustine and the vision of God. Gerald Boersma grew up in the Netherlands and in Canada. He completed his Ph.D. studies at Durham University (UK).

DR. HILARY FINLEY received her Bachelor of Arts in Humanities from the Franciscan University of Steubenville and her Doctorate in Literature from the University of Dallas. Dr. Finley has taught Catholic Literature for Holy Apostles College Seminary, and is now serving as both the Coordinator of the Catholic Studies Centre at Saint Louis University, as well as its Fellow in Catholic Literature.

JOSEPH GRONE is a doctoral candidate in the Department of Theological Studies at Saint Louis University. He works on Christology, ecclesiology, sanctification, and the liturgy in late antique Christianity, especially in the Latin West. For his dissertation, he is studying Augustine's understanding of liturgical worship, in its many forms, as a locus for the formation, exercise, and manifestation of ecclesial identity.

FR. ANDREW HOFER, OP, is Associate Professor of Patristics and Ancient Languages as well as Director of the Doctoral Program at the Pontifical Faculty of the Immaculate Conception, Dominican House of Studies in Washington, DC. He is the author of *Christ in the Life and Teaching of Gregory of Nazianzus* (Oxford University Press, 2013), editor of *Divinization: Becoming Icons of God through the Liturgy* (Hillenbrand Books, 2015), co-author of *A Living Sacrifice: Guidance for Men Discerning Religious Life* (Vianney Vocations, 2019), and co-editor of *Thomas Aquinas and the Greek Fathers* (Sapientia Press, 2019) and *Thomas Aquinas and the Crisis of Christology* (Sapientia Press, 2021).

DR. JOHN PETER KENNEY is Professor Emeritus of Religious Studies at Saint Michael's College. He is the author of *Mystical Monotheism: A Study in Ancient Platonic Theology* (Brown University Press, 1991), *The Mysticism of Saint Augustine: Rereading the Confessions* (Routledge, 2005), *Contemplation and Classical Christianity: A Study in Augustine* (Oxford University Press, 2013), *On God, the Soul, Evil, and the Rise of Christianity* (Bloomsbury, 2018), and co-editor of *Christian Platonism: A History* (Cambridge University Press, 2021).

DR. ERIKA KIDD is Associate Professor of Catholic Studies at the University of St. Thomas in St. Paul. Kidd studied philosophy, Latin, and Great Texts at Baylor University in Texas and received her PhD in philosophy from Villanova University in Pennsylvania. She writes and speaks on Augustine and the Augustinian tradition, and teaches courses on happiness, conversion, and taking the Incarnation seriously. She is currently at work on a book about how we can learn to hear the voice of God in our conversations with one another.

DR. JEFFREY S. LEHMAN is is Professor of Humanities, director of the graduate program in Classical Education, and executive director of the St. Ambrose Center for Catholic Liberal Education and Culture at the University of Dallas. Among his publications are *Augustine: Rejoicing in the Truth* and *Socratic Conversation* (both published by Classical Academic Press) as well as numerous articles on Plato, Aristotle, Vergil, Augustine, Boethius, and Thomas More. He is the founding director of Arts of Liberty (artsofliberty.udallas.edu), an online compendium of resources whose mission is to educate students, teachers, and lifelong learners in the purpose and power of the liberal arts and liberal education.

DR. JOHN W. MARTENS is professor of Theology at University of St. Thomas and director of the MA in Theology at the St. Paul Seminary School of Divinity. His research focuses on the emergence of Christianity within Judaism and its intersections within the Greco-Roman world, specifically in the lives of ancient children, sexuality, and marriage. He is the author, with Cornelia Horn, of *"Let the Little Children Come to Me": Childhood and Children in Early Christianity* (Washington, D.C.: Catholic University Press, 2009) and most recently the editor, with Kristine Henriksen Garroway, of *Children and Methods: Listening to and Learning From Children in the Biblical World* (Brill's Series in Jewish Studies, 2020).

FR. DAVID VINCENT MECONI, SJ, is Professor of Patristics as well as the Director of the Catholic Studies Centre at Saint Louis University; he is also the editor of *Homiletic and Pastoral Review*. He holds the pontifical license in Patrology from the University of Innsbruck in Austria, as well as his doctorate in Ecclesiastical History from the University of Oxford. Fr. Meconi has published widely on the early Church. His most recent works include the *Sermons of Peter Chrysologus* (Routledge), *The Cambridge Companion to Augustine's City of God* (Cambridge University Press), and *Augustine on Self-Harm, Narcissism, Atonement and the Vulnerable Christ* (Bloomsbury Press, 2019).

DR. VERONICA ROBERTS OGLE is Assistant Professor of Philosophy at Assumption University, where she teaches in the core curriculum and directs the LEX (Law, Ethics and Constitutional Studies) Program. Her research focuses on the intersection between theology and political philosophy in Augustine's thought. She has published in journals such as *Journal of Religious Ethics*, *Augustinian Studies*, and *Studia Patristica* and has most recently authored *Politics and the Earthly City in Augustine's City of God* (Cambridge University Press, 2020).

PAUL RUFF is a Licensed Psychologist who is currently the Director of Counseling Services and Assistant Director of Human Formation at The Saint Paul Seminary, St. Paul, Minnesota. His therapeutic framework is most influenced by phenomenological approaches that focus on the integration of mind, body, and spirit. Mr. Ruff also serves as a guest faculty member for the Institute for

Priestly Formation at Creighton University in Omaha, and the Seminary Formation Council Certification Program for Seminary Formators hosted by Saint Vincent de Paul Seminary, Boynton Beach, Florida.

DR. CHRISTOPHER J. THOMPSON serves as the academic dean of The Saint Paul Seminary School of Divinity. He teaches, writes and reflects on the intersection of Thomistic and Augustinian thought, especially in the areas of creation, the moral law and the ecological imperative to steward His earth. Dr. Thompson also serves on the Board of Directors for Catholic Rural Life as well as on the Board of the International Catholic Rural Association for the Pontifical Council for Justice and Peace.

Index of Names and Subjects

Index of Scripture References